The Innovation Imperative

The Innovation Imperative

National Innovation Strategies in the Global Economy

Edited by

Göran Marklund

VINNOVA, Swedish Governmental Agency for Innovation Systems, Sweden

Nicholas S. Vonortas

The George Washington University, USA

and

Charles W. Wessner

US National Academies, USA

Edward Elgar

Cheltenham, UK • Northampton, MA, USA

Published by
Edward Elgar Publishing Limited
The Lypiatts
15 Lansdown Road
Cheltenham
Glos GL50 2JA
UK

Edward Elgar Publishing, Inc.
William Pratt House
9 Dewey Court
Northampton
Massachusetts 01060
USA

A catalogue record for this book
is available from the British Library

Library of Congress Control Number: 2008937414

Mixed Sources
Product group from well-managed
forests and other controlled sources
www.fsc.org Cert no. SA-COC-1565
© 1996 Forest Stewardship Council

ISBN 978 1 84720 192 8

Printed and bound in Great Britain by MPG Books Ltd, Bodmin, Cornwall

Contents

Figures

Tables

Contributors

William Aspray, the Rudy Professor of Informatics and Special Advisor on Information Technology and Professional Partnerships, Indiana University, Bloomington, IN, USA.

David B. Audretsch, Professor, Indiana University, Bloomington, IN, USA and Max Planck Institute of Economics, Jena, Germany.

Susana Borrás, Associate Professor, International Center for Business and Politics, Copenhagen Business School, Copenhagen, Denmark.

Cristina Chaminade, Associate Professor, Centre for Innovation, Research and Competence in the Learning Economy (CIRCLE), Lund University, Sweden.

Christopher J. Currens, Associate Director, Building and Fire Research Laboratory, National Institute of Standards and Technology (NIST), Gaithersburg, MD, USA.

Charles Edquist, Professor, CIRCLE, Lund University, Lund, Sweden.

Thomas R. Howell, Partner, Dewey Ballantine LLP, Washington, DC, USA.

Åsa Lindholm Dahlstrand, Professor, R&D, Innovation and Dynamics of Economies (RIDE), Halmstad University, Halmstad, Sweden.

Göran Marklund, Associate Professor, Uppsala University and Director, Strategy Development Division, VINNOVA, Stockholm, Sweden.

Frank Mayadas, Program Director, Sloan Foundation, New York, NY, USA.

Evan S. Michelson, Research Associate, Project on Emerging Nanotechnologies, Woodrow Wilson International Center for Scholars, Washington, DC, USA.

Marc G. Stanley, Director, Technology Innovation Program, NIST, Gaithersburg, MD, USA.

Moshe Y. Vardi, the George Professor in Computational Engineering and Director of the Computer and Information Technology Institute at Rice University, Houston, TX, USA.

Nicholas S. Vonortas, Professor, Center for International Science and Technology Policy and Department of Economics, George Washington University, Washington, DC, USA.

Charles W. Wessner, Director, Program on Technology, Innovation and Entrepreneurship, US National Academies, Washington, DC, USA.

Abbreviations and acronyms

ACI	American Competitiveness Initiative
ACM	Association for Computing Machinery
ACS	Australian Computer Society
AFM	atomic force microscope
AML	anti-monopoly legislation
ATP	Advanced Technology Program
BANG	bits, atoms, neurons, genes
BEA	Bureau of Economic Analysis
BRS	business reporting system
CA	coordinated actions
CBEN	Center for Biological and Environmental Nanotechnology
CERN	European Organization for Nuclear Research
CNSI	California NanoSystems Institute
CNT	Center for Nanotechnology
COTS	commercial off-the-shelf
CPS	current population survey
CSO	corporate spin offs
CTEKS	converging technologies for the European knowledge society
DARPA	Defense Advanced Research Projects Agency
DOD	Department of Defense
DOE	Department of Energy
EC	European Commission
EIS	European innovation scoreboard
EMBL	European Molecular Biology Laboratory
EMBO	European Molecular Biology Organization
EPA	Environmental Protection Agency
ERA	European research area
ERC	European Research Council
ERSO	Electronics Research and Service Organization
ESO	European Organization for Astronomical Research in the Southern Hemisphere
ETC	erosion, technology and concentration
EU	European Union
FDI	foreign direct investment
FP	framework programme(s)

GATT	General Agreement on Tariffs and Trade
GDP	gross domestic product
GPA	government procurement agreement
HEA	high-expectation entrepreneurial activity
HLEG	high level expert group
ICT	information and communication technology
IMF	International Monetary Fund
IP	integrated projects
IPO	initial public offering
IPR	intellectual property rights
ISN	Institute for Soldier Nanotechnologies
ISO	indirect university spin-offs
IST	information society technologies
IT	information technology
ITO	International Trade Organization
ITRI	Industrial Technology Research Institute
JTI	joint technology initiative
JV	joint ventures
MFN	most favoured nation
MNC	multinational corporations
NBIC	nano-bio-info-cogni
NBTC	Nanobiotechnology Center
NTBF	new technology-based firms
NCI	National Cancer Institute
NCMT	numerically controlled machine tools
NEST	new and emerging science and technologies
NIH	National Institutes of Health
NIST	National Institute of Standards and Technology
NNI	National Nanotechnology Initiative
NoE	non-observed economy
NSF	National Science Foundation
NSI	national system(s) of innovation
NSTS	nanoscience and technology studies program
NTBF	New technology based firms
OECD	Organisation for Economic Co-operation and Development
OES	occupational employment statistics
PPP	purchasing power parity
R&D	research and development
RTD	research and technological development
S&T	science and technology
SAC	Standards Administration of China
SAIC	state administration of industry and commerce

SBIR	small business innovation research
SIPO	State Intellectual Property Organization
SME	small and medium enterprises
SMIC	Semiconductor Manufacturing International Corporation
SO	selecting official
SSA	specific support actions
STRePs	specific targeted research projects
TBT	technical barriers to trade
TEA	total entrepreneurial activity
TRIPS	Trade-Related Aspects of Intellectual Property Rights
UCLA	University of California-Los Angeles
UCSB	University of California-Santa Barbara
UN	United Nations
UNESCO	UN Educational, Scientific and Cultural Organization
USDA	United States Department of Agriculture
USO	university spin offs
USPTO	US Patent and Trademark Office
VAT	value–added tax
WEF	World Economic Forum
WiCC	widening the circles of convergence
WTO	World Trade Organization

Foreword

This volume reflects the proceedings of a conference arranged by VINNOVA and George Washington University in cooperation with the US National Academies in Stockholm in the Spring of 2006. The title of the conference was 'The innovation imperative – globalization and national competitiveness' and focused on policy challenges and policy measures related to innovation and economic growth in a rapidly globalizing world. In this volume, different authors contribute to deepening our understanding of globalization and innovation policy challenges and developing insights of innovation policy strategies and measures that are important in fostering national competitiveness.

We would like to thank John Forrer, George Washington University, for his support to the conference and to this volume. Our warmest gratitude goes also to Kruna Madunic, VINNOVA, for her excellent and tireless work with arranging and managing the conference in 2006 and to Cynthia Little for her marvelous work with the different texts and turning them into a printable manuscript. Finally, we would like to thank all the authors for their excellent contributions to the conference and to this volume.

Göran Marklund, Nicholas Vonortas
and **Charles Wessner**

Preface

The changes that are affecting firms and industries, people and competencies, nations and economies as a consequence of globalization have been noted by business, academic, public institution and policy actors. Globalization is an intangible force that is impinging on almost all areas of society; however, its drivers and consequences are generally not well understood, either by the general public or in policy circles.

Globalization is creating new policy challenges and opportunities for all countries of the world. Global wealth has increased, and more and more countries are being affected by globalization as a consequence of economic growth. While the expansion of trade and investment has played a major role in driving this growth, the chapters in this volume suggest that there are new challenges that need to be addressed, as well as a growing recognition of the importance of national innovation policies as a differentiator in international competition. Successful innovation policies can and do affect national conditions for work and wealth generation in fundamental ways.

Innovation is essential to economic growth and job creation. Globalization both creates increasing opportunities for innovation and puts competitive pressure on a country's innovative capacity. As a consequence, strategies aimed at investment in innovation capabilities have rapidly gained in importance. And the role and challenges for policy have changed considerably in relation to investments in research and in the mechanisms and incentives designed to ensure sustainable returns on such investments.

Policy makers need to constantly renew their understanding of the key policy challenges. Globalization and the innovation imperative towards sustained economic growth require a major renewal of public policy thinking and strategies. The design and introduction of new policy measures to stimulate innovation in order to keep pace with global competition and to reap the benefits of global opportunities are critical for sustainable wealth generation, job creation and growth.

This book focuses on these policy challenges, and the policy strategies and policy measures needed for innovation and growth in a globalizing world. The objective is to provide guidance for policy strategies and measures. The chapters in the book reflect the proceedings of a conference 'The innovation imperative – globalization and national competitiveness' jointly organized by VINNOVA and George Washington University in coopera-tion with the US National Academies, which was held in Stockholm in Spring 2006. The conference and its findings continue to be of great rele-vance to today's challenges.

The editorial team for this volume has been led by Dr Göran Marklund, Director of Strategy Development at the Swedish Government Agency for Innovation Systems (VINNOVA), Sweden, supported by his co-editors Dr Charles Wessner, Director, Programme on Technology, Innovation and Entrepreneurship, the US National Academies, and Dr Nicholas Vonortas, Professor, George Washington University, USA.

Per Eriksson
Director General, VINNOVA

1. Introduction

Göran Marklund, Nicholas S. Vonortas and Charles W. Wessner

1.1 GLOBALIZATION

Globalization is rapidly changing the conditions for social interactions, economic processes and political agendas. In particular, globalization is affecting economic opportunities and economic competition. As a consequence, it has important impacts on the conditions for economic growth, wealth distribution and social welfare.

In its most general sense, globalization refers to the worldwide integration of humanity and the compression of both the temporal and spatial dimensions of worldwide human interactions. However, it is more often discussed in the more limited sense of the increasing economic integration and economic interdependence of countries. Globalization is the consequence of the deeply intertwined and mutually interdependent evolution of economic, technological and social processes.

The processes of spatial integration of production and technologies started in the earliest days of human history. It is only relatively recently, however, that these processes have had such an impact on the economic, technological and social integration of regions worldwide that the term globalization is warranted. Although a quite modern phenomenon, globalization is considerably older than is generally discussed in the now abundant literature on its size and consequences.

Globalization, in terms of global flows of capital and, thus, of technology, productive capacity and economic power, is at the heart of the capitalist economic system. Hence, the roots of the driving forces of modern economic globalization go back to, at least, the late nineteenth century. The first significant wave of globalization took place in the period 1870–1913, when most of Western and Northern Europe and the USA went through industrialization. It was characterized by rapid expansion of international trade, investment and migration. The second wave of globalization occurred after World War II and reached a peak in the early 1970s. It was interrupted by the 1973–76 energy crisis. The third and present wave of globalization began in the late 1970s and has been ongoing for about three decades. The pace of globalization processes has been increasing since the mid 1990s.

It is often argued that national borders have decreased in importance and will continue to do so as a result of the global integration of world economies. However, this to a large extent is based on confusions among different processes and logics in global economic development. It is certainly true that globalization has considerably changed the logics of value systems, business models and technological development. For business logics then, and accordingly also for business behaviour, the importance of national borders has continuously decreased. This is a core driving force of capitalist development and hence a key explanation of the evolution of economic globalization and the resulting decreasing importance of national borders for business processes. It is likewise true that the importance of national borders for technological logics, which are closely tied to business logics, has decreased. And, since knowledge and technology are difficult privately to appropriate completely, they have a tendency to diffuse more rapidly and more widely than capital. Hence, they have been a major contributor to economic globalization and, thus, to the decreasing importance of national borders for technological and economic development.

However, this is not the case for political logics. Political logics are, and will always be, geographically constrained by the mission to provide the conditions for wealth generation and welfare distribution among citizens. Hence, as long as national administrative borders remain the basis for policy power, they will remain of key importance for political logics. Although globalization has not fundamentally changed the nature of political geography, it has greatly transformed policy challenges and opportunities. First, it has greatly increased the importance to nations of being internationally competitive, both industrially and technologically. Second, it has dramatically changed and considerably increased the policy challenges related to this competitiveness. Third, in generating a series of fundamental institutional changes in terms of international agreements on policy measures, it has considerably changed the scope of and boundaries to policy measures.

Increases in interactions, mobility and trade across borders are generating increases in overall wealth. However, there are winners and losers in these processes. Global developments do not evolve evenly. They do not distribute evenly either the sources or the outcomes of economic development among continents, nations, regions or citizens. Hence, reaping the benefits of global growth is not automatic; instead, there are fundamental strategic challenges associated with globalization.

1.2 INNOVATION

Globalization increases many different kinds of opportunities. In particular, it enhances the opportunities for wealth generation. Simultaneously, the competition for these opportunities increases considerably. This dynamic competition accelerates the pressures for constant business renewal in order to maintain or increase profitability. Innovation is about exploring new combinations to respond to future challenges. Innovation is essential to economic life, as it is the main determinant of economic productivity and productivity growth in firms, sectors, regions and nations. It is therefore the underlying basis of long-term economic growth. As global competition and opportunities accelerate as a consequence of the rapidly globalizing world, international competitiveness increases in importance for both businesses and nations. Hence, the innovation imperative for wealth creation becomes an essential strategic issue for business firms and public policy.

For business firms, the essential issue is how to continue to be prosperous in evolving and emerging markets. Innovating for business renewal is of fundamental importance for competitiveness. Innovativeness is about internal innovation capabilities and also network relationships, which enable external innovation capabilities to be tapped. Of particular significance are relationships with customers, as innovation is intimately related to the commercialization and sale of new ideas. Innovation networks and markets for innovations are inherently tied to geographies of capabilities and customers. Hence, as globalization is markedly changing geographical structures and resource distributions, this is strongly affecting the locations of business innovation.

For nations, a key challenge is how to maintain or increase standards of living in an increasingly competitive world. In nations and regions where economic renewal and structural change are slow or insufficient, economic competitiveness will gradually decline. Innovation is at the heart of renewal processes. Opportunities for and challenges to innovation have become of paramount importance for national wealth creation and welfare generation. As the geographies of business innovation are rapidly changing due to globalization processes, attracting business innovation investment has become increasingly important for regions and nations. As a result, improving innovation competitiveness has become a major focus of policy for most countries and regions, and international organizations including the European Union (EU), the Organisation for Economic Co-operation and Development (OECD) and the United Nations (UN).

1.3 POLICY

As the importance to nations of attracting innovation investments and innovation based businesses has increased, policy competition among countries and regions has emerged. Different policy strategies and measures are being adopted by different governments. Yet, despite the importance of innovation policy for national and regional wealth creation and welfare generation, most governments do not consider it to be a specific policy field. Public policy is inherently embedded in economic and social activities. Hence, policy institutions and measures strongly condition the incentive structures and opportunities for innovation. Policies affecting innovation conditions and the competitiveness of business firms and nations are not restricted purely to the economic area. Policies in most fields have impacts on innovation competitiveness. Innovation policy, therefore, runs through public policy, without necessarily being explicitly addressed either in overall policy making or in relevant policy fields.

Policy discussions around innovation, innovation policy and national competitiveness still often lack structure and rigour. As a consequence, the challenges and opportunities related to innovation competitiveness, and the options and alternatives for policy are often unclear in much policy debate. And in election campaigns, innovation policies are rarely a major issue, despite their critical importance for welfare generation.

The purpose of this book is to contribute to the development of innovation policy thinking and policy making in a globalization perspective. The focus will be on policy challenges related to maintaining and improving national competitiveness in a globalizing world. As innovation is imperative for long-term national competitiveness, the theme that runs through the contributions to this book is the policy challenges related to innovation.

1.4 OUTLINE

Susana Borrás, Cristina Chaminade and Charles Edquist discuss the challenges of globalization and the strategic choices for policy in Chapter 2. The main message of this chapter is that globalization has increased the importance of innovation policy for national wealth generation, while the conditions for such policy have changed considerably. Innovation policy needs to consider both the rapid changes in global markets and the innovation activities and the specific conditions of each national innovation system.

In Chapter 3 William Aspray, Frank Mayadas and Moshe Y. Vardi analyse the trends in offshoring related to software research and development (R&D) and production. Their chapter is based on a study undertaken by a major task force through an initiative of the Association for Computing Machinery (ACM). The study discusses a major difference in globalization patterns from those previously observed, as offshoring is now also affecting key high-technology service industries such as software. The overall conclusion of the authors is that offshoring, like winter, is inevitable – and its consequences can only be countered by ambitious innovation and competitiveness policies.

Thomas R. Howell discusses international trade regulations as key institutions of market formation in a world of globalizing economies in Chapter 4. This chapter addresses the shortcomings of the World Trade Organization (WTO) and other international trade conventions in failing to establish effective regulation of the competition among countries through incentives for business investments and trade. He emphasizes the necessity for policy makers to recognize the world of incentive competition for how it really is rather than how it ought to be.

In Chapter 5 David Audretsch discusses the implications for innovation of the shift towards a service economy, in which ideas, people and knowledge are the key assets. He emphasizes the importance of the entrepreneur penetrating the 'knowledge filter', that is, the obstacles to commercializing different kinds of knowledge. He concludes that entrepreneurship performs the function of 'creative construction', while globalization is the main force of destruction of old businesses and industries.

Åsa Lindholm Dahlstrand, in Chapter 6, discusses the critical links between the emergence of new technology-based ideas and entrepreneurship generating innovation and growth. Lindholm-Dahlstrand has studied large numbers of new technology-based firms (NTBF) in Sweden, and her chapter focuses on the challenges of reaping the economic potentials of these NTBF. Her main conclusion is that innovation policies should focus on linking innovation, competitiveness, internationalization, entrepreneurship and education.

In Chapter 7 Charles Wessner discusses the key issues and policy challenges generated by globalization. His main conclusion is that innovation is imperative for competitiveness, and policies generating the most favourable innovation conditions are essential for long-term national economic competitiveness. He draws attention to innovation award programmes to improve innovation performance in the USA and in Sweden. He particularly highlights the targeting of and impacts on small business innovation.

Marc Stanley and Christopher Currens in Chapter 8 present the impact logics of the US Advanced Technology Program (ATP) in stimulating innovation. The ATP, which has been in place since 1992, focuses on critical challenges to radical innovation. The authors' main conclusion, based on continuous impact evaluations, is that ATP successfully addresses the fundamental challenges of early stage financing of innovation. The ATP logic could thus serve as an inspiration to policy strategies and measures of other countries.

In Chapter 9 Evan S. Michelson discusses the business, policy and social implications of the convergence of nanotechnology. Convergence of technologies at the nanoscale has already started to emerge, but has yet to reach its peak. As nanotechnology probably will bring considerable technological changes for future innovation systems, following and understanding the emerging nanorevolution should be of key importance to innovation policy.

Nicholas Vonortas, in Chapter 10, analyses the impacts of the EU framework programmes for research, technology and development (RT&D) to promote European competitiveness. His chapter is based on an evaluation of past framework programmes, and concludes that they have played an important role in developing the knowledge base of the EU. However, as globalization generates considerable competitiveness challenges for Europe, future framework programmes will have to be more clearly focused on EU competitiveness.

In Chapter 11 Göran Marklund discusses some critical dimensions and targets of innovation policy. He argues that innovation policy needs to be based on a multidimensional focusing on four sets of general formation processes: market formation, business formation, technology formation and science formation. In the EU and Sweden special emphasis should be put on market and business formation, as innovation policy traditionally has tended to focus strongly on inputs, targeting levels of R&D investments.

The final chapter brings the different chapters and lines of thought together in an attempt to draw conclusions. These concern on the one hand critical *foci* in innovation policy and on the other hand key innovation policy targets.

2. The challenges of globalization: strategic choices for innovation policy

Susana Borrás, Cristina Chaminade and Charles Edquist

2.1 INTRODUCTION

The vast literature on systems of innovation is rich in theoretical and empirical studies on the complexity and institutionally embedded processes of interaction and learning at regional, sectoral and national level (Asheim and Gertler, 2005; Edquist, 1997, 2005; Loasby, 2001; Lundvall, 1992, 2005; Malerba, 2004; Nooteboom, 2000). So far, however, this literature has not studied, in a comprehensive manner, the nature and types of strategic choices that public actors in systems of innovation are facing in the ever-changing social, economic and technological contexts (Lundvall and Borrás, 1998).

This chapter is a first step in this direction. It discusses the implications of globalization for the strategic choices for innovation policy. The specific point of departure is the set of challenges that the process of globalization has been posing to systems of innovation in industrialized and developing countries, past and present. During recent decades, research and innovation activities are becoming increasingly global. While new actors have emerged in the global innovation arena (notably some Asian countries) the nature of the globalization process is changing from the international exploitation of nationally produced goods to the global generation of innovation (Archibugi and Michie, 1995). As a consequence, the geographical pattern of innovation activities is shifting and the boundaries between local, national and global innovation systems are becoming blurred. This new global context is posing great challenges for policy makers with regard to the nature and types of strategic choices they need to make. When and how to intervene in the system of innovation when innovation activities are global becomes crucial, pointing to the importance of rationales for public intervention (Chaminade and Edquist, forthcoming).

Hitherto, discussion of the rationales for public intervention seems to have been at a rather abstract and theoretical level, based on the properties of knowledge and the nature of knowledge production systems, and not embedded in specific social, economic and institutional contexts (Metcalfe, 1995). As a result, the literature serves only as broad guidance for public actors, and is too abstract to support them in the highly contextualized, reality embedded practice of policy making. This chapter attempts to fill this research gap by discussing the impact of the recent globalization of innovation patterns on the strategic choices that public actors currently face.

The chapter is structured as follows. First, we highlight recent changes in the global distribution of innovation activities. Section 2.3 and 2.4 discuss the implications of globalization for innovation policy and provide a brief review of the policy-related literature in the field, highlighting missing elements and overlooked issues. Particular attention is paid to the impact of globalization on the rationales behind the two dominant approaches. Sections 2.5 and 2.6 investigate the issue of uncertainty and selectivity, two core aspects of strategic choices. The last section concludes discussing systemic problems in the context of globalization, and addresses the design of a method to help public actors spell out objectives and instruments, which is critical to the unfolding of specific strategic choices for systems of innovation.

2.2   CHANGES IN THE GLOBAL CONTEXT

Economic globalization is not a new phenomenon, but it is rapidly changing in nature. It involves the global trade of goods and services, the international mobility of labour and capital, the global location of production and, more recently, innovation activities. Generally speaking there are three forms of innovation globalization (Archibugi and Michie, 1995): international exploitation of nationally produced innovations; global and techno-scientific strategic alliances and collaborations between firms; and global generation of innovations (global distribution of innovation activities). Firms commercialize nationally generated innovations to increase their return on investment, to internationalize their innovation activities to respond to different demand and market conditions and adapt their products to local demand (Narula and Zanfei, 2005). Universities and other research organizations collaborate internationally to access and disseminate new knowledge. The increasing internationalization of innovation activities during the past two decades suggests a change in the geographic patterns of innovation processes.

The global character of innovation activities has been widely analysed in the innovation literature (Archibugi and Michie, 1995; Archibugi and Iammarino, 1999; Archibugi and Lundvall, 2001; Cantwell, 1995, 2000; Johansson and Lööf, 2006; Narula, 2000). Despite the important consequences in terms of knowledge spillovers and capacity building that the global location of research and development (R&D) and innovation activities has (Marin and Bell, 2006), it is still a fairly limited phenomenon in terms of aggregate numbers. Only 12 per cent of multinational companies' R&D is performed outside their home countries, showing that the international relocation of knowledge creation activities is a marginal phenomenon. Moreover, the global distribution of innovation activities is a phenomenon that is almost exclusive to the developed world. Analysis of the evolution of technology clubs worldwide confirms the geographical concentration of innovative activity in the developed world and its stability over time (Castellacci, 2006).

Despite this territorial concentration and the relatively small degree of knowledge production relocation, the rapid growth of some Asian countries is challenging the traditional patterns of economic globalization, including the global distribution of innovative activities.[1] According to Schmitz (2006), there are three indications of these quite dramatic changes. First, China's participation in world trade is increasing rapidly. Exports from China have escalated and it is estimated that by 2050, half of the world trade will be Chinese. Second, there are important changes in the organization of production because an increased number of Chinese companies is coordinating global supply chains and influencing global standards. And third, the relocation of innovation activities is provoking important changes. An increasing number of industry and firm based cases are suggesting that some Asian regions and sectors are starting to move up the value chain, from competing in costs to competing in knowledge and innovation (Altenburg et al., 2006; Chaminade and Vang, 2006a, b; Parthasarathy and Aoyama, 2006). Furthermore, it should be remembered that in 2005 China was ranked third in the world after the USA and Japan for gross domestic expenditure on R&D in absolute terms (although as a percentage of GDP this is only 1.4) and second after the USA for numbers of researchers (OECD, 2006).

Some countries and regions in the developing world seem to be catching up in terms of innovation, and are rapidly increasing the knowledge value added to their activities (Parthasarathy and Aoyama, 2006). The most visible consequence of this dramatic change is that an increasing number of developed country firms are locating their R&D departments in Asian countries, notably China and India, in order to tap into their large knowledge bases, not simply to adapt existing products to local markets. In 2005, 252 new

R&D foreign direct investment (FDI) projects were located in China and India, and India was considered to be the second most preferred R&D location in the world after the USA (Economist Intelligent Unit, 2007).[2]

This trend is very significant in some industries and regions, such as the software industry in India, and the biotech industry and automotive industries in China (Altenburg et al., 2006). Asian firms are moving rapidly up the value chain and starting to provide R&D services to transnational corporations and locating R&D departments in the developed world. This is clearly the case of the software industry in Bangalore, India (Parthasarathy and Aoyama, 2006; Chaminade and Vang, 2006b). The extent and scope of this phenomenon needs further research. From the evidence available, it seems clear that there is a new emerging trend characterized by the rapid increase in the knowledge base of some developing economies. However, some case studies suggest that the innovation systems in these countries suffer from many weaknesses that might seriously limit their growth (Chaminade and Vang, 2006b; Vang et al., forthcoming).[3]

The motivation for location of R&D activities abroad seems to be different from that in the past when adaptation to local markets was the main driver. The current localization of innovation activities is driven mainly by the need to gain access to local competencies and knowledge (Narula and Zanfei, 2005; Economist Intelligent Unit, 2007).[4] The consequences of this emerging trend on the global location of innovation activities has yet to be analysed more systematically. However, it can be expected that the globalization of innovation activities, and thus innovation systems, will pose new challenges to policy makers in terms of strategic choices.

2.3   PUBLIC ACTION IN THE NEW GLOBAL CONTEXT

As we can see from the above, the globalized distribution of innovation processes is changing. So, what are the implications of this globalization for innovation policy? And is the relevance and importance of innovation policy eroding as a result of growing global innovation dynamics? In an increasingly borderless world where the flux of knowledge and information is growing rapidly, what is the logic behind government investment in capacity building or government efforts to regulate knowledge appropriation if that knowledge is going to vanish into global-related processes?

Innovation policy is action by public organizations that influence innovation processes, that is, the development and diffusion of (product and process) innovations.[5] By 'influence' we mean improvement of some kind to these processes, for example, by trying to solve or mitigate problems related to innovation processes. To influence and govern is the *raison d'être* of policy, as well as politics in general. The objectives of innovation policy are politically determined and can be economic, military, environmental or social. In practice, innovation policy initiatives are attempts to solve or mitigate 'problems' in the innovation system. Such problems exist when the actions of private actors do not automatically lead to the fulfillment of their objectives. This implies that public action should not replace or duplicate private action, but should supplement it (additionality) and address specific problems associated with the incentives for innovation (appropriability, among others).

Traditionally, governments have an important role in the development of innovation systems. Systems of innovation are based on competence building and learning in those areas where markets alone cannot provide the conditions conducive to learning and the acquisition of competences. This is mainly because learning and adaptation do not happen in a vacuum; they normally involve specific social dynamics embedded in an overall institutional design. Formal and informal institutions, such as rules, norms, routines or informal social patterns of behaviour, shape the interactions of the different organizations in the system of innovation (Nooteboom, 2000). Policy also tries to tackle collective problems, including grasping the opportunities that are being left unexploited by private actors.

These tasks are far removed from the individual firm's sphere of action, and hence require government intervention. Furthermore, it is precisely these tasks that render innovation policy a key element in shaping responses to globalization in the innovation system. In an increasingly globalized context firms are more exposed to changing market and technological conditions. In such a context innovation policy is an important part of the system's response because innovation policy aims at shaping the conditions for learning and the overall capacity of firms and other organizations to attract external knowledge and to innovate. In other words, strategically designed policy to enhance learning and adaptability in general, and that of firms in particular in the context of globalization, is an important component of the system's ability to cope with new challenges and rapid change.

The next question, therefore, is how to design such a strategy, including how to respond to the specific systemic bottlenecks vis-à-vis the globalizing economy, and how to make the most of future chances and challenges. This calls for a reconsideration of the specific premises and rationales upon which innovation policy should be designed and articulated. The rich literature on innovation policy rationales has so far not dealt directly with these matters. However, interesting, current analysis of the implications of globalization for redesigning innovation policy have addressed the issue of new rationales in a rather superficial way (Lundvall and Borrás, 1998; Archibugi et al., 1999; Cantwell, 1999). What do the different approaches to innovation policy say in relation to policy rationales? How do they address the issue of globalization? To what extent do the rationales and logics underlying innovation policy design need to be reconsidered given the major challenges mounted by the increasing globalization of innovation processes? Section 2.4 provides a succinct review of the way in which the existing approaches to innovation policy have addressed these issues, and considers the need to revisit some aspects in view of the changing conditions of globalization.

2.4   TAKING STOCK OF INNOVATION POLICY APPROACHES

There is a large economics literature dealing with the rationales of innovation policy. The bulk of scholarly work on this topic has generally followed two distinct deductive approaches. The first is based on the traditional economic rationale, which focuses on achieving optimal Pareto equilibrium with regard to the allocation of resources to innovation (or invention in the early literature).[6] Within this approach the main objective of public intervention is to address the different types of market failures that prevent the achievement of Pareto optimality. Early seminal works by economists, such as Arrow (1962), Nelson (1959) and Machlup (1980), defined the lines of enquiry in this approach.

One of the building blocks of the neoclassical approach to technology policy is that knowledge cannot be appropriated by the inventor due to its indivisibility and quasi public good nature (Nelson, 1959). This is considered to be a market failure because the market alone cannot generate the incentives to invest in innovation. The problem of knowledge appropriability can be solved through state intervention in the form of patent regulations, which grant short-term monopolies to inventors and, hence, secure private returns to the inventor's investment. More generally, though, these authors argue, the role of the state is primarily to secure the market conditions that allow for an optimal level of private investment in innovation. This entails addressing both the issue of knowledge appropriability mentioned above, and the issues of perfect competition and market dynamics in terms of technological diversity and selectivity. In other words, and to put it bluntly, for this school the role of the state is to create Pareto-optimal market conditions to achieve the highest possible level of private investment in innovation, which in turn will generate overall social welfare and social returns to the economy.

From the perspective of this approach to innovation policy, the process of globalization combined with increased digital communication poses a further problem for the appropriability of knowledge. The advancement of digital technologies has facilitated hugely the copy and transfer of information and data across the globe. In addition, the globalized patterns of innovation processes mean that more and more knowledge is being transferred across borders. Knowledge, particularly information, is becoming borderless. A problem then arises when the protection of intellectual property rights (IPR), and in particular of patents, is defined strictly in terms of national jurisdictions. In other words, the problem of appropriability is reopened in a global context where the solution to that problem (patents) does not apply to all the relevant geographical areas. States have reacted by signing international agreements, the most important of which is the TRIPS (Trade-Related Aspects of Intellectual Property Rights) agreement. However, enforcement and compliance are proving to be difficult and limited. In the neoclassical approach innovation policies generally focus on the provision of national solutions to problems. When activities become global neoclassical assumptions of, for example, perfect competition and perfect information become even more critical.

Growing dissatisfaction in the 1980s with the static and optimality-oriented economic premises of the equilibrium school led to the articulation of a new approach to the economics of innovation and to innovation policy. For the evolutionary school, technological change is not an exogenous aspect, but is endogenous to and the main explanatory factor in economic growth (Nelson and Winter, 1982; Dosi and Orsenigo, 1988). For evolutionary economists, the innovation process is the fruit of firm behaviour in an ever-changing context characterized by a high level of complexity and institutionally embedded processes of interaction and learning (Metcalfe, 1995). The evolutionary policy maker, therefore, is not interested in optimizing the conditions for achieving Pareto-equilibria of societal investment on technology, but in the innovation system's ability to adapt to changing conditions in order to maintain and enhance the knowledge and technological capabilities accumulated by firms and individuals through time. While for the equilibrium economists the role of technology policy is essentially to secure adequate levels of investment in technology, for the evolutionary and institutional economists technology policy also deals with the constant adaptability and learning abilities of firms and institutions. Therefore, rather than market failure, the evolutionary policy maker focuses on a series of systemic failures or problems, such as infrastructure provision, technological lock-ins, network problems and transition problems (Smith, 2000; Woolthius and Lankhuizen, 2005).

From the perspective of the evolutionary approach, globalization is putting important pressures on the adaptability of firms and systems in a rapidly changing context. The problem is not so much one of appropriability, since tacit knowledge, despite the greater mobility of firms and labour, is geographically 'sticky' and remains embodied in people and locally based organizations. The problem is more one of the adaptability of the actual innovation system, which is the aggregate result of firms' and other organizations' and institutions' adaptability (rules of the game). Reaping the benefits offered by globalization requires a new set of skills and resources on the part of firms, in a context where their competitive advantages might no longer be an advantage in the short term. The ability to establish global networks in order to tap into resources from other places might be one way of keeping ahead of the rapid obsolescence of competitive advantage based on 'static' assets. Hence, innovation policy should address the institutional and organizational bottlenecks that hinder adaptability.

These two approaches to innovation policy provide interesting and alternative ways of deciding on the roles of governments and their public actors in the innovation process, and identifying the challenges and problems posed by globalization. However, each has its own limitations. The problem with the existing literature is that there are significant blind spots in analyses of the relationship between innovation and public action, in particular the virtual absence of links between the rather abstract theoretical rationales of equilibrium and evolutionary economics, and the real world of innovation policy making. As Metcalfe (1995, p. 410) put it: 'Setting priorities, designing instruments, developing new institutional arrangements, monitoring and evaluating current policies are connected in only a general way to the literature [of policy rationales]'. It is true that during the past several decades the logics spelled out in the aforementioned equilibrium and evolutionary rationales have served policy makers as broad guidelines for public involvement. However, the rather abstract nature of these rationales (focusing on the 'why' of public action) provide relatively poor guidance to the questions of 'what' (strategic choices for the system) and 'how' (designing objectives and instruments). Bridging the gap between economic theory and real world policy making requires an understanding that innovation policy strategic choices, objectives and instruments are part of the equation, rather than an add-on aspect of the innovation process. Policy makers are part of the innovation system. This raises important issues that are deserving of attention, two of which are coming to grips with the learning dimension of policy itself, and defining specific criteria for the problems of selectivity and additionality in conditions of permanent uncertainty and evolution (Chaminade and Edquist, forthcoming).

2.5 POLICY IS ALWAYS SELECTIVE

In important parts of any modern economy the prime means of competition is innovation, not price (Baumol, 2002; Schumpeter, 1943). These innovations may be, for example, new products (material goods or intangible services) or new processes (technological or organizational). Pursuing these innovation processes is plagued by uncertainty. In real time the actors involved in innovation processes – individuals, organizations such as firms and public agencies, etc. – do not know whether a specific innovation will be successful, how large the market for a new product will be or if a new production process will really decrease the cost of production or even function. Genuine uncertainty prevents potential actors from acting at all, since they cannot calculate the risk of doing so – or relate it to possible benefits at a later stage. If firms and other private organizations do become involved in pursuing innovation processes, they try to do so in a focused manner. They concentrate on transforming specific combinations of ideas and knowledge into specific products and processes, and on actions that they believe will achieve this. In other words, they are highly selective in their strategies. They make 'strategic choices'. Attempts by private organizations to innovate may be successful or not. This depends largely on whether they choose to do the 'right' things or not. If they choose the right things in the right way, the benefits can be very large. On the other hand, if they choose to do the wrong things – or do not do them well, all the resources invested may be wasted. These are two outcomes of selective action. It is important that society provides rewards for doing the right things and does not brand or stigmatize failure too severely.

In order to design innovation policy initiatives the policy maker needs to know the main causes or determinants behind the 'problems' that afflict the economy and the innovation process. Innovation policy aims at influencing innovation processes through their determinants. Hence, policy makers, voluntarily or not, explicitly or implicitly, are constantly making 'strategic choices', and doing so in a context where public resources are always limited. It is for this reason that actions by public organizations (that is, policy – in the general sense) should focus on solving or mitigating problems that are not solved by private actors (see Section 2.3). However, the public resources available for innovation policy are so limited that public organizations can certainly not be involved in all kinds of innovation processes, or in all stages of their development. This means that the public resources allocated to innovation policies are generally used selectively, by means of implicit or explicit strategic choices. Any public policy that is intended to solve or mitigate a societal problem must focus on the nature of the problem and on its causes – and thus be selective in defining the 'what', the object, of public action.

The real world of innovation policy making is full of examples of how governments select policy instruments, the 'how' of innovation policy. R&D policy instruments involve public financing of research, which means allocating economic resources across different research fields. An increase in public funding of R&D of 1 billion (crowns or euros) requires a decision about which field of R&D should benefit from the additional resources. Should they be used for electronics research or for research in the life sciences? Decisions typically are made in complex political and administrative institutional set-ups, in the understanding that those allocations will serve to stimulate and enhance levels of innovative and knowledge capacity in the economy, in areas where private investment was inadequate. Another conventional innovation policy instrument, tax deduction for R&D expenditure by private firms, tends to favour those firms that have (large) R&D expenditures, and industries with high R&D intensity. It is, therefore, a selective instrument. Likewise, public technology procurement is a much targeted innovation policy instrument, which focuses upon a certain function, such as air force attacking, high-voltage electricity transportation or telephone call exchanging. It then subsidizes the development of a system that can fulfill this function. Hence, this type of instrument is highly selective. Last, but not least, innovation-related regional policies are – by definition – selective because they make important innovation-related economic development strategies for a particular territory. These are only a few of the many examples of such policies, but they demonstrate that public policies are normally selective in some sense. They may be selective with regard to problems, regions, sectors, products, firms, instruments and so on.

Globalization adds an additional dimension to the discussion on selectivity, particularly when resources invested in innovation might not generate externalities in the particular country or region, but elsewhere. As Archibugi and Iammarino (1999, p. 326) acknowledge, with increasing globalization, the choices of public actors 'are strongly limited by processes they are not entirely in control of'. Should governments encourage foreign firms to establish R&D facilities in their countries or should they instead support R&D in domestic firms (that might later become global players)? How can governments decide which interventions might have a larger positive impact in their territories when innovation activities are becoming increasingly global?

These and other issues are addressed in a forthcoming book (Edquist and Hommen, 2008), which reports on the findings from a comparative study of ten national systems of innovation (NSI) in small countries in Europe and Asia. Theoretically, the book employs an 'activities-based' framework for studying and comparing NSI. This means that it focuses strongly on what 'happens' in the systems – rather than on their constituents or elements – and, in this way, takes a more dynamic perspective. The introductory and concluding chapters address rival conceptions of NSI with differing perspectives on their systemic properties. Empirically, the book deals with the determinants of the development and diffusion of innovations, innovations and growth, and globalization and innovation policy in the NSI of Denmark, Finland, Hong Kong, Ireland, the Netherlands, Norway, the Republic of Korea, Singapore, Sweden and Taiwan. To increase comparabililty, we used the same conceptual and theoretical framework – and even a common table of contents – for the ten case studies.

2.6 UNCERTAINTY DIFFERS, AS DO POLICY INSTRUMENTS

We have noted that innovation processes are plagued by uncertainty. But the level of uncertainty is greater or smaller for different fields or sectors, for different kinds of innovations and in different stages of the innovation process. Uncertainty seems to be greater for innovation processes in new fields (compared to mature sectors/industries), for radical innovations (compared to incremental innovations), and in the early stages of innovation processes (compared to the late stages of those processes). Empirically, it seems to be the case that private organizations perform least well in situations where uncertainty is greatest.

Publicly funded R&D in combination with public technology procurement has played a crucial role in developing new high-technology sectoral systems of innovation in the USA – and thereby in the world. Examples are numerically controlled machine tools (NCMTs), commercial aircraft, semiconductors, computer hardware, computer software, lasers and the Internet (Carlsson and Jacobsson, 1997; Mowery, 2005). In the USA this is regarded as defence policy rather than innovation policy, and is financed by the US Department of Defense and the US Department of Energy (which are in charge, for example, of nuclear-related technologies and large scientific infrastructural establishments). Hence, public intervention seems to be the rule in *new* fields and new industries. All emerging fields of innovation are potentially interesting from a military point of view, and the US government has the resources to bet on all the horses in the race.

Radical technological shifts can also occur in mature industries. In these situations the picture is rather complicated. Sometimes the incumbent private actor is able to transform its activities along the new trajectory. Sometimes it fails. If these failures can be identified or foreseen, then public intervention to secure the transformation can be considered. There also seems to be a close connection between the situations just discussed and the early stages of innovation. For example, the supply of financing from private sources is much more limited for the very early stages of the innovation process. The gap between the end of an R&D project and the development of a product prototype is sometimes referred to in the USA as 'the valley of death'. Public organizations supply seed capital for the early stages in the USA and in many other countries simply because private capital is not available. The uncertainty is simply too great.

Globalization also poses new challenges to the issue of uncertainty. We argued earlier that policy intervention might be more desirable in the early stages of the innovation process or in emerging new fields where uncertainty is higher, when public support might create the incentive for firms to engage in high risk activities. But with globalization, the risk that a region or country will not reap the full benefits from its initial investments is increasing, as firms might choose to relocate their activities in a different country later on. Two positions seem to dominate the current debate on innovation policies in the global economy. On the one hand, there are those that argue that government policies to maintain competitive advantage are irrelevant and governments have no control over the behaviour of international firms and research activities. On the other hand, there are those that maintain that policy options should focus on adaptability to the new context, since all successful innovations necessarily entail organizational change and market success, requiring investment in the capabilities of the system of innovation to deal with uncertainty (Archibugi and Iammarino, 1999).

2.7   CONCLUDING REMARKS: IMPLICATIONS FOR INNOVATION POLICY

In this chapter we have discussed the impact of globalization on the rationales for public intervention. Globalization challenges some of the underlying assumptions of both the neoclassical and the evolutionary approaches to innovation policy, particularly those based on national-only sets of conditions. Furthermore, globalization adds a new perspective to the discussion of the issue of uncertainty in the innovation process. This chapter has indicated that a large degree of uncertainty may prevent private actors from getting involved in the innovation process, given the rapidly changing market conditions at the global level and the intrinsic uncertainties associated with operating in international markets with underdeveloped institutional frameworks. This is particularly so for activities that require substantial initial investments, such as the early stages of the innovation process or innovation in new fields.

In other words, globalization is not decreasing the need for innovation policy; on the contrary, it is increasing it. Firms are encountering rapidly changing and highly uncertain market and institutional conditions in the international context, on top of the technological uncertainties associated with inventive and innovative activities. For these reasons, public action needs to focus on the adaptability of the innovation system, with the overall objective of generating a national framework that is conducive to adaptability and efficient exploitation by firms of the opportunities offered by globalization. This means that public action should focus on the different systemic elements and their real bottlenecks vis-à-vis globalizing dynamics and, in particular, the deficient and/or missing aspects in the national institutional set-up that enhance firms' capabilities to operate in a globalized context.

Since public resources are scarce, systemic problems and bottlenecks are country-specific and opportunities are limited, innovation policy makers need to make important 'strategic choices' regarding how best to enhance the adaptability of the system in order to stimulate firms to grasp upcoming prospects. Innovation policy should serve as the midwife – not the end of life support. While investment in new fields and early stage activities seems appropriate for the type of policy instruments related to the allocation of R&D resources, there are many other innovation policy instruments that could focus on other issues. Examples are policies supporting the balance between individual and social returns (IPR), policies that create an adequate institutional framework to facilitate local interactions (regional development) or policies transforming low-technology industries into higher added value activities for the economy.

Strategic selectivity implies that policy makers should review existing and new policy instruments thoroughly, and carefully examine the extent to which those instruments are really and successfully addressing the problems and bottlenecks mentioned above. This thorough revision of policy instruments should not be undertaken on the basis of intuition, or as a mere 'copy' of what other countries have done. It has to be undertaken on the basis of a more sophisticated set of policy rationales anchored in an ample theoretical discussion. A new rationale for innovation policy must address the blind spots in previous theoretical discussions, provide a clear set of guidelines for policy makers' selection of instruments in specific contexts, and be able to generate an overall view of the causal mechanisms between real bottlenecks, possible policy responses to them and innovative output. Establishing this new set of rationales is an ambitious project, both in theoretical and in practical terms.

Therefore, there are mainly two conclusions of this chapter. First, the process of globalization imposes new demands on innovation policy, because firms are confronted with a new and rapidly changing international market and new institutional conditions. Innovation policy, therefore, should focus on improving the adaptability of the system of innovation, which in turn should help firms to acquire the competences and resources required to face global challenges. Second, the definition of rationales for public intervention (why, how and when should governments intervene) needs to be developed further and needs to be embedded in the specific social, economic and institutional context of each country. But, above all, a renewed framework of policy rationales should attempt to bridge the gap between policy makers' practice and the theoretical discussion of government intervention in the innovation system. In this vein, further theoretical and empirical research is needed to address the critical issue of designing a method to help public actors spell out objectives and instruments, and identify specific strategic choices for adapting systems of innovation.

NOTES

1. For example, according to the last World Investment Report (UNCTAD, 2006), in 2005, 57 of the transnational corporations listed by Fortune 500 were from developing countries compared to 19 in 1990.
2. There are no aggregated statistics available that capture this tendency, only anecdotal evidence of firms that have located R&D departments abroad.
3. Although in the previous lines we have emphasized the emerging trend of the changing role of some regions and industries in developing countries, it should be noted that the globalization of innovation is a phenomenon that affects both developed and developing regions. Furthermore, and as indicated in the introduction to this section, most of the flows continue to be north–north. At the same time, a large number of developing countries, for example, in Africa and Latin America, are not a part of this emerging trend.
4. The case of Novo Nordisk, a large Danish biotech corporation, illustrates this change. The firm has established a large R&D laboratory in China, which conducts basic research for a complete line of business worldwide to tap into the large pool of highly qualified researchers in that field available in China and to respond to the increasing scarcity of researchers in that particular scientific field in Denmark (Novo Nordisk, 2007; Boel, 2006).
5. It may be useful to distinguish between direct innovation policies, which are designed to influence innovation processes, and indirect innovation policies, which are designed to achieve other things – but influence innovation policies anyway (Edquist, 2001).
6. Note that in the 1950s and 1960s the main focus was on invention and the conditions for the production of knowledge. See Metcalfe (1995) for an excellent review of this matter.

REFERENCES

Altenburg, T., H. Schmitz and A. Stamm (2006), 'Building knowledge-based competitive advantages in China and India: lessons and consequences for other developing countries', paper presented at the Asian and Other Drivers of Global Change, Global Development Network Annual Conference, St Petersburg, Russia, January.

Archibugi, D. and S. Iammarino (1999), 'The policy implications of the globalisation of innovation', *Research Policy*, **28**(2–3), 303–16.

Archibugi, D. and B.-Å. Lundvall (2001), *The Globalizing Learning Economy*, Oxford: Oxford University Press.

Archibugi, D. and J. Michie (1995), 'The globalisation of technology: a new taxonomy', *Cambridge Journal of Economics*, **19**(1), 121–40.

Archibugi, D., J. Howells and J. Michie (1999), 'Innovation systems and policy in a global economy', in D. Archibugi, J. Howells and J. Michie (eds), *Innovation Policy in a Global Economy*, Cambridge: Cambridge University Press, pp. 1–18.

Arrow, K. J. (1962), 'The economic implications of learning by doing', *The Review of Economic Studies*, **29**(3), 155–73.

Asheim, B. T. and M. S. Gertler (2005), 'The geography of innovation: regional innovation systems', in J. Fagerberg, D. Mowery and R. Nelson (eds), *The Oxford Handbook of Innovation*, Oxford: Oxford University Press, pp. 291–317.

Baumol, W. J. (2002), *The Free-market Innovation Machine – Analysing the Growth Miracle of Capitalism*, Princeton, NJ: Princeton University Press.

Boel, E. (2006), 'Novo Nordisk R&D strategy in China', paper presented at the International Conference New Asian Dynamics in Science, Technology and Innovation, Gilleleje, Denmark, September, accessed 30 July 2007 at www.asian-dynamics.niasconferences.dk.

Cantwell, J. (1995), 'The globalisation of technology: what remains of the product cycle model?' *Cambridge Journal of Economics*, **19**(1), 155–74.

Cantwell, J. (1999), 'Innovation as the principal source of growth in the global economy', in D. Archibugi, J. Howells and J. Michie (eds), *Innovation Policy in a Global Economy*, Cambridge: Cambridge University Press, 225–41.

Cantwell, J. (2000), 'The role of multinational corporations and national states in the globalization of innovatory capacity: the European perspective', *Technology Analysis & Strategic Management*, **12**(2), 243–62.

Carlsson, B. and S. Jacobsson (1997), 'Diversity creation and technological systems: a technology policy perspective' in C. Edquist (ed.), *Systems of Innovation: Technologies, Organisations and Institutions*, London: Pinter, pp. 266–94.

Castellacci, F. (2006), 'Convergence and divergence among technology clubs', paper presented at the DRUID Conference, Copenhagen, Denmark, June, accessed 30 July 2007 at www.druid.dk/wp/pdf_files.org/06–21.pdf.

Chaminade, C. and C. Edquist (forthcoming), 'Rationales for public policy intervention in the innovation process: a systems of innovation approach', in S. Kuhlman, P. Shapira and R. Smits (eds), *The Co-evolution of Innovation Policy*, Oxford: Oxford University Press.

Chaminade, C. and J. Vang (2006a), 'Innovation policy for Asian SMEs: an innovation systems perspective', in H. Yeung (ed.) *Handbook of Research on Asian Business*, Cheltenham, UK and Northampton, MA, USA: Edward Elgar, pp. 381–408.

Chaminade, C. and J. Vang (2006b), 'Globalisation of knowledge production and regional innovation policy: supporting specialized hubs in developing countries', CIRCLE electronic working paper 2006/15.

Dosi, G. and L. Orsenigo (1988), 'Coordination and transformation: an overview of structures, behaviour and change in evolutionary environments', in G. Dosi,

D. Teece and J. Chytrys (eds), *Technical Change and Economic Theory*, London: Pinter, pp. 13–37.

Economist Intelligence Unit (2007), 'Sharing the idea: the emergence of global innovation networks', accessed 30 July 2007 at www.eiu.com.

Edquist, C. (1997), 'Systems of innovation approaches – their emergence and characteristics', in C. Edquist (ed.), *Systems of Innovation: Technologies, Organisations and Institutions*, London: Pinter, pp. 1–35.

Edquist, C. (2001), 'Innovation policy – a systemic approach', in D. Archibugi and B.-Å. Lundvall (eds), *The Globalizing Learning Economy*, Oxford: Oxford University Press, pp. 219–39.

Edquist, C. (2005), 'Systems of innovation – perspectives and challenges', in J. Fagerberg, D. C. Mowery and R. R. Nelson (eds), Oxford: Oxford University Press, pp. 181–208.

Edquist, C. and L. Hommen (2008) *Small Country Innovation Systems: Globalisation, Change and Policy in Asia and Europe*. Cheltenham, UK and Northampton, MA, USA: Edward Elgar.

Johansson, B. and H. Lööf (2006), *Global Location Patterns of R&D Investments*, CESIS electronic working paper series, April 2006, accessed 30 July, 2007 at www.infra.kth.se/cesis/documents/WP60.pdf.

Loasby, B. J. (2001), 'Time, knowledge and evolutionary dynamics: why connections matter', *Journal of Evolutionary Economics*, 11(4), 393–412.

Lundvall, B.-Å. (ed.) (1992), *National Systems of Innovation. Towards a Theory of Innovation and Interactive Learning*, London: Pinter.

Lundvall, B.-Å. (2005), 'Interactive learning, social capital and economic performance', paper presented at the Advancing Knowledge and the Knowledge Economy Conference, Washington, DC, 10–11 January, accessed 30 July 2007 at www.business.aau.dk/ike/upcoming/ Washington_paper.pdf.

Lundvall, B.-Å. and S. Borrás (1998), *The Globalising Learning Economy: Implications for Innovation Policy*, Brussels: European Commission.

Machlup, F. (1980), *Knowledge: Its Creation, Distribution, and Economic Significance. Vol. 1, Knowledge and Knowledge Production*, Princeton, NJ: Princeton University Press.

Malerba, F. (2004), *Sectoral Systems of Innovation: Concepts, Issues and Analysis of Six Major Sectors in Europe*, Cambridge: Cambridge University Press.

Marin, A. and M. Bell (2006), 'Technology spillovers from foreign direct investment (FDI): the active role of MNC subsidiaries in Argentina in the 1990s', *Journal of Development Studies*, 42(4), 678–97.

Metcalfe, S. (1995), 'The economic foundations of technology policy: equilibrium and evolutionary perspectives', in P. Stoneman (ed.), *Handbook of the Economics of Innovation and Technological Change*, Oxford: Blackwell, pp. 409–512.

Mowery, D. (2005), 'National security and national innovation systems', paper presented at the PRIME/PREST workshop on Re-evaluating the Role of Defence and Security R&D in the Innovation System, University of Manchester, 19–21 September.

Narula, R. (2000), 'Industrial development, globalization and multinational enterprises: new realities for developing countries', *Oxford Development Studies*, 28(2), 141–67.

Narula, R. and A. Zanfei (2005), 'Globalization of innovation: the role of multinational enterprises', in J. Fagerberg, D. C. Mowery and R. R. Nelson (eds), *The Oxford Handbook of Innovation*, Oxford: Oxford University Press, pp. 318–47.

Nelson, R. R. (1959), 'The simple economics of basic scientific research', *Journal of Political Economy,* **67**(3), 297–306.
Nelson, R. R. and S. Winter (1982), *An Evolutionary Theory of Economic Change,* Cambridge, MA: Harvard University Press.
Nooteboom, B. (2000), 'Learning by interaction: absorptive capacity, cognitive distance and governance', *Journal of Management and Governance,* **4**(1–2), 69–92.
Novo Nordisk (2007), accessed 26 April 2007 at www.novonordisk.com/jobs/ working_at_novo_nordisk/ novo_nordisk_geographical_sites/china_uk.asp.
OECD (2006), *Main Science and Technology Indicators 2006–2,* Paris: OECD.
Partharasarathy, B. and Y. Aoyama (2006), 'From software services to R&D services: local entrepreneurship in the software industry in Bangalore, India', *Environment and Planning A,* **38**(7), 1269–85.
Schmitz, H. (2006), 'Asian drivers: typologies and questions', *IDS Bulletin,* **37**(1), 54–61.
Schumpeter, J. (1943), *Capitalism, Socialism and Democracy,* New York: Harper & Row.
Smith, K. (2000), 'Innovation as a systemic phenomenon: rethinking the role of policy', *Enterpries and Innovation Management Studies,* **1**(1), 73–102.
United Nations Conference on Trade and Development (UNCTAD) (2006*), World Investment Report,* Geneva: UNCTAD.
Vang, J., C. Chaminade and L. Coenen (forthcoming), 'Learning from the Bangalore experience: the role of universities in an emerging regional innovation system', in G. Parayil and A. D'Costa (eds), *New Asian Dynamics in Science, Technology and Innovation,* Technology, Globalization and Development book series, Basingstoke, Hampshire: Macmillan.
Woolthius, R. K. and M. Lankhuizen (2005), 'A system failure framework for innovation policy design', *Technovation,* **25**, 609–19.

3. Globalization and offshoring of software

William Aspray, Frank Mayadas and Moshe Y. Vardi

3.1 INTRODUCTION[1]

Computer science and technology (S&T) have been stunningly successful in forging a global market. These tools have enabled the information technology (IT) industry to create innovations that have driven down data and voice communication costs almost to zero; added Web features that provide information to anyone – anywhere, anytime; driven hardware costs so low that this technology is affordable in developing countries; developed standardized curricula and made educational material widely available; and produced agreed upon software standards that enable different machines and systems to interoperate. Globalization has resulted in billions of people joining the world free market, and dozens of countries joining the World Trade Organization (WTO). This trend has produced a world where not only goods, but also labour are tradeable, and can be sent over a wire rather than physically relocated.

The Association of Computing Machinery's (ACM) Job Migration Task Force undertook an in-depth study of software offshoring, including its extent and magnitude, perspectives of key countries and companies, globalization of research activities, risks and exposures and counter-balancing steps underway or contemplated in key countries. The findings of the study, which was published in 2006, point to continuing growth in the IT sector in both developing and developed countries and that, in contrast to media predictions, offshoring is not having an adverse impact on IT employment in developed countries.[2] At the same time, the study highlights intensifying competition within the global IT market and suggests the need for increased national investments in education and innovation to sustain competitive edge and technological leadership.

3.2 SOFTWARE GLOBALIZATION: THE BIG PICTURE

Over the past decade, low-wage countries, such as India, have developed vibrant, export-oriented software and IT service industries. Attracted by available talent, quality work and, most of all, low cost, companies in high-wage countries, such as the US and the UK, are increasingly offshoring software and service work to these low-wage countries. Since 1970, trade (together with automation) has caused many jobs in the manufacturing sector to be lost from the West and many developing nations in East Asia to increase their wealth and industrial prowess. Changes in technology, work organization, education systems and many other factors have caused service work – previously regarded as immune to these forces – also to become tradeable. This trade in services, led by the trade in software and IT-enabled services, presents many opportunities and challenges for individuals, firms and policy makers in both developed and developing nations.

Many people in the US and Western Europe fear that sending software work offshore will cause wage and job suppression in the high-wage countries. Others believe that the process of getting good labour at lower prices will make the economy more productive, enabling the creation of new wealth and new jobs. Many people in the low-wage countries are excited by the economic development that their software and service industries are bringing, while some are concerned about side effects such as congestion, pollution and loss of traditional cultural values. One thing that is clear is that the globalization of software is here to stay, so that policy makers, educators and employers all need to address the realities of offshoring. This includes, for example, how to help people whose jobs are shipped to another country to get assistance with their careers, how to create innovative environments that help to create new jobs and how to revamp education systems for the realities of a globalized world.

There are at least six types of work sent offshore related to software and IT: (1) programming, software testing and software maintenance; (2) IT research and development (R&D); (3) high-end jobs such as software architecture, product design, project management, IT consulting and business strategy; (4) physical product manufacturing – semiconductors, computer components, computers; (5) business process outsourcing/IT enabled services – insurance claims processing, medical billing, accounting, bookkeeping, medical transcription, digitization of engineering drawings, desktop publishing and high-end IT enabled services such as financial analysis and reading of X-rays; and (6) call centres and telemarketing. Our primary interest is with the first three of these categories, which are the ones most closely associated with the transfer of software work across national boundaries.

The countries that send work offshore are primarily developed nations. The US followed by the UK have been the largest offshorers, but other countries in Western Europe, Japan, Korea, Australia and even India send work offshore. The countries that receive the work fall into four categories: (1) those that have a large workforce of highly educated workers and a low-wage scale (e.g., India, China); (2) those that have special language skills (e.g., the Philippines, being proficient in both languages, can serve the English and Spanish customer service needs of the US); (3) those with geographic proximity ('nearsourcing'), familiarity with the work language and customs, and relatively low wages compared to the country sending the work (e.g., Canada accepting work from the US, the Czech Republic accepting work from Germany); and (4) special high-end skills (e.g., Israel's strengths in security and anti-virus software).

There are many drivers and enablers of offshoring. (1) The dot-com boom years witnessed a rapid expansion of telecommunications systems, making ample, low-cost broadband available at attractive rates in many countries. This made it possible to readily transfer the data and work products of software offshoring. (2) Software platforms were stabilized, with most large companies using a few standard choices: IBM or Oracle for database management, SAP for supply chain management and so on. This enabled offshoring suppliers to focus on acquiring only these technologies and hiring people who were knowledgeable about them. (3) Companies were able to use inexpensive commodity software packages rather than customized software, which produced some of the same advantages from standardization as applied to software platforms. (4) The pace of technological change was sufficiently rapid and software investments were becoming obsolescent so quickly that many companies considered it better to outsource IT rather than invest in technology and people that would soon have to be replaced or retrained. In addition, companies that saw their competitors switch to offshoring felt a compulsion to follow suit. (5) Influential industrialists, such as General Electric's Jack Welch, became champions of offshoring, while venture capitalists were pushing entrepreneurial startups to use offshoring as a means to reduce the burn rate of capital. (6) New firms began to emerge to serve as intermediaries, to make it easier for small and medium-sized firms to send their work offshore. (7) Work processes were digitalized, routinized and broken into separable tasks by skills sets – some of which were easy to outsource. (8) Education became more available globally, with model curricula provided by the professional computing societies, low capital barriers to establishing computer laboratories following the spread of personal computers and packaged software, national plans to strengthen undergraduate education as a competitive advantage and greater access to Western graduate education as immigration restrictions were eased. (9) Citizens of

India and China, who had received their graduate education in the US or Western Europe and initially worked there, began to return home in large numbers, creating a reverse diaspora that provided these countries with highly educated and experienced workers and managers. (10) In the case of India, there was and is a large population familiar with the English language – the language of global business and law, and its accounting and legal systems are similar to those in the UK and the US. (11) Global trade is becoming ever more prevalent, with individual countries, such as India and China, liberalizing their economies, the fall of communism lowering trade barriers and many more countries participating in international trade organizations.

At first it was believed that the only software work that would be off-shored was low-level work, such as routine maintenance and testing, routine business office processes and call centres. Offshoring suppliers, however, have made strong efforts to move up the value chain and provide services with higher value added because this is where there is the greatest opportunity for profit. R&D, project integration and knowledge process outsourcing, such as reading X-rays and checking patents, are increasingly being offshored. And some people believe that any kind of software or IT-enabled work can be offshored. While there is some foundation for this belief, there are some important caveats, and there are some types of work that have not been offshored.

Even if it were possible to offshore a particular type of work, it does not mean that every job of that type would be offshored. In fact, there are a number of reasons why a company might not wish to offshore work:

- The job process has not been made routine.
- The job cannot be done at a distance.
- The infrastructure in the offshore country is too weak.
- Offshoring would impact negatively on the client firm, for instance, the client firm could lose control over an important element, it might lose all its in-house expertise in an area and it runs the risk of severely reduced morale among its workers.
- Risks to privacy, data security and intellectual property (IP) are too high.
- There are no workers in the supplier firm with the requisite knowl-edge for the work; this can occur when a job requires application domain as well as IT knowledge.
- The costs involved in opening or maintaining an offshore operation are too high.
- There are cultural differences that act as a barrier between client and vendor.

- The company can achieve the benefits of offshoring by outsourcing within the home country or consolidating its business operations.

One might wonder whether IT is still a good career choice for students and workers in countries that offshore software and IT services work. Despite all the publicity in the US about jobs being lost to India and China, the size of the IT employment market in the US in 2007 is higher than it was at the height of the dot-com boom. IT, aggregated across all industry sectors, is likely to be a growth area at least until 2015, and US government projections are that several IT occupations will be among the fastest growing occupations in this period. There are some things that students and workers in this field could and should do to prepare themselves for the globalized workplace. They should get a good education that will serve as a firm grounding for understanding the rapidly changing field of IT. They should expect to participate in life-long learning, which means learning intensively in the workplace, as well as participating in more formal kinds of education and training. They should hone their 'soft skills' involving communication, management and teamwork. They should familiarize themselves with application-specific domains in particular industries, especially in growth fields such as health care, in addition to acquiring core technical computing skills. They should learn about the technologies and management issues that underlie the globalization of software, such as standard technology platforms, methods for reusing software, and the tools and project management for geographically distributed work.

3.3   THE ECONOMICS OF OFFSHORING

Much of the economic debate on offshoring centres around whether the theory of comparative advantage applies to the offshoring of software and IT services. Economists have argued on both sides. The arguments are sophisticated and nuanced, and the outcomes often depend on whether the underlying assumptions hold in the current context. While a majority of economists believe that free trade 'lifts all boats' equally, the underlying question is an empirical one and can be answered by analysing reliable data as they become available.

The theory of comparative advantage states that if each of two countries specializes in the production of goods in which it has a comparative (relative) advantage, then both countries will enjoy greater total consumption and well-being in aggregate, by trading with each other. Offshoring, for example, enables US firms to lower costs and save scarce resources for activities in which they have a relative advantage, while at the same time it provides significant employment and wage gains for Indian workers and rapid profit and revenue increases for Indian businesses.

What the theory of comparative advantage does not mean is that all members of society will benefit from trade. In general, imports of an 'input' have economic effects that are similar to those of an increase in the supply of the input, namely, lower returns to the suppliers of the input, lower costs of production and lower prices for consumers. If the input were a service, the wages and salaries of those producing the service would fall, but so also would the costs for the firms that are the buyers of the service. In the exporting country the opposite is true. That is, the returns to the owners or suppliers of the service or input increase, and the wages of the service providers' employees increase due to higher demand.

Economists believe that trade generally leads to significant benefits for the trading countries. These gains are not inconsistent with employment losses in specific sectors that cause economic pain for the workers affected. To achieve an equitable result, many analysts believe that it is important to establish a safety net that provides income and training opportunities to affected workers. Components of the safety net might include extended unemployment benefits, wages insurance and retraining.

A key assumption underlying the theory of comparative advantage is that the economy enjoys full employment. Thus, this theory is best thought of as a theory of the long term, in which workers displaced by imports or offshoring find work in other sectors. By contrast, most popular discussions of the offshoring phenomenon tend to focus on questions such as 'where will the new jobs be created' and 'can the workers be retrained for these new jobs'. In general, peering into a crystal ball to predict where and what types of new jobs will be created is both difficult and unrewarding. A dynamic economy, such as that of the US, creates and destroys millions of new jobs in response to changes in tastes and, more importantly, in response to innovations and advances in technology. There is no guarantee that the economy will continue to create these new jobs, but policy makers can take some comfort from the historical evidence that, thus far, it has managed to do so. The key to job creation is, of course, the ability of the economy to rapidly generate and adopt innovations – new types of goods and services, and productivity-enhancing process improvements.

In general, trade stimulates innovation and economic growth in both trading partners. Some, such as Ralph Gomory and William Baumol, have argued that completely free trade can create possible new conflicts of interest between trading partners. For example, insofar as in countries such as China, offshoring stimulates innovation and productivity growth in goods and services where developed countries such as the US enjoy a comparative advantage, this will cause the 'terms of trade' to become less favourable over time for the US. In other words, even if free trade is the best policy, it may well be that free trade, by stimulating innovation overseas, may impose long-term losses. However, Gomory and Baumol's (Gomory and Baumol, 2000) analysis shows that this conflict of interest (deriving from unequal benefits of free trade) is most pronounced when the two trading partners are at similar stages of development. Since most current offshoring involves countries at very different levels of development, this conflict of interest is still in the future.

In the IT services sector there is a related concern. Currently, it is efficient to offshore 'low-end' IT services, such as coding or maintenance, to a low-wage country while 'high-end' activities, such as requirements analysis, design and R&D, remain in the high-wage country. The concern is that eventually the high-end IT activities would also move offshore. Were this to happen, the current technology leaders (US, Germany, Japan, UK and so on) may lose that leadership role. There is some anecdotal evidence that some IT process innovations are moving to low-wage, offshoring operations.

However, most economists argue that the current technology leaders will not lose their technological leadership positions. Even if production moves to other countries, history shows that in many industries the locus of production and the locus of invention are physically separated. There are two key resources required to remain at the centre of innovation in software: access to talented designers, software engineers and programmers, and proximity to a number of large and technically sophisticated users. Current technology leaders, and the US in particular, dominate on both counts. More broadly, the US has other important capabilities, including the best universities and research institutions, highly efficient capital markets, flexible labour markets, the largest consumer market, business-friendly immigration laws and a large and deep pool of managerial talent. As a result, the evolution of business in the US has followed a consistent pattern: launch innovative businesses at home, grow the business and, as products and services mature, over time migrate lower value-added components and intermediate services to lower-cost countries. Nevertheless, there are those who argue that globalization will diminish the comparative advantage of the current technology leaders, leading to a loss of their current dominant position and creating a long period of adjustment for their workers.

3.4 UNDERSTANDING OFFSHORING FROM A NATIONAL PERSPECTIVE

The first countries to develop software industries primarily for export rather than domestic purposes were Ireland and Israel. The big player to come in a little later was India, beginning in the mid 1970s and growing rapidly from the late 1990s. To some degree, a global division of labour is beginning to form: India serving the English-speaking world, Eastern Europe and Russia serving Western Europe, and China serving Japan. But India also provides services to Western Europe, and China serves the US. In addition, there are many smaller supplier countries. The ACM report focuses greatest attention on the US and India, the two biggest players.

The US historically has dominated and continues to dominate the software and services industry, with about 80 per cent of global revenue. It is also dominant in the packaged services industry with 16 of the top 20 companies worldwide, and slightly less commanding, but still dominant, in the software services sector, with 11 of the top 20 companies. This dominance is based on a number of factors, including a legacy of government funding of R&D, computer science research in the open US higher education system, a skilled workforce created by a strong university system, a culture of risk taking and the capital to finance risks, early adoption by sophisticated users, the world's largest economy and market, and leading semiconductor and data storage industries that have helped to spread the use of computing. The centrality and dominance of the US industry has been a given since the 1950s. What is emerging is the globalization of the software and software services industry. This creates opportunities around the world for people and companies in both developed and developing countries to participate in this profitable industry. It also creates challenges for the former leaders, notably the US, Western Europe and Japan.

Software services is India's largest export. As a large developing nation, India faces many challenges including: high rates of poverty, corruption and illiteracy; a substandard infrastructure; excessive government regulation; and various other problems typical of a poor nation. These challenges are offset by a number of strengths, especially for software and services production. It has a long history of developing capable mathematicians. India is unique in terms of the large number of individuals with adequate English language capability and the large cadre of Indian management and technical professionals working in North American and, to a lesser degree, in European high-technology occupations and organizations. For those that can afford it, India has a strong and highly competitive primary and secondary education system emphasizing science and mathematics. Despite its democratic socialist tradition, which involved huge amounts of bureaucracy and state regulation, it has been a market economy and has a history of management education and competence. These assets have given India many advantages in establishing a software export industry.

India's software export industry began in 1974, when it started sending programmers to the US to do work for the Burroughs Corporation.

Political liberalizations related to trade in the 1970s and again in the early 1990s helped to support the development of the Indian software industry. Offering solutions to the Y2K problem helped the industry to grow substantially; it expanded beginning in the late 1990s, first by bringing back to India much of the software development, maintenance and testing work previously done on the client's premises, then developing an export trade in business process offshoring, call centres and R&D. India is moving up the value chain and is seeking people considerably more skilled than low-level programmers to do these higher value jobs. Software and service export firms in India are growing at 20 per cent to 25 per cent per year according to the best statistics available, and the three leading Indian software firms (Infosys, TCS and Wipro) already employ over 40 000 people.

India's software industry is likely to continue to grow in scale, scope and value added. There is little reason to believe that offshoring as a process will end in the foreseeable future, but it could slow down. The enormous investment by leading software multinationals will expand the number of Indian project managers with strong managerial skills. This, together with the relocation of portions of startup firms to India, is likely to result in greater levels of entrepreneurship and produce firms able to sell their skills on the global market. The offshoring of IT services and software for export will dominate the near future of the Indian software industry. There are several possible trajectories. Custom projects could become more complex and large, leading Indian software professionals to move from programming into systems integration and systems specification and design. The average size of the projects that Indian firms are undertaking has already grown from 5 person years in 1991 to 20 person years in 2003. As multinationals deepen their Indian operations, domain skills are developing in India and some other nations, so that managed services are likely to become more important; this will match global trends in the outsourcing of applications management and business processes.

Despite the fact that India's software production for the US market exceeds that of any other nation, it holds only a small share of the global market for all software value added. The only part of the software value chain in which India has made substantial inroads is in applications development, where it has captured 16.4 per cent of the world market. But applications development is only approximately 5 per cent of the entire global software services market. This implies that there is much room for growth. In order to grow, the Indian industry will have to shift to more complex activities by securing larger projects, undertaking engineering services, integrating and managing services or bidding for projects that include transforming a client's entire work process. India, however, will have some difficulty in achieving this growth unless it strengthens its R&D capability.

Software offshoring to India is likely to grow; indigenous Indian firms are continuing to grow and foreign software firms are increasing their employment in India in product development and particularly in software services. Competition is likely to grow between multinationals based in developed countries, such as Accenture, IBM and Siemens Business Services, and the large Indian firms, such as HCL, Infosys, TCS and Wipro, as the multinationals expand their operations in low-cost countries and the Indian companies expand their global reach. The Indian subsidiaries of multinationals are playing an important role in the development of India's software capabilities, because they are more willing to undertake high value-added activities, such as software product development, within their own subsidiary in India than they are to send the work to an independent Indian firm. For at least the medium term, India should be able to retain its position of primacy for software offshoring from the English-speaking world. In the longer term, unless India makes an even greater effort to upgrade its universities and the technical capabilities of its graduates, China may become an important alternative destination.

China's software and services industry currently does not have a major impact on the world economy. The industry is highly fragmented into many small companies, few of which are big enough to take on large projects for developed nations. The hardware industry is well established in China, and in the future it may drive the software industry to a focus on embedded software. Unlike India, where the multinationals are focused mainly on serving the world market, in China multinationals are focused more on positioning themselves to serve the enormous, emerging Chinese domestic market.

Japan has the second largest software and services industry in the world after the US, and it is the fastest growing industry in Japan. Japan makes games software and custom software for the world market, and packaged software for its domestic market. It imports a significant amount of systems and applications software from the US, and it calls on China and India to provide custom software. There are three typical patterns of Japanese offshoring. Most commonly, a Japanese firm will identify a need for custom software, contract with a Japanese IT company to provide the software, and this IT company in its turn will contract with a Japanese subsidiary of a Chinese firm to do the programming work. This programming was once done almost exclusively in Japan, but as the cost of locating Chinese workers in Japan has grown, more and more programming is being done in China. A second, more recent approach is for Japanese firms to invest in China to form wholly owned subsidiaries or joint ventures with Chinese firms. A third approach is for multinational corporations to move the programming and back-office functions of their Japanese subsidiaries to lower-cost locations, often in China. The Dalian software park in China is growing rapidly as a result of this emerging Japanese business. The amount of offshoring from Japan is still small, but cost pressures are likely to cause it to increase; and since Japan has such a large software industry, the opportunities for offshoring are considerable.

The European Union (EU) represents the second largest market in the world for software and IT services after the US. There are many differences, however, from country to country, and the EU cannot be viewed as a unified, homogeneous market. The European software industry and employment patterns are different from those of the US, with much more software production done in-house and embedded in physical products. This does not prevent offshoring, and certainly many leading European industrial firms are establishing offshore facilities to produce embedded software. Much of this employment is subsumed under R&D and other activities such as application-specific integrated circuit design.

About two-thirds of the work offshored from Europe is from the UK. Continental European firms continue to lag behind UK firms in sending software work across their borders. The Germanic and Nordic nations have only recently begun to build offshore software and software service delivery capabilities, but firms with global practices, such as SAP, Siemens and others, are moving rapidly to build their own offshore capabilities in Eastern Europe, China and India. The geography of European offshoring will be somewhat different from that of the US in that Nordic and Germanic firms will use Eastern Europe and Russia in addition to India. Latin (Romance-language-speaking) Europe has been slower to begin offshoring, but now its major firms are sending work to Romania, Francophone Africa (particularly Morocco) and Latin America in addition to India. Despite these geographical differences, there is no reason to believe that the pressures to offshore software-related work will be substantially different than in the Anglophone nations. In part this is because the US-based multinationals with strong global delivery capabilities, such as Accenture, EDS, Hewlett-Packard and IBM, are present and competitive in all European markets. European firms may continue to experience a lag due to union and government opposition to offshoring, but their cost and delivery pressures are similar to those experienced by US firms.

In Russia software was a relatively neglected field during the Soviet era, but in the 1990s, with the transition to a market economy, many Russian scientists and engineers moved from low-paid government and university positions into entrepreneurial firms and Russian subsidiaries of multinationals; and some of these people entered the software field. So far there are relatively few programmers in Russia. Wages are low. The technical skills level is high, but there is little project management experience. Software firms are typically small, and unable to take on large international software integration projects. Nevertheless, the high skills level of the Russian research community, a legacy of its Soviet history, has led Intel and a few other multinationals, including Boeing, Motorola, Nortel and Sun, to open R&D facilities in Russia.

3.5   UNDERSTANDING OFFSHORING FROM A COMPANY PERSPECTIVE

Instead of examining offshoring by country, it is possible to examine it by type of company. We will consider five types of firms. The first are large, established software firms, headquartered in developed nations, that make and sell packaged software. Examples include Adobe, Microsoft and Oracle. As a general rule, the largest and most successful packaged software firms are headquartered in the US, the notable exception being SAP in Germany.

Most large packaged software firms have global operations. In many cases their offshore operations are for localization work for the local domestic market. However, particularly in the case of India, and also to some degree in Russia, offshoring work is for the development of their worldwide software packages. Locating in these low-wage countries gives these firms access to lower-cost programmers, many of whose skills are comparable to those of the companies' workers in the developed nations. This is not the only benefit. Having facilities in other time zones can speed up production by facilitating round-the-clock operations. These opportunities are encouraging major packaged software firms to expand their workforce in India and other lower-cost nations.

The effect of offshoring on packaged software firms will be complex. First, it might and likely will put pressure on developed nations' software firms to decrease employment in the developed countries. On the other hand, the lower cost and faster production enabled by offshoring could allow the development of new features in old software and could contribute to the creation of new, well-priced software products, which could in turn increase income for these firms and perhaps lead to increased hiring.

Next we consider large, established software firms headquartered in developed nations that are major providers of software services. These companies may also provide packaged software, though not all of them do so. Examples include Accenture, EDS and IBM. Software services firms are among the fastest growing firms in the IT sector and, in general, they are far larger than the packaged software firms. Firms on the software side (e.g. Hewlett Packard, IBM) and on the services side (e.g. Accenture) are converging. In the case of IBM, this has occurred through direct hiring and through IBM's recent acquisition of the Indian service firm Daksh (and its approximately 6 000 employees). Hewlett Packard has built its global non-IT services to over 4 000 persons in the last three years, largely through in-house hiring.

Software services is in most respects a headcount and labour cost business; these companies grow their revenues by hiring more people. The multinational software services firms have been experiencing increasing pressure on costs due to competition from developing nation producers, particularly from the Indian service giants, such as Infosys, TCS and Wipro. This has forced the multinationals themselves to secure lower-cost offshore labour. Service firms, such as Accenture, ACS, EDS, IBM and Siemens Business Services, operate globally, but only in the last five years have they found it necessary to have major operations in developing nations to decrease their labour costs. The larger service firms, including Accenture and IBM, are rapidly increasing their headcount in a number of developing nations, particularly India. At the same time, these firms are holding steady on their developed nation headcount or gradually reducing it. Given the ferocious competition in software services, there is little possibility that prices will increase substantially. This suggests that, for the large multinationals, the offshoring of services will continue to increase both in absolute numbers and percentages of their global workforce.

Next we consider firms headquartered in developed nations that have software operations, but are not part of the software industry sector. This is the enormous and eclectic group of companies that provide all the non-IT goods and services in the economy. Software is now at the heart of value creation in nearly every firm, from financial firms, such as Citibank, to manufacturing firms, such as General Motors. Customizing, maintaining and updating IT systems has become an increasingly significant expenditure for businesses in developed countries, and thus firms are actively trying to lower these cost. One way to lower them is to offshore the work to nations with lower labour costs.

It is difficult to estimate the amount of software work that is offshored by these companies. Businesses often do not break out this particular kind of expense, and if work is transferred to an overseas subsidiary, this is considered an internal transfer and may not be reported at all. However, it is clear who does the work. If it is not an overseas subsidiary of the company, then it is likely to be one of two other kinds of firms that provide the service: a large service firm from a developed nation (e.g. Accenture, CapGemini, IBM or Siemens Business Services) or a firm from a developing nation (e.g. Infosys or TCS in India, Luxoft in Russia or Softech in Mexico).

It is not certain whether offshoring will lead to a decline in the number of software service employees employed in the developed nations. In the current economic recovery, the firm headcount throughout the IT sector in the US appears to be stagnant. For other sectors, limited data are available. For example, in financial services it is not known whether the increasing headcount in developing nations has had any impact on employment in the developed nations. The most that can be said is that non-IT firms are increasing their IT employment in developing nations to serve the global market, and this trend is underway across many different firms, including industrial firms, such as General Electric and General Motors.

The next group of firms is the software-intensive small firms, particularly startups, based in developed nations. For small startups, offshoring is often a difficult decision, although recently a number of firms in the US have been established with the express purpose of facilitating offshoring for access to skilled engineers at lower cost. For many smaller firms, an offshore facility can be demanding on management time. This is especially true for offshoring to India where hiring and retaining highly skilled individuals is difficult. The protection of IP, which is typically the most important asset of a technology startup, is problematic in India and more especially China. There is substantial anecdotal evidence that, despite these challenges, under pressure from their venture capital backers and the need to conserve funds, small startups are establishing subsidiaries abroad, particularly in India, to lower the costs and increase the speed of software development.

A pattern is emerging for US startups. They may initially use outsourcing, say, to an Indian firm, as a strategy, but many soon establish a subsidiary in place of the Indian firm. They do this for a variety of reasons, including worries about IP protection, control of the labour force and management efficiency. The minimum size of an offshored operation can reportedly be as few as ten persons. If such reports are accurate, then it may be possible for many more small firms than have done so thus far to establish subsidiaries in developing nations. Unfortunately, data on the scale and scope of offshoring by startups are unavailable.

It is tempting to view offshoring by startups (whether to an Indian firm or to their own overseas subsidiary) as an unmitigated loss of jobs for US workers. However, the real situation is more complicated. Lowering the cost of undertaking a startup could mean that the barriers to entry are lowered, thus encouraging greater entrepreneurship. The jobs created by this entrepreneurship should be counted against those lost to offshoring. So, correctly estimating the employment net effect of offshoring in the case of startups is very difficult.

Finally, we consider firms in developing nations providing software services to firms in the developed nations. The availability of capable software programmers in developing nations provided an opportunity for entrepreneurs and existing firms to offer programming services on the global market.

It was in India where this practice first began in a significant way. Because telecommunications links were less sophisticated, the Indian programmers initially were placed in the US customer's premises. This practice was profitable and gradually expanded to include remote provision of services – often to do Y2K work – when telecommunications improved and demand heated up in the late 1990s. These developments created an environment where major corporations were willing to experiment with overseas vendors, and a sufficient number of these experiments proved satisfactory. The result was that offshore vendors, particularly Indian firms, were validated as candidates for software-related projects. These projects also enabled offshore vendors, again Indian firms especially, to grow in headcount, experience and financial resources, allowing them to undertake larger and more complicated projects.

Software services firms from a number of the developing nations have become players in the global economy. The large Indian firms (HCL, Infosys, Satyam, TCS and Wipro) are at present the global leaders. However, in China, Mexico and Russia there are software service firms employing 1 000 to 5 000 people. Currently, the firms from other nations are not large enough to compete with either the multinationals headquartered in developed nations or the large Indian firms. Medium-sized firms in other countries, however, can reduce the risk for customers of having all their offshore work done in one country, where it might be interrupted by a natural disaster or by political or military problems. The larger multinationals and Indian firms are also establishing facilities in other geographic areas, particularly Eastern Europe and, more recently, Mexico.

Firms are leading a global restructuring of the geography of software and software services production. They are experimenting with a variety of strategies meant to utilize workers that have become available in the global economy. This is true of software product firms as well as multinational and developing nation software service providers. The impact of firms outside the IT sector with large internal software operations transferring some of their software operations to lower-cost environments has been less remarked upon; however, should the current trend continue, it will have a substantial effect on IT employment. These firms have already relocated a significant amount of work from high-cost to lower-cost environments, and this process appears likely to continue and possibly accelerate, as firms become more comfortable working in developing nations. The offshoring of startup employment bears particular observation because the US high-technology economy in particular is dependent upon the employment growth provided by small startups.

3.6 EDUCATION AND RESEARCH IN LIGHT OF OFFSHORING

Offshoring creates major changes in the demand for workers. Some countries need more workers, others fewer. Offshoring also causes the set of skills and knowledge of workers to change. Education is a tool that enables a country to provide the skilled workers that it needs, and thus it can be the centrepiece of a national policy on offshoring. Developing countries that are building up their software service export markets, such as India and China, need to prepare growing numbers of people to work in this industry. The developed countries are facing questions about how to revise their education systems to prepare their citizens for the jobs that will remain when other jobs have moved to lower-wage countries. These developed countries also have to find ways of making their education systems serve to increase the technological innovation that has historically driven productivity gains, new employment and new wealth for nations.

The US has a well-established and complex IT education system. The bachelor's degree is the primary degree for people entering a computing career. While degree programmes appear under many names, five majors cover most of the programmes: computer science, computer engineering, software engineering, information systems and IT. Although there are some differences among these five types of programmes, they have many similarities in terms of providing foundational knowledge related to computer programming, the possibilities and limitations of computers, how computers and computing work in certain real world applications, various skills related to communication and teamwork and other topics. Non-degree programmes also play an important role in US IT education.

Recent changes in Europe, following the Bologna Declaration, are aimed at unifying European education systems along the lines of the American system of separate bachelors and masters degrees. The Bologna process provides for a standardized sequencing of degree programmes, makes it less time consuming to obtain the first undergraduate degree, and makes the system more open for students who received their baccalaureate degrees in developing nations to enter masters programmes without having to repeat some of their earlier training. The Bologna initiative has stimulated new interdisciplinary and specialized studies in computing within European universities, especially those incorporating domain-specific knowledge such as bioinformatics and media-informatics, and has also created separate programmes in software engineering and telecommunications. The increasing uniformity of IT education across Europe will provide additional incentives for offshoring work from higher to lower-wage countries within Europe; in the long run it may lead to a levelling of IT wages across Europe.

India, as the largest supplier of exported software services, faces a different set of education challenges from the US or Europe, namely to ramp up its higher education system to staff its rapidly expanding software industry. The higher education system in India is extensive and rapidly expanding. In 2006 it included more than 300 universities, 15 000 colleges and 5 000 training institutions. Nevertheless, only 6 per cent of the college-age (18–23 year old) population is enrolled in college or university. Some of the schools, such as the Indian Institutes of Technology and the Indian Institutes of Management, are world-class; but the quality falls off rapidly after the top 15 schools. Total bachelors and masters degree production in the computing and electronics fields is approximately 75 000 per year. There are also some 350 000 students in other science and engineering fields at universities and polytechnics receiving degrees each year, and many of them enter the IT industry upon graduation.

China faces the same educational challenges as India in building a trained workforce for its software industry, but its approach is different, through centralized planning. As in the case of India, enormous numbers of students graduate from Chinese universities every year. In 2001, 567 000 students received first degrees, including 219 000 in engineering and 120 000 in science. The quality of these graduates varies dramatically, but the sheer volume means that China has a large reservoir of technically trained individuals. Until 2001, Chinese universities neglected software studies as an academic discipline. At the end of the 1990s, the Chinese government recognized that it had a shortage of trained software personnel and called for improvements in Chinese software capabilities as part of its central planning efforts. In response, 51 Chinese universities established masters degrees in software engineering, which quickly attracted students. Including all the different kinds of curricula, China is now training about 100 000 people per year for the software industry. There are internal criticisms of the education, including overemphasis on theory, insufficient attention to practice and lack of familiarity with international standards.

IT research is concentrated in only a few countries. About a third of total computer science papers come from the US. A few additional traditional centres of concentration of IT research (Australia, Canada, France, Germany, Israel, Italy, the Netherlands, Sweden, Switzerland and the UK) account for about another third. This is not surprising considering the large part of the world Gross Domestic Product (GDP) that is concentrated in these same countries. There is a correlation between Purchasing Power Parity (PPP) adjusted GDP and computer science publication. However, the share of computer science papers published by scientists in the traditional centres of concentration of IT research is more than 60 per cent greater than their share of world PPP GDP (65 per cent vs 40 per cent) while Brazil, China, India, Indonesia, Mexico and Russia together account for 27 per cent of world PPP GDP, but only 7 per cent of computer science paper production. IT research was even more concentrated in the past than it is today. The initial bloom of IT research occurred in a few select locations in the US and a few other countries, in the aftermath of World War II. This concentration has been perpetuated by the natural tendency of strength to build on strength. Particularly in the US this growth was driven by ample government funding and a significant migration of scientific talent from the rest of the world. In fact, there is little doubt that in most countries government funding has played an important role.

Research-driven innovation is seen by many countries as a way to increase national wealth and standards of living. Both developed and developing countries are attempting to build up or shore up their research capabilities. This means greater competition among nations in the research area, and in the market for talent. Until recently, the US was winning the research talent competition, but that situation is changing. Due to strong efforts to foster research on the part of a number of national and local governments outside the traditional centres of research, IT research is slowly but steadily, and almost certainly inevitably, becoming more global. This globalization of IT research has been accompanied by a significant increase in the production of PhDs outside the traditional centres of concentration, and a reduction in the migration of researchers to these centres. In the long run, there is no obvious reason why IT research should be any more concentrated than world economic activity in general.

Globalization allows more and better people to participate in IT research. It provides improved opportunities for people who live outside the traditional centres of concentration of IT research. It also provides improved opportunities for the best researchers, due to increased global competition for their services. It may, however, limit opportunities for other researchers in the traditional centres of concentration, for whom global competition may mean declining wages or even the loss of jobs.

3.7   IS IT STILL A GOOD CAREER CHOICE FOR PEOPLE IN DEVELOPED COUNTRIES?

Almost every day there is a story in the US press about people losing IT jobs because positions have been sent to a low-wage country. Many of these stories quote talented young people who are choosing careers in other fields because they believe there are no longer opportunities in IT. There are fears that it will not only be low-level programming jobs that are sent to low-wage countries, but also jobs that require higher skill levels and which are more

highly compensated. If the world really is flat, as Thomas Friedman pro-
claims, and a job can as easily be done in Bangalore or Beijing as in Boston,
then even if the job remains in Boston, eventually the wages will fall in
order to remain competitive with wages in other parts of the world.

All of this sounds bleak, but consider some interesting statistics on jobs
(Table 3.1) and salaries (Table 3.2). Both these tables are based on data from
the US Bureau of Labor Statistics, one of the most reliable sources available. There is some lag in collecting and analysing data so the most recent
data are from May 2004. Note what David Patterson, a computer scientist
from Berkeley who is president of the ACM, has to say about these
numbers:

> Moreover, most of us believe things have gotten much better in the year since the
> survey was completed. Does anyone besides me know that U.S. IT employment
> [in 2004] was 17% higher than in 1999 – 5% higher than the bubble in 2000 and
> showing an 8% growth in the most recent year – and that the compound annual
> growth rate of IT wages has been about 4% since 1999 while inflation has been
> just 2% per year? (Patterson, 2005, p. 26)

How could it be that at the same time that jobs are being shipped overseas
the number of IT jobs in the US is growing rapidly and is even higher than
at the height of the dot-com boom? There are several possible explanations,
but we do not have adequate data to identify the one at play. One explanation might be that the very companies that are sending jobs overseas are
prospering from the lower costs of overseas labour, which is enabling them
to grow and create new jobs in the US and elsewhere. Another explanation
is unrelated to offshoring except that the background factors that make it
possible are the same background factors that make offshoring possible,
namely, that many industries are being reorganized to make them more productive through the use of IT. Catherine Mann, an economist from the
Institute for International Economics, has conducted a study of Bureau of
Economic Analysis (BEA) data for the years 1989–2000. (More specifically,
her data are from BEA Digital Economy, 2002, Table A.4.4.) She found a
strong correlation among industry sectors between high productivity
growth and high investment in IT (Mann, 2004). She also identified a
number of sectors that still have low IT intensity and thus are poised to take
off as IT is introduced. These include health care, retail trade, construction
and certain services. As IT becomes more pervasive in society, there are
more jobs involving either pure IT skills or combinations of IT skills and
skills associated with a particular domain, such as finance or health care.
Most forecasts suggest that perhaps 2 per cent to 3 per cent of US IT jobs
on average will be lost annually to offshoring over the next decade. With the
expanded use of IT in society, it is very possible that the total number of

Table 3.1: Professional IT employment in the US

Occupations	Employment							Change, May 2003 to May 2004	
	1999	2000	2001	2002	May 2003	Nov. 2003	May 2004	#	%
Computer and Information Scientists, Research	26 280	25 800	25 620	24 410	23 210	23 770	24 720	1 510	6.50
Computer Programmers	528 600	530 730	501 550	457 320	431 640	403 220	412 090	-19 550	-4.50
Computer Software Engineers, Applications	287 600	374 640	361 690	356 760	392 140	410 580	425 890	33 750	8.60
Computer Software Engineers, Systems Software	209 030	264 610	261 520	255 040	285 760	292 520	318 020	32 260	11.30
Computer Support Specialists	462 840	522 570	493 240	478 560	482 990	480 520	488 540	5 550	1.10
Computer Systems Analysts	428 210	463 300	448 270	467 750	474 780	485 720	489 130	14 350	3.00
Database Administrators	101 460	108 000	104 250	102 090	100 890	97 540	96 960	-3 930	-3.90
Network and Computer Systems Administrators	204 680	234 040	227 840	232 560	237 980	244 610	259 320	21 340	9.00
Network Systems and Data Communications Analysts	98 330	119 220	126 060	133 460	148 030	156 270	169 200	21 170	14.30
Computer and Information Systems Managers	280 820	283 480	267 310	264 790	266 020	257 860	267 390	1 370	0.50
Computer Specialists, All Other							130 420	130 420	
TOTAL (Excluding 'Computer Specialists All Other')	2 627 850	2 926 390	2 817 350	2 772 740	2 843 440	2 852 610	2 951 260	107 820	3.79
Computer Hardware Engineers	60 420	63 680	67 590	67 180	72 550	70 110	74 760	2 210	3.00
TOTAL, including Computer Hardware Engineers (Excluding 'Computer Specialists. All Other')	2 688 270	2 990 070	2 884 940	2 839 920	2 915 990	2 922 720	3 026 020	110 030	3.77

Source: US Bureau of Labor Statistics. Occupational Employment Statistics, 2005.

Table 3.2: IT mean annual wages

	1999	2000	2001	2002	May 03	Nov 03	May 04	CAGR (1999–May 2004)	May 2003–May 2004
Computer and Information Scientists. Research	$67 180	$73 430	$76 970	$80 510	$84 530	$85 240	$88 020	5.60%	4.10%
Computer Programmers	$54 960	$60 970	$62 890	$63 690	$64 510	$65 170	$65 910	3.70%	2.20%
Computer Software Engineers. Applications	$65 780	$70 300	$72 370	$73 800	$75 750	$76 260	$77 330	3.30%	2.10%
Computer Software Engineers. Systems Software	$66 230	$70 890	$74 490	$75 840	$78 400	$79 790	$82 160	4.40%	4.80%
Computer Support Specialists	$39 410	$39 680	$41 920	$42 320	$42 640	$43 140	$43 620	2.10%	2.30%
Computer Systems Analysts	$57 920	$61 210	$63 710	$64 890	$66 180	$67 040	$68 370	3.40%	3.30%
Database Administrators	$52 550	$55 810	$58 420	$59 080	$61 440	$62 100	$63 460	3.80%	3.30%
Network and Computer Systems Administrators	$50 090	$53 690	$56 440	$57 620	$59 140	$60 100	$61 470	4.20%	3.90%
Network Systems and Data Communications Analysts	$55 710	$57 890	$60 300	$61 390	$62 060	$62 220	$63 410	2.60%	2.20%
Computer and Information Systems Managers	$74 430	$80 250	$83 890	$90 440	$95 230	$95 960	$98 260	5.70%	3.20%
Computer Hardware Engineers	$66 960	$70 100	$74 310	$76 150	$79 350	$82 040	$84 010	4.60%	5.90%

Source: US Bureau of Labor Statistics (2002).

IT jobs will grow at a rate of more than 3 per cent over the decade. Thus it is not surprising that the US Bureau of Labor Statistics forecasts that three IT occupations will be among the ten fastest growing occupations over the coming decade (US BLS, 2002).

Even if the IT job market is a growth area over the next decade, some types of jobs are likely to fall off, probably including routine programming jobs. As explained above, there are many reasons why companies do not send work offshore so there are likely to be jobs in almost every IT occupation to be found somewhere in the US; but, perhaps in some of these specific occupations, there will be fewer jobs than there are today. It is very unlikely that the US will be completely devoid of even the most at risk, routine programming jobs ten years from now.

The US BLS has two sources of occupational employment data that can be used to estimate the number of IT workers in the US. There are the Occupational Employment Statistics (OES), based on semi-annual surveys of 1.2 million employers which are the basis of Table 3.1.

And there are the Current Population Survey (CPS) data, based on monthly surveys of around 50,000 households. The surveys are complementary; each has its strengths and weaknesses. During the period of interest – 1999 to 2005 – the occupational classification systems in these two programmes were in the process of being changed. The changes made it more likely for workers to shift among occupations within the IT sector than to move in or out of IT occupations; thus the aggregate data are less likely than the figures for individual occupations to be affected by the changes in the occupational classification schemes. As an alternative to the OES data, some BLS staff suggested we use also the CPS data beginning in 2000 because the occupational classification data are reasonably consistent over this period. Using the CPS data for aggregate time-series analysis for 2000 to 2005 produced the same comparative results: there are more IT workers in the US at the end of this period – a period of increasing offshoring – than there were at the height of the dot-com boom in 2000. (Here, also, time-series analysis should not be used for individual job categories.) For more detail on OES and CPS data, see www.bls.gov/oes/home.htm and www.bls.gov/cps/home.htm (both accessed 14 July 2007). These two datasets support the claim that IT employment in the US had recovered by 2005 from the decline of the early 2000s, in spite of increasing offshoring.

3.8   FINDINGS AND RECOMMENDATIONS

Globalization and offshoring are primarily driven by business economics and the drive to maintain or improve profitability and shareholder value, which, in turn, comes from the increasingly competitive global business environment. Some important conclusions follow.

1. Globalization of, and offshoring within, the software industry are strongly connected and both will continue to grow. Key enablers of this growth are IT itself, the evolution of work and business processes, education and national policies. The world has changed. IT is largely now a global field, business and industry. There are many factors contributing to this change, much of which has occurred since 2001. Offshoring is a symptom of the globalization of the software systems services industry.

   This rapid shift to a global software systems services industry in which offshoring is a reality has been driven by advances and changes in four major areas:

   - Technology – including the wide availability of low-cost, high-bandwidth telecommunications and the standardization of software platforms and business software applications.
   - Work processes – including the digitalization of work and the reorganization of work processes so that routine or commodity components can be outsourced.
   - Business models – including early-adopter champions of offshoring, venture capital companies that insist the companies they finance use offshoring strategies to reduce capital burn rate, and the rise of intermediary companies that help firms to offshore their work.
   - Other drivers – including worldwide improvements in technical education, increased movement of students and workers across national borders, lowering of national trade barriers, and the end of the Cold War and the concomitant increase in the number of countries participating in the world market.

2. Both anecdotal evidence and economic theory indicate that offshoring between developed and developing countries, on the whole, can benefit both, but competition is intensifying. Economic theory of comparative advantage argues that if countries specialize in areas where they have a comparative advantage and freely trade goods and services over the long run, all nations involved will gain greater wealth. As an example, the US and India have deeply interconnected software industries. India benefits from generating new revenue and creating high-value jobs; the US benefits from having US-based corporations achieve better financial performance as a result of the cost savings associated

with offshoring some jobs and investing increased profits in growing business opportunities that create new jobs. This theory is supported to some extent by data from the US BLS. According to BLS reports, despite a significant increase in offshoring over the past five years, more IT jobs are available today in the US than at the height of the dot-com boom. Moreover, IT jobs are predicted to be among the fastest growing occupations over the next decade.

Some economists have argued recently that in certain situations offshoring can benefit one country at the expense of another. While debate continues about this aspect of theory/policy, the majority of the economic community continues to believe that free trade is beneficial to all countries involved, though some argue that globalization may lead to technology leaders' losing their current dominant position. In any event, there is agreement amongst economists that even if the nation as a whole gains from offshoring, individuals and local communities can be harmed. One solution to this potential negative impact is for corporations or their governments to provide programmes that help these individuals and their related communities to regain their competitiveness. The cost of such 'safety net' programmes can be high and, thus, difficult to implement politically.

3. While offshoring will increase, determining the specifics of this increase is difficult given the current quantity, quality and objectivity of the data available. Scepticism is warranted regarding claims about the number of jobs to be offshored and the projected growth of software industries in developing nations. It is very difficult to determine how many jobs are being, or will be, lost due to offshoring. The best data available are for the US. Some reports suggest that 12 million to 14 million jobs are vulnerable to offshoring over the next 15 years. This number is, at best, an upper limit on the number of jobs at risk. To date, the annual job loss attributable to offshoring is approximately 2 per cent to 3 per cent of the IT workforce. But this number is small compared with the much higher level of job loss and creation that occurs every year in the US.

4. Standardized jobs are more easily moved from developed to developing countries than are higher skill jobs. These standardized jobs were the initial focus of offshoring, but global competition in higher-end skills, such as research, is increasing. These trends have implications for individuals, companies and countries.

The ACM report considers several case studies of firms and how they are addressing offshoring, including software services firms in low-wage nations and four types of firms in high-wage nations – packaged software firms, software services firms, entrepreneurial startup firms and established firms outside the IT sector. These cases show that the amount and diversity of work being offshored is increasing; and companies, including startups, are learning how to access and use higher skill levels in developing countries.

People are by far the most important asset in research. The historic advantage held by Western Europe and the US is not as strong today as in the past, given the developments in the graduate education systems in China and India, increased opportunities for research careers in those countries and the rising national investment in research. The US, in particular, faces a challenge in its inability to recruit and retain foreign students and researchers in the numbers it did in the past. Its dominance in the research area, therefore, is likely to be challenged.

5. To remain competitive in a global IT environment and industry, countries must adopt policies that foster innovation. To this end, policies that improve a country's ability to attract, educate and retain the best IT talent are critical. Educational policy and investment is at the core. Building a foundation to foster the next generation of innovation and invention requires:

    -   sustaining or strengthening technical training and education systems
    -   sustaining or increasing investment in R&D
    -   establishing government policies that eliminate barriers to the free flow of talent.

Developed nations can use education as a response to offshoring in order to protect national interests. There are some general principles that all countries can follow to mount an effective education response to offshoring:

-   Evolve computing curricula at a pace and in a way that better embraces the changing nature of IT.
-   Ensure computing curricula prepare students for the global economy.
-   Teach students to be innovative and creative.
-   Design curricula to achieve a better balance between foundational knowledge of computing, on the one hand, and business and application domain knowledge, on the other.
-   Invest to ensure the education system has good technology, good curricula and good teachers.

3.9 CONCLUSIONS

Globalization of and offshoring within the software industry will continue and will increase. This increase will be fuelled by IT as well as by government action and economic factors, and will result in more global competition in both lower-end software skills and higher-end endeavours such as research. The business imperatives – profits, shareholder value and inter-company competitiveness – will continue to play dominant roles. Current data and economic theory suggest that despite offshoring, career opportunities in IT will remain strong in the countries where they have been strong in the past even as they grow in the countries that are targets of offshoring. The future, however, is one in which the individual will be situated in a more global competition. The brightness of the future for individuals, companies or countries is centred on their ability to invest in building the foundations that foster invention and innovation.[3]

NOTES

1. The material in this chapter is based on *Globalization and Offshoring of Software*, W. Aspray, F. Mayadas and M. Y. Vardi (eds) (2006) and reprinted with the permission of the Association of Computing Machinery (ACM), New York, NY, accessed 2006 at www.acm.org/globalizationreport/.
2. 'Offshoring' is the term used in this chapter. It is a term that applies best to the US because, even though the US does outsource work to Canada and Mexico, most of its work is sent overseas – mostly to India, but also to China, Malaysia, the Philippines and many other places. Germany, for example, also sends work across its borders, including to Eastern Europe, but there is no water – no shore – to cross. Some of the work that is offshored is sent to entrepreneurial firms established in these low-wage countries.
3. A rich bibliography is provided at www.acm.org/globalizationreport/bibliography.htm, accessed 2006.

REFERENCES

Gomory, R. E. and W. J. Baumol (2000), *Global Trade and Conflicting National Interests*, Cambridge, MA: MIT Press.
Mann, C. (2004), 'What global sourcing means for US IT workers and for the US economy', *Communications of the ACM Archive*, **47** (7) (July), 33–5.
Patterson, D. A. (2005), 'Restoring the popularity of computer science. President's letter', *Communications of the ACM* (September), 25–8.
US Bureau of Economic Analysis (BEA) (2002), accessed at www.esa.doc.gov/2002.cfm.
US Bureau of Labor Statistics (BLS) (2002), 'Fastest growing occupations, 2002–2012', Labor Review Table 3 (February), accessed 27 December 2007 at www.bls.gov/emp/emptab3.htm.

4. The multilateral trading system and transnational competition in advanced technologies: the limits of existing disciplines

Thomas R. Howell

4.1 INTRODUCTION[1]

Globalization is bringing unsettling change in the world economy. Dramatic advances in information technology and transportation and reductions in trade and investment barriers have enabled corporations to locate manufacturing and services functions in virtually any country possessing the right combination of factor advantages. A rapidly increasing range of production, design, logistics, research and development (R&D) and services can be outsourced to other countries, bringing cost savings, relief from regulatory burdens, access to local labour pools and many other advantages. Factories, corporations and entire industries are decamping from their countries of origin to relocate in other parts of the world. Individuals, particularly those possessing special skills and training or entrepreneurial ability, are leaving their countries of birth in pursuit of better opportunities. These developments have made available to the world's consumers a vast array of new goods and services, often at progressively declining prices, but at the same time have been profoundly destabilizing. Companies and industries that do not adapt to the realities of globalization risk extinction and even highly skilled workers that are not mobile, in global terms, are finding that their jobs are not secure. National and local governments must grapple with the economic and political complications arising out of industrial 'hollowing out', the abrupt migration of industries and people to other parts of the world offering greater advantages (Aspray et al., 2006).

For centuries national governments have intervened in economic affairs to shape market outcomes to enhance national advantage, and it is unsurprising that they are now introducing policies for the same purpose in the era of globalization. Countries are competing through the use of policy measures to develop, attract and hold high value-added, knowledge-intensive manufacturing, research, design and services industries, which offer the greatest long-run prospects for national economic well-being. They are seeking to capture not only foreign technology, but the innovation, research, design and developmental activities that give rise to new technology, and advanced manufacturing and the high-skill jobs associated with it. This transnational competition is being waged in the absence of clear-cut rules, reflecting the fact that the existing system of multilateral trade and monetary agreements has not kept pace with the realities of global economic change.

4.2 LIMITS OF THE MULTILATERAL SYSTEM

The existing rules-based multilateral trading system was established to bring to an end the commercial anarchy that characterized the world economy prior to World War II and which was seen by many as an important precipitating cause of the war itself.[2] In the preparatory work for what eventually became the General Agreement on Tariffs and Trade (GATT) one participant referred to the pre-war environment as the 'jungle stage of international relations . . . a stage when countries lay in wait and pounced on the commerce of other countries without even giving the roar of warning which the lion gives before he springs on his prey.'[3]

A testament to the vision and efforts of their post-war founders, the GATT, the International Monetary Fund (IMF) Agreement, the Organisation for Economic Cooperation and Development (OECD) and various subsequent ancillary multilateral bodies, agreements and codes came into being after the World War II with the objective of reducing tariffs, exchange controls and other barriers to international trade and investment in order to facilitate increased global prosperity. Rules were established to govern such controversial trade practices, such as subsidies, dumping, import quotas, state trading and discriminatory taxation, and the original rules have been progressively refined and expanded down to the present day. Since the mid 1950s the success of the multilateral institutions in fostering the liberalization of trade and investment flows has made possible a veritable explosion in international trade, rising global living standards and the phenomenon of globalization itself. Since 1948 the average tariff rate of industrialized countries has fallen from 40 per cent to 4 per cent, and world exports of goods have grown from $US50 billion annually to $US9 trillion (Office of the US Trade Representative, 2006). Not surprisingly, given this success, the widespread impression exists that today international competition is governed by a comprehensive and rational set of rules, enforced, when necessary, by appropriate international bodies. Regrettably, this is only partially so.

From their inception the multilateral economic institutions were never as complete or comprehensive as their framers had intended. The founding generation sought to create an International Trade Organization (ITO) with a sweeping charter to regulate world trade, restrictive business practices and transnational labour issues. But the ITO was stillborn, primarily due to opposition from the US business community.[4] The GATT, which was more narrowly focused on certain government measures affecting trade, came into being to form one piece of what had been envisioned as the larger ITO framework – but with the collapse of the ITO scheme, the GATT was left to evolve on its own. Since this shaky start the 'incomplete work' of the system's original founders has been moved forward in periodic rounds of multilateral negotiations, which have reduced tariffs and other barriers and expanded the scope and effectiveness of multilateral disciplines. In 1994 the Uruguay Round of Multilateral Trade Negotiations resulted in the creation of the World Trade Organization (WTO) and the establishment of multilateral rules for services, investment and intellectual property (IP). The GATT/WTO system has continued to add new members, including the People's Republic of China in 2002.

These very real achievements should not obscure weaknesses intrinsic in the system. The institutional machinery of the GATT/WTO system is cumbersome and slow. Multilateral rounds take many years to negotiate, and tend to address issues agreed upon by the parties at the inception of each round. International dissensus has prevented or sharply limited the establishment of multilateral disciplines in a number of key areas. There is no practical way to 'legislate' changes in rules between rounds. By their very nature the multilateral institutions lag behind trends in the international economy, a phenomenon which is becoming more pronounced as the tempo of global economic and technical change accelerates, and the time span between multilateral rounds widens.

Reflecting these shortcomings some of the most controversial and significant current trends in the international economy – particularly developments arising out of rapid technological change – are simply not covered by existing multilateral rules. Certain complex trade practices in technology-intensive sectors defy any attempt to subject them to rules of general applicability.[5] Many of the most contentious and strategically significant international economic disputes revolve around intellectual property rights (IPR), but the WTO TRIPS (Trade-Related Aspects of Intellectual Property Rights) Agreement provides only a very loose institutional framework for addressing such issues and the Doha Round of multilateral trade negotiations, even if brought to a successful conclusion, will not change this reality.[6] The use of government incentive programmes to capture manufacturing operations from other countries is not the subject of any multilateral codes or rules. Similarly, there are no rules governing government policies aimed at luring skilled foreign manpower in a world labour market which, at the high end, is increasingly global. Anti-competitive private practices, such as cartels, fall entirely outside the scope of WTO disciplines, and have resisted every attempt to bring them into the system since the inception of the GATT.[7] (See also Wolf, 1994, pp. 195–216.)

In order to function properly, the GATT/WTO system depends upon voluntary compliance of its members, and the system has worked as well as it has because most WTO members comply with their obligations most of the time. However, the scope of WTO obligations allows considerable leeway for government intervention to influence market outcomes in a manner that, at least arguably, is consistent with WTO rules, and in many key areas which are subject to government intervention, members' obligations are poorly defined or non-existent. Where significant national interests or political sensitivity exists, members – including key players such as the US, Japan and the EU – have demonstrated that they will take actions that fall in these grey areas of the rules, or even completely outside them. The WTO Dispute Resolution system offers potential redress under some circumstances, but only to a limited degree.

Notwithstanding its many achievements the Uruguay Round may actually have weakened disciplines in some of the grey area practices not clearly covered by WTO rules. The system of multilateral agreements traditionally has been significantly reinforced through bilateral agreements negotiated by the main players in the system addressing issues that were not covered by multilateral rules. Historically, the US and, to a lesser extent, the European Community negotiated bilaterals providing for market access as well as disciplines on certain market distorting practices. The US, in particular, proved successful in negotiating market access bilaterals using the implicit or explicit threat of sanctions, for example, exclusion from the large US market pursuant to Congressional action and/or Section 301 of the 1974 Trade Act. Market access achieved bilaterally benefited all GATT members because pursuant to GATT Article I, any market-opening benefits inuring the parties to such bilaterals are required to be extended to all other signatories on a Most Favoured Nation (MFN) basis. The use of bilateral US pressure to open markets was widely decried as bullying 'unilateralism', but it did succeed in prising open national markets to the commercial benefit of all GATT signatories.[8]

The US commonly used its trade remedies, principally the anti-dumping and countervailing duty laws and Section 301 of the Trade Act of 1974, to challenge market-distorting practices that existed outside the scope of multilateral disciplines (see Howell, 1998). These included various non-tariff barriers, private restraints of trade, subsidies and a variety of IP concerns. However, the Uruguay Round established a system of binding dispute resolution which now ensures that any attempt by the US to impose sanctions pursuant to Section 301 or any other statute can be successfully challenged in the WTO (see Wolf and Magnus, 1998). Section 301 has fallen into disuse, and decisions by WTO panels have sharply curtailed the scope of the anti-dumping and countervailing duty laws. Although most, if not all, WTO members welcome these new constraints on 'US unilateralism', the fact remains that the Uruguay Round effectively removed the single most significant discipline on market-distorting practices outside the scope of multilateral discipline – bilateral US pressure – without putting anything in its place (Bayard and Elliott, 1994).

4.3 NEW FORMS OF TRANSNATIONAL COMPETITION ON ADVANCED TECHNOLOGIES

The system of WTO rules was fashioned to regulate traditional forms of government market intervention, which sought to promote domestic enterprises through the use of mechanisms, such as subsidies, trade protection, restrictions on inward foreign investment and tax preferences. However, recent government initiatives in advanced technology sectors have taken forms not contemplated by the framers of the system – for example, measures to lure rather than exclude foreign production and research functions, proprietary technology, capital, trained people and entrepreneurial talent. The objective of such policies is not the traditional protectionist goal of shutting foreign products and enterprises out, but rather of drawing foreign production in on terms that suit the developmental objectives of the host country. Multilateral rules have proven marginally relevant – if that – to this dynamic. Some recent developments in East Asia offer perspective on the forms that competition between nations for technological and industrial leadership are likely to take in the twenty-first century.

4.3.1 Taiwan's Ascendancy in Microelectronics

Taiwan has implemented industrial development policies which have transformed the island from an agrarian plantation economy to one of the foremost centres of high technology manufacturing and R&D in the world. Rather than pursuing the common, developing country practice of excluding or constraining foreign multinationals, Taiwan has aggressively courted them. The government offered the multinationals financial incentives, created a modern infrastructure, and educated and trained its own population to ensure that foreign firms could draw upon a skilled local workforce. The multinationals brought capital, technology, talent, training and career opportunities for the Taiwanese, many of whom ultimately drew on their experience of working with foreign firms and went on to found their own companies. Taiwanese industrial policies appear to have violated no multilateral rules, yet have produced destabilizing effects on industries in other countries more profound than most practices circumscribed by WTO rules.[9]

Several aspects of Taiwan's high technology promotional policies are worthy of particular note. First, rather than pursuing technological and economic autarky, Taiwan sought to integrate its own economy into the development and production strategies of foreign multinationals by assuming tasks that the latter found particularly costly, burdensome or risky. The most dramatic example of this dynamic was Taiwan's pioneering of the semiconductor 'foundry', a manufacturing enterprise, which does not produce its own products for sale in the market, but manufactures semiconductors designed by other firms for sale under their labels in return for a service fee. The foundry business model is based on the reality that semiconductor manufacturing facilities have become so costly – $US2 billion or more – that only a very small and rapidly declining number of private enterprises is able to bear the costs and risks associated with such investment. The foundry (with government backing) assumes this huge investment risk and relieves semiconductor device-making firms of increasingly unsustainable investment costs.[10] In return the semiconductor device firm surrenders the manufacturing function to its foundry partner, shares its proprietary designs and other know-how and becomes, either partially or wholly, a pure design-oriented 'fabless' firm.

From a developmental perspective semiconductor foundries entailed major advantages for Taiwan. Advanced manufacturing activities that otherwise would have continued in California, Europe or Japan were effectively shifted to Taiwan, creating thousands of local, skill-intensive jobs for graduates from Taiwan's universities. The unique demands of foundry manufacturing, which require flexibility to produce many types of products, enabled two Taiwanese firms, TSMC and UMC, to emerge as perhaps the most versatile and efficient semiconductor manufacturing firms in the world. By producing the designs of the world's leading semiconductor firms, the foundries absorbed and refined manufacturing process technology and developed design capabilities and cell libraries of their own. Taiwan's foundries used their relationships with semiconductor multinationals to build global networks of technological alliances with those firms.[11] Because R&D and design functions tend to gravitate toward sites where manufacturing takes place, Taiwan's expansion as a semiconductor manufacturing centre spurred the development of the local design industry and helped to attract talent from abroad.[12]

Assumption of the wafer fabrication function by Taiwanese foundries proved to be only the first step in what has become a much broader disaggregation of production in the global semiconductor industry. 'If it made business sense to rely on an outside foundry for chip manufacturing, then the obvious next question was what other portion of the supply chain could be shed?' Assembly, testing, packing and product development could also be outsourced and, with Taiwan's growing competency in design, it became evident that these too could be sourced abroad. At present, in an anomalous symmetry, as semiconductor multinationals outsource an increasing number of functions to Asia to cut costs and reduce risks:

> East Asia [is] eagerly snapping up everything it can. '[D]isaggregation' on the one side has led to 'reaggregation' on the other. The ultimate question posed by these trends for other countries is obviously 'what happens when you've disaggregated everything . . . what's left for Silicon Valley? Lunches with venture capitalists? Meetings with reporters? Or empty office buildings?'[13]

Given the impact the foundry model has had on the global semiconductor industry, the fact that the world's first 'pure-play' foundry could not have come into being without government support is noteworthy. TSMC received 44 per cent of its original capitalization from the Development Fund of the Executive Yuan, which supports projects that the private sector would not otherwise undertake by itself. The foundry concept could not have attracted private capital – the risks were too great. Instead TSMC was created by spinning off a large segment of a government research organization, the Electronics Research and Service Organization (ERSO).[14] TSMC took over a pilot manufacturing facility for advanced semiconductors which had been built by ERSO (Mathews, 1997).

The Taiwanese government deployed other measures to attract inward investment. Pursuant to several special promotional statutes, Taiwan offered tax incentives and holidays to firms that invested in designated advanced technologies and/or which located in high technology industrial parks.[15] Although many countries offer such incentives, Taiwan's were so lavish that, in effect, they created a business environment for semiconductor production that was tax free. Indeed the cumulative effect of the various tax incentives was so dramatic that for many years TSMC, Taiwan's largest semiconductor producer, had a higher after-tax income than its pre-tax income, reflecting the cumulative effects of credits from prior years. Taiwan's tax policy also rewarded individual employees. Managers, engineers and other skilled employees in Taiwan's semiconductor enterprises commonly received company stock and/or options as part of their compensation. Under Taiwanese tax law they were taxed based on the face value of the stock at the time of receipt not the market value, which was commonly many times higher.[16] When the shares were sold the individuals paid no capital gains tax because Taiwan does not tax capital gains.[17] Moreover, Taiwanese returning from overseas who brought with them capital gains on options or venture capital investments in the US or other countries were not taxed on those gains. These tax rules were 'a big reason why Taiwan can attract the best talent in the high tech industry from at home and abroad'.[18]

Finally the government established science-based industrial parks designed to replicate the innovative and entrepreneurial dynamics of Silicon Valley and Boston's Route 128 (Mathews, 1997, pp. 26–54). Many countries have attempted to create 'new Silicon Valleys' but few of those efforts have achieved the degree of success of Taiwan's Hsinchu Science Based Industrial Park (Howell, 2003, pp. 221–3). Hsinchu offered investors who located in the park an array of financial and tax incentives, but also the complete infrastructure needed to support semiconductor manufacturing. What is perhaps the best institute of applied industrial research in the world, ITRI, is located in the park, and two excellent research universities and microelectronics research centres are located nearby. The park itself has drawn an entire semiconductor industry chain, including not only wafer fabrication operations, but suppliers of semiconductor manufacturing equipment and materials, logistics and assembly, and testing and packaging facilities.[19]

Taiwan's industrial policy in microelectronics drew technology and skills from abroad which could never have been developed by Taiwan alone. The government purchased some technology outright (Mathews, 2000, pp. 165–9). It encouraged Taiwanese expatriates with managerial and technological skills to return home, and it drew on foreign – particularly American – advice and talent (Squires Meaney, 1994, pp. 170–92). Taiwan's foundries established a mechanism through which multinational firms would willingly disclose their proprietary designs to Taiwanese manufacturing partners, enabling the latter to hone their manufacturing skills and also to enhance their own design capabilities.

Although a number of countries have been disconcerted by the rapid displacement of production functions and skilled manpower from other regions of the world to Taiwan, Taiwan's promotional policies were not inconsistent with multilateral rules either before or after Taiwan's accession to the WTO in 2002. The WTO *Agreement on Subsidies and Countervailing Measures* (signed 15 April 1994, entered into force 1 January 1995), which governs the use of subsidies, does not prohibit any of the programmes employed by Taiwan. While that agreement offers a right of redress when non-prohibited subsidies by one member have harmful effects on another member, WTO panels have set a high bar to finding such harm and to date no member has successfully brought a challenge against Taiwan. Taiwan thus offers a blueprint for building a world-class high technology industry in a manner consistent with existing trade rules – and in the twenty-first century other countries, most notably China, are copying or adapting various Taiwanese policies in the hope of emulating Taiwan's high technology success.[20] As a result, nations seeking to establish or merely retain advanced technology industries are being drawn into an incentives free for all, an intergovernmental rivalry relatively unconstrained by multilateral rules.

4.3.2 The Rise of China

While Taiwan's dramatic ascendancy in advanced technologies has revolutionized a number of industries, notably semiconductors, China's rise is profoundly affecting the entire global economy, a reflection of its sheer size and the single-minded commitment of its leaders to national development. China's recent rapid strides in high technology reflect not only the adaptation of Taiwanese developmental models, but increasingly, the direct participation of Taiwanese executives, former government officials, scientists and engineers in the development of China's technology-intensive industries.

Since the inception of a sweeping programme of national economic reform in 1978, China has moved from a marginal role in the world trading system to becoming one of its most central and rapidly growing players. China's phenomenal economic growth has been driven by government planners animated by an abiding attitude of economic nationalism. The government has employed a sweeping array of policy measures to encourage technology transfer from developed countries and to achieve economic self-sufficiency, particularly in industries seen as strategically important. Chinese leaders have commonly sought to use the prospect of access to the large and growing Chinese market as leverage for securing technology from foreign enterprises.

China became a WTO member in 2002, and among other things it undertook a commitment not to require the transfer of technology as a condition for investment or import licensing.[21] Reversing prior policies, it began to encourage foreign direct investment and reduced tariffs and other border measures. China's leadership, formerly driven by communist ideology, carefully studied foreign industrial systems and adapted selected practices and policies.[22] Since 2000 the Chinese government has abandoned many of the command economy policy tools associated with socialist central planning in favour of Western-style industrial policy measures, such as subsidies, procurement preferences, infrastructural investment and tax incentives.

Nevertheless many aspects of China's trade and industrial policy have drawn criticism from abroad. The underdevelopment of China's institutions for protecting IPR and the extensive pirating of foreign proprietary technologies in China are among the most contentious issues in the international economic arena.[23] Foreign-invested enterprises complain that they are still under pressure to transfer technology to Chinese enterprises and to 'localize' their global R&D activities within China. China's government procurement policies are used with the frank purpose of promoting domestic industries. At the same time China's leaders have emphasized the importance of compliance with WTO rules, and most Chinese policies and practices which gall China's trading partners and are decried as 'unfair' do not clearly violate any WTO or other multilateral rule[24] or the terms of China's protocol of accession to the WTO. Moreover, even in the handful of situations in which an apparent violation of WTO rules has occurred, the practical effect of the rule has been limited by the length of the time frame required to enforce it. An example is the recent dispute over China's preferential value-added tax (VAT) for domestic semiconductor enterprises.

The semiconductor VAT preference
China's semiconductor industry traditionally lagged far behind the world's leading companies by every measure of technological competitiveness.[25] A series of government-driven promotional efforts between 1978 and 1999 closed the gap slightly, but at the end of the 1990s Chinese industry was still several technology generations behind the state of the art. With the advent of China's Tenth Five Year Plan, however, China abandoned many of its traditional promotional policies in microelectronics in favour of measures emulating Taiwan's successful effort. China implemented financial, tax and infrastructure programmes based on the Taiwanese model and hired former Taiwanese government officials and executives to provide expertise.[26] The Chinese government courted Taiwanese entrepreneurs who founded new mainland-based semiconductor enterprises, most notably Richard Chang, the CEO of the Semiconductor Manufacturing International Corporation (SMIC), a semiconductor foundry enterprise established by Taiwanese entrepreneurs.

China also implemented a border measure, which had a dramatic effect in attracting inward foreign investment in the semiconductor industry. In mid 2000 it implemented a VAT, which discriminated in favour of China-based semiconductor manufacturing and design enterprises.[27] China's VAT was normally 17 per cent, an amount paid at the border when semiconductors were imported. Domestically designed and/or manufactured semiconductors, however, were entitled to a refund of that portion of the VAT which exceeded 6 per cent (later reduced to 3 per cent). This scheme functioned effectively as a tariff, protecting domestic semiconductor manufacturing in China, which was at the time the most rapidly growing major market for semiconductors in the world.[28] One of SMIC's directors, speaking of his company's appeal to foreign chip makers, said: 'China offers the tax advantages. Chips made outside China are subject to a value-added tax of 17% when sold in the local market, while those produced within China are only taxed at 3%. Right there, using SMIC brings a 14% tax savings.'[29]

China's deployment of incentives triggered an extraordinary exodus of Taiwanese capital and talent to the mainland, a phenomenon that gave rise to terms, such as 'Shanghai fever' and 'high-technology-moving-westward fever' (*gaokeji canye xijing re*).[30] According to one 2001 report: 'The flow of high technology talent has become a deluge. "It was amazingly abrupt – a year ago, suddenly everybody wanted to work in China", says Manuel Lopez, who runs one of Taipei's top head-hunting firms.'[31] Mid-level managers and engineers at Taiwan's established semiconductor companies saw new opportunities on the mainland and migrated in large numbers to the Shanghai area, the epicentre of the new investments. Entire new communities of Taiwanese expatriates sprouted, with local Chinese government authorities helping to provide housing, schools, parks and new transportation links. Some individuals received generous fiscal incentives from local administrations.[32] '[Taiwanese semiconductor personnel] are voting with their feet and moving to the mainland to staff the new chip companies.'[33] Semiconductor investment that had been planned in Taiwan was significantly scaled back, while Taiwanese investments on the mainland grew at an explosive rate.[34]

Confronting what appeared to be the abrupt hollowing-out of its microelectronics industry and infrastructure, Taiwanese government planners scrambled to devise policies to adapt to the new realities. Taiwan already maintained strict prohibitions on direct investment in and technology transfer to the Chinese information industry, and restricted the extent certain key individuals could seek employment in China. However, in 2001–02 these restrictions were being widely circumvented and had little apparent effect on the talent exodus. The Taiwanese government prepared to adopt regulations to prevent 'mainland Chinese companies illegally funded by Taiwan people on the mainland from head hunting Taiwanese high tech experts'.[35] But the proposal ran into a firestorm of public criticism; the regulations were eventually watered down to restrictions limited to personnel involved in semiconductor water fabrication lithography.[36]

One Taiwan-based observer commented that 'you cannot control talent . . . if they want to go to China, they can go by various channels'.[37] It is unlikely that the adoption of comparable or more stringent restrictions on the outflow of high technology talent – if implemented by other countries – would have a different outcome.

The traditional economic explanation of the displacement of semiconductor production from Taiwan to China was that China offered entrepreneurs a lower cost manufacturing environment.[38] In fact, however, in the 2001–02 period there was virtually no cost difference between Taiwan and China for the construction of 200 mm or 300 mm semiconductor wafer fabrication facilities.[39] With respect to operating costs, China enjoyed a 9 per cent advantage with respect to 200 mm fabs and a 6 per cent edge with the more advanced 300 mm fabs – hardly enough to account for the wholesale shift in location of production which actually occurred. Virtually all of China's slender cost edge was attributable to lower labour costs, and labour did not account for a significant proportion of semiconductor manufacturing costs.[40] 'Cost is not the major issue', said a spokesman from TSMC, Taiwan's largest foundry operator, in 2001, speaking of the Taiwanese industry's move to the mainland.[41] The VAT preference was the decisive factor – as one industry observer commented in 2002, 'without the VAT break, much of the justification for the existence of the high end Chinese foundries would go away'.[42]

The displacement of Taiwanese semiconductor investment to the mainland in and after 2001 can best be viewed as a contest of government incentives in which China's incentives proved sufficiently powerful to draw substantial capital and skilled manpower away from Taiwan. China roughly matched the incentives Taiwan offered to its own semiconductor industry, offering comparable tax holidays, subsidized infrastructure, financial support and incentives and perks for individuals. In addition, with the preferential VAT, China offered an incentive that Taiwan could not match – the prospect of preferential access to its potentially vast semiconductor market to those who invested in local manufacturing facilities. It should be noted that continental-sized trading powers (the US and EU) have in the past made similar successful use of actual or prospective preferential market access to induce inward foreign investment, employing methods which, like China's, may well have been inconsistent with their GATT commitments.[43]

With respect to China's VAT, in 2004 the US government took the position that the domestic preference was inconsistent with GATT Article III, which prohibits discriminatory internal taxes. In 2004 the US initiated WTO dispute resolution procedures against China's VAT, at which point China announced that the measure would be withdrawn at the end of

2004.[44] This outcome could easily be cited as an example of how the existing WTO system operated successfully to eliminate a discriminatory and market-distorting measure involving an industry on the technological frontier.

But the dispute can also be viewed from the Chinese perspective prioritizing national development. In mid 2000, when China implemented the VAT policy, it had no world-class semiconductor companies and no immediate prospect of creating them. Most of its semiconductors were produced on obsolete 4, 5 and 6 inch wafer fabs. However, three and a half years later, at the end of 2004, China had given rise to one world-class semiconductor enterprise, SMIC, and had attracted a number of other promising foreign-invested semiconductor firms. Nine new fabs had been established, all at the 8 inch level or above. One 12 inch fab, the current global state of the art in terms of wafer size, was operational, and more were planned.[45] China was emerging as 'a real power-house in foundry production.'[46] Thus, arguably, by the time the US resort to WTO procedures induced China to revoke the discriminatory VAT measure, that measure had already achieved its objective.

More recently Chinese government authorities have deployed new incentives to attract inward investment in the semiconductor industry, which do not raise WTO issues as the VAT rebate did. Regional and local governments are offering foreign investors in semiconductor facilities massive financial aid which relieves them of much of the risk normally associated with large-scale investment in a volatile and cyclical industry. In mid 2006 SMIC announced plans to participate in the establishment of a 300 mm fab in Wuhan and a 200 mm fab in Chengdu, both of which, according to early reports, would be 'owned' by local governments, but operated by SMIC, which could also 'book the operating profit'.[47] Similarly, in 2007, the Taiwanese producer ProMOS, which manufactures semiconductor memory devices, announced that it would build a 200 mm wafer fab in Chongqing. The project would receive $360 million in loans from state controlled banks, and the Chongqing government reportedly will provide $200 million to build the fab, which it will lease to ProMOS.[48]

Use of preferential procurement to promote 'indigenous innovation'
In 2005 and 2006 the government of China released a number of comprehensive plans for promoting the nation's development of science and technology,[49] which were paralleled by comparable plans issued by some regional and local governments.[50] These plans emphasized promotion of 'indigenous innovation', absorption of foreign technology,[51] and an end to dependency on foreign technologies and technology-intensive products.[52] In 2007 the government began to promulgate specific policy measures to

achieve these objectives, most notably the use of preferential government procurement.

China's *Long Term S&T Plan to 2010*, released in 2006, provides among other things that 'Rules governing government procurement should be adopted so that the government will give priority to purchasing high-tech equipment and products that domestic manufacturers own their independent IPR.'[53] In December 2006 three Chinese ministries jointly released the *Provisional Measures for Accreditation of National Indigenous Innovation Products (Interim) ('Accreditation Measures')*.[54] The measures provide that 'domestic innovative products' can be accredited through an administrative process and that products so accredited 'shall be given priority in procurement projects for government and in national key projects that will spend treasury funds.'[55] The IP underlying the product in question must be Chinese.[56] The *Accreditation Measures* stipulate that consideration be given as to whether the applicant's products can be substituted for imports.[57] Given the pervasive role of the government in China's economy, the impact of preferential procurement practices is potentially very substantial.

At the time of writing the *Accreditation Measures* have not yet been officially adopted and numerous ancillary measures are pending, and as a result many important questions about the measures and the policy thrust which they embody have yet to be answered.[58] For example, it is not clear whether or not a technology which was invented by a foreign firm in another country but subject to a Chinese patent obtained by the foreign firm's Chinese subsidiary would qualify for procurement preferences. However, the purpose of the measures appears to be to encourage R&D activity within China using preferential government procurement as an inducement. This goal would be fully consistent with a range of other Chinese measures designed to encourage the localization of research functions, whether by Chinese or foreign enterprises.

The *Accreditation Measures* appear likely to establish a system of government procurement practices, which, on the face of it, discriminates in favour of domestic products embodying 'indigenous innovation'. The WTO *Government Procurement Agreement* (GPA) establishes disciplines on this type of discriminatory procurement, but China is not a signatory to the GPA and thus not subject to those disciplines. China holds observer status with respect to the GPA and has committed to becoming a signatory at some unspecified point in the future.[59] It has also stated that all government entities at national and sub-national levels will conduct procurement transparently and on a MFN basis, meaning that no foreign supplier will be treated more favourably than another foreign supplier.[60] But China is under no international legal obligation to refrain from government procurement practices which favour domestic products and producers.

The 'perfect storm?'

China's adoption of plans to foster 'indigenous innovation' has been paralleled by the pendency of draft laws and measures, which are intended to play an important role in advancing China's developmental objectives in high technology. These include an Anti-Monopoly Law, new regulations on standards setting and a series of measures to foster indigenous enterprise designated sectors. These activities have led some observers in the US to warn of a looming 'perfect storm' – a scenario in which new Chinese measures could be used in concert as levers to extract proprietary technologies from foreign multinationals under threat of criminal liability, and in a manner at least arguably consistent with China's WTO commitments.

The WTO TRIPS Code provides that under certain limited and carefully defined circumstances, member governments can appropriate patented technologies from private parties without their consent for 'use by the government or third parties authorized by the government'.[61] Among other things the government must first make 'efforts to obtain authorization from the right holder on reasonable terms and conditions'.[62] The use of such technology 'shall be authorized predominantly for the supply of the domestic market of the Member authorizing such use'.[63] However neither of these constraints apply where appropriation of the technology 'is permitted to remedy a practice determined after judicial or administrative process to be anti-competitive'.[64] In addition, the TRIPS provision, which requires the appropriating government to pay the rights holder 'adequate remuneration',[65] is circumscribed in cases involving anti-competitive practices – 'the need to correct anti-competitive practices may be taken into account in determining the amount of remuneration in such cases'.[66]

Because patents and other IPR confer exclusivity on the rights holders, they are often criticized as 'anti-competitive'. Patents, which establish a monopoly for the patent holder, may open the holder to charges of monopolization or abuse of a dominant position under various national competition law regimes. The prospect exists that various countries may utilize competition law to achieve industrial developmental objectives by compelling foreign monopolists or dominant enterprises to transfer their key technologies to domestic entities.

China has been preparing anti-monopoly legislation (AML) since the 1980s, and in 2007 it enacted the law, effective 1 August 2008.[67] Among other things, the legislation prohibits abuse of dominant market position.[68] Factors for determining dominance include market share,[69] the 'ability to control the sales market', the 'reliance on the entity by other entities' and the 'degree of difficulty for other undertakings to enter the relevant market'.[70] These indicia are rather nebulous and could be read to apply to foreign firms holding IPR which gives them 'dominant' shares of advanced technology product markets. Examples of abuse of dominance include 'selling products at unfairly high prices', which could be read to embrace licensing fees for technologies that competition authorities regard as too high.[71] Abuse may also include 'without valid reasons, refusing to trade with relative trading parties', a provision that might be applied to situations in which a rights-holder refused to license proprietary technology to domestic enterprises.[72] Article 55 of the AML provides, with respect to IPR, that:

> This law is not applicable to conducts by undertakings to protect their legitimate intellectual property rights in accordance with the IP law and relevant adminis- trative regulations; *however, this law is applicable to the conduct of undertakings to eliminate or restrict market competition by abusing intellectual property rights stipulated in the IP law and administrative regulations.* (emphasis added)[73]

While the language of the AML is ambiguous and subject to varying interpretations, the policy background of China's AML indicates that the new law is seen by some Chinese policy makers as a tool for compelling multinational corporations to surrender proprietary technology to China. A 2004 article by the State Administration of Industry and Commerce (SAIC) cited a long list of abuses of dominant market position by multi- national corporations, and called for 'countermeasures'.[74] Abuses included 'refusal to deal through the abuse of intellectual property' and refusal to share proprietary patented protocols and business secrets. SAIC stated that 'it is necessary to . . . enact the Anti-Monopoly Law in order to complete the competition law system and stop the anticompetitive practices of multi- national companies in a timely manner'.[75] In 2005 Lu Wei, an official working within the State Council, stated that 'We shall strengthen the Antimonopoly [protections] related to IPR and prohibit multinationals from shutting domestic enterprises out of the market using IPR.'[76] Wang Xiaoye, one of the main authors of the AML, stated that although the law does not specifically target foreign companies, 'foreign concerns are more likely to be [under surveillance] by regulators'[77] and that 'the adoption of an anti-monopoly law will serve as an important tool for China to check the influence of multinationals'.[78] The prevention of abuse of IP is also a recurrent theme in China's other economic plans.[79]

Related to China's AML, at the time of this writing the Standards Administration of China (SAC) and the State Intellectual Property Organization (SIPO) are in the process of jointly drafting regulations applicable to the formulation of regulations applicable to owners of patents that are 'essential to the implementation' of Chinese national industrial standards. According to drafts circulated in 2005, the regulations contem- plated a scheme pursuant to which Chinese industrial working groups developing standards could request a patent holder to grant 'irrevocable' licences to any Chinese firm adopting the standards on either a royalty-free basis or reasonable and non-discriminatory terms. If the patent-holder refused, the State Council could grant a compulsory licence, and if the patent-holder 'intentionally conceals the patent information and this results in losses in the formulation or implementation of the standard, the patent rights holder shall bear corresponding liability in accordance with the law'. These developments have been paralleled by other actions taken by the Chinese government based on the view that foreign IP which is implicated in standards is problematic and an appropriate subject for government remedial measures.[80]

These measures, taken together, could result in various scenarios under which China directs a foreign multinational to surrender critical proprietary technology or face criminal penalties. For example, under the draft standards regulation previously noted, a patent rights holder refusing to cooperate with a Chinese standards-setting group by transferring patent information might be subject to 'corresponding liability in accordance with law', specifically, a finding under the AML that the rights holder had 'abused IP' by refusing to transfer it. The Chinese government could plausibly contend that criminal and civil penalties assessed under the AML, as well as the compulsory transfer of the technology itself, are exempt from the limits set by TRIPS Article 31 as compulsory technology transfer because such measures would be taken 'to correct anticompetitive practices'.

Whither China?

Significant divisions exist within China's policy making circles and bureaucracy over the future course of the country's international economic relations. A strong current of support exists for aligning China's industrial and trade policies more closely with those of other industrialized countries and further liberalization of China's economic policies. Advocates of this approach utilized the process of China's accession to the WTO to press successfully for elimination of many elements of the old command economy and the reduction of trade and investment barriers. The drafters of China's Anti-Monopoly Law have gone to extraordinary lengths to solicit foreign commentary on the draft law and have incorporated many foreign recommendations, reflecting a desire to establish a law that will reflect well on China in the international community. Should such policy perspectives emerge as dominant, a number of the concerns noted in this chapter are likely to prove unfounded as China moves toward accommodation with its trading partners.

At the same time there are strong elements of economic nationalism – or 'techno-nationalism', as it is often called – throughout the Chinese government. Those who share this perspective tend to view economic laws and measures as tools to be used in a concerted fashion to achieve developmental objectives, including national autonomy in strategic technology-intensive sectors. They do not necessarily advocate policies that are clearly inconsistent with China's WTO obligations, but are prepared to undertake policies with frankly nationalist or mercantilist objectives within the boundaries of the WTO rules.[81] The basic point of this chapter is that there is plenty of room for such manoeuvres within that framework. A number of manifestations of the 'techno-nationalist' perspective have appeared in recent months in the form of new policies and measures favouring domestic interests, and at the time of this writing the WTO implications are, at best, ambiguous.

4. 4 CONCLUDING PERSPECTIVE

The fact that an unruly and intensifying government-driven competition to capture technology-intensive industries and IP is unfolding 60 years after the formation of the GATT should be a matter of concern to all who recognize the benefits the GATT/WTO system has brought to the post-war world. Whether the WTO regime can play a role in preventing or at least inhibiting a high technology regression into 1930s-style mercantilism is an open question. The cases cited in this chapter suggest that while the multilateral rules may establish certain broad outer boundaries of acceptable behaviour, national governments can find ample space within those boundaries to intervene in the market to pursue national developmental objectives. The Doha Round of Multilateral Trade Negotiations – should they ever be brought to a successful conclusion – will do little to change this reality, given that there is little in the Doha agenda that would affect measures of the type described in this chapter. With respect to IP, a tension exists between the desire of the advanced industrial countries to protect their proprietary technologies and that of newly-industrializing countries to pursue developmental objectives in which technology transfer – voluntary or otherwise – plays a central role. It is unclear that such divergent objectives can be reconciled and conflicts contained, through the adoption of mutually agreed rules.

Given these realities any country that seeks to establish or maintain an economy characterized by technology-intensive, innovative industries and the skilled jobs and other benefits associated with such industries, must confront the world as it is, rather than as they might wish it to be. If government incentives are decisive in determining the location of key industries, countries that seek to retain such industries must deploy incentives of their own or find some other way to counteract or offset the incentives of others – and for the most part the basis for such counteraction will not be found at the WTO. If a government seeks to force the transfer of strategically key proprietary technology from a foreign enterprise through the use of formal or informal measures, as a matter of national interest, that enterprise's government must respond, if not within the institutional framework of the WTO, then outside of it, or surrender the technology and all of the advantages associated with it.

Certainly, the fact that the WTO institutions have significant limitations does not mean that they have no role in resolving high technology conflicts. The US successfully utilized WTO procedures to bring about elimination of the preferential semiconductor VAT; although limited in its effect this outcome was preferable to a continuation of the discriminatory measure. In 2007 the US initiated a series of WTO dispute settlement procedures with respect to China's export subsidies, alleged lax enforcement of trademark and copyright laws, and restrictions on the sale of US movies, music and books in China.[82] This process has already brought about at least some amelioration of the circumstances that led the US to take these steps.[83]

Nevertheless the prospect of a proliferation of bilateral brawls, incentives races and WTO dispute resolution proceedings involving high technology industries is certainly a bleak one. It remains preferable to seek common ground and new rules to govern the new issues that are arising out of globalization and technological change. The WTO system may be too cumbersome to meet this challenge fully, and if a minimum of rational order is to be maintained in the advanced technologies, it may best be achieved through bilateral and plurilateral negotiations among the leading players, perhaps under the auspices of the OECD or some other multilateral forum. In the past multilateral consensus arrangements governing issues, such as export financing, sale of commercial aircraft and the treatment of delinquency on official loans, have been reached in this way. Such arrangements have been manifestly imperfect in many respects, but they have also clearly exercised a normative effect on government actions and represent a first rather than a final step.

NOTES

1. The author is indebted to Rachel Howe for the substantial contributions her research made to this chapter.
2. Clair Wilcox, the US economist and statesman who chaired the International Trade Conference which led to the creation of the GATT, described the pre-World War II international trading environment as follows: 'The attention of governments turned inward . . . .. Each for himself and the devil take the hindmost became the general rule. . . .

Exports were forced; imports were curtailed. All of the weapons of commercial warfare were brought into play; currencies were depreciated, exports subsidized, tariffs raised, exchanges controlled, quotas imposed, and discrimination practiced through preferential systems and barter deals. Each nation sought to sell much and buy little,' cited in Hudec (1975, p. 5).

3. UN Doc. EPCT/A/PV.5 (1947, p. 8), cited in Jackson (1969, p. 179).

4. The ITO's charter was agreed upon at a UN conference held in Havana in 1948 ('Havana Charter'). The US government in 1950 declared that it would not seek Congressional ratification of the ITO, precluding the formation of the organization. The GATT, originally established as a provisional instrument pending adoption of the Havana Charter, formed the foundation for subsequent multilateral initiatives to ensure a rules-based system of international commerce.

5. Laura D'Andrea Tyson, presenting a case study on obstacles encountered by Motorola in its attempts to sell advanced telecommunications equipment in Japan, observed that 'it is hard to imagine an effective "fixed-rule" approach for dealing with the kinds of market barriers at play in this case. No set of rules, however detailed, could have anticipated the methods employed to thwart Motorola's repeated attempts to sell its products. Certainly, most of these methods fell outside the purview of GATT regulations, since they involved structural impediments rather than trade barriers. Moreover, the impediments in question were specific to the organization of the telecommunications industry in Japan. A general set of rules that abstracted from industry and national specificity would have been largely irrelevant' (D'Andrea Tyson, 1992, p. 73).

6. The Canadian economist and senior government official Sylvia Ostry noted in 1997 that 'the U.S. [innovation] system favors creation of intellectual property over its diffusion and [the EU and Japan] tilt in the opposite direction. The compromise negotiated in TRIPS did not resolve the matter.' Ostry also noted that the disagreements which presented a more comprehensive TRIPS agreement related only to the status quo; 'rapid and ongoing technological change in [information, computer and communication technology] and biotechnology are raising a host of new issues that will require major adaptation of the existing IPR architecture' (Ostry, 1997, p. 316).

7. See F. Jenny, 'The impact of globalization on competition', www.compcom.co.za/events/last%20year%20conference%20speeches%202001/Frederic%Jenny.htm (accessed 29 August 2007). While it is sometimes contended that such private restraints are addressed by national competition authorities, that is true only in a very limited sense, particularly when cartels and other anti-competitive measures are a tacit expression of government policy.

8. For example, the series of bilateral US–Japan agreements in semiconductors initiated in 1986 succeeded in opening the Japanese semiconductor market. One of the principal beneficiaries was Korea, which was able to expand significantly its exports of semiconductor memory devices as a result of the agreements.

9. Taiwan did not join the WTO until 2002 and was thus technically not subject to GATT/WTO disciplines until that point. However, from the point at which it formally applied to join the GATT (1 January 1990) it rapidly moved to conform its trade and industrial policies to GATT requirements. It also pledged to participate in all subsequent GATT tariff reductions and to implement the results of the Uruguay Round whether or not it was admitted to the GATT, 'Government of Taiwan, memorandum on foreign trade regime of the customs territory of Taiwan', *Penghu, Kinmen and Matsu*, submitted by the Republic of China, 17 January, 1992, *Chinese Yearbook of International Affairs*, (1992), **10**, 206–70. Taiwan Board of Foreign Trade, 'The trade policy of the Republic of China as Taiwan', mimeo by 3rd Department staff, 1990.

10. The world's first foundry, TSMC, was partially capitalized by Taiwan's Development Fund of the Executive Yuan, a special fund used to support projects that the private sector would not undertake on its own. TSMC and another Taiwanese firm, UMC, emerged as the world's dominant semiconductor foundry producers.

11. 'Collaborations underscore Taiwan's cutting edge foundries', *Solid State Technology*, August 2002.

12. 'Taiwan's design projects', *Nikkei Microdevices*, January 2003.
13. The quoted passages in this paragraph are drawn from A. Leonard, 'The world in the iPod(2)', *Spiegel Online International*, www.spiegel.de/international/0,1518, 368763–2,00.html, 8 August 2005. A symbol of the profound change that the advent of Taiwan's foundry model has wrought in the global semiconductor industry was the January 2007 announcement by Texas Instruments (TI) that it would no longer manufacture digital CMOS devices at the 45 nanometre and below node and would outsource those manufacturing functions to foundries in Taiwan and China. TI is credited with the original co-invention of the integrated circuit and has always been one of the world's leading semiconductor manufacturers. TI will continue to design digital semiconductors, but one observer commented that 'it seems unlikely that TI would ever construct a leading-edge wafer fab again and is set to let its own manufacturing of digital CMOS wither on the vine' (P. Clarke, 'Texas Instruments exits process development race', *Electronics Supply & Manufacturing*, 24 January 2007). This and other similar disinvestment moves by semiconductor makers in the US suggest that 'If you are a cutting-edge engineer interested in working with innovative new techniques for chip manufacturing, you will be drawn not to Silicon Valley but to the scores of brand new fabs being built in Asia . . . that is where engineers are being trained to use the newest tools, and that is where further innovations in technology are likely to spring from,' A. Leonard (2005), 'The world in the iPod', www.spiegel.de/international/0,1518,368763-2,00.html (accessed 17 September 2007).
14. 'The private sector was still fearful of risk and could not raise enough money. Once again the government put up money, this time to start TSMC . . .. [T]he technology and all the people came from ERSO, including about 130 engineers, the 2-micron CMOS developed at ERSO, and its latest 6-inch wafer fab' (Hu, 2003, p. 154).
15. Tax holidays were made available pursuant to the Statute for Upgrading Industries and the rules establishing incentives for investors in Taiwan's science-based industrial parks. See http://investintaiwan.nat.gov.tw/en/opp/incentives.tax_incentives/ (accessed 29 August 2007), Government of Taiwan, 'The Republic of China (Taiwan) in 2003 APEC: investment incentives in Taiwan, R.O.C.', www.gio.gov.tw/taiwan-website/5-gp/apec/ap 3_11.htm (accessed 17 September 2007); TSMC Financials (1994–2000). These tax incentives, which ensured that some of Taiwan's most profitable firms paid no taxes, were unpopular and politically controversial in Taiwan, and contributed to the downfall of the KMT Party in the 2000 national elections. However, the DPP, the new party in power, having campaigned against tax holidays for the semiconductor industry, concluded that industrial policy considerations required that they be retained.
16. 'Plan to tax employee bonus stocks bases on their market value', press release, Taiwan Tax Collection Bureau, 10 August 2000, www.mof.gov.tw/news/read.asp?num=1963, accessed 17 September, 2007, See also Taiwan Ministry of Finance, eTax portal, 'Employees get the bonus from the company will pay individual income tax for the over value part according to the newly implement Alternative Minimum Tax (AMT)' (sic), http://english.etax.nat.gov.tw/wSite/ct?xItem=429168ctNode=11300 (accessed 17 September 2007).
17. Taiwan *Income Tax Law*, Art. 4–1.
18. 'Investment in 300 mm plants heating up, 32 new lines to be built', *Nikkei Microdevices*, June 2000.
19. Hsinchu Park no longer has sites available and the overspill of semiconductor activity has been directed toward a new site, Tainan Science-Based Industrial Park.
20. 'Chips and the China syndrome', *Taipei Times*, 1 January 2002.
21. World Trade Organization (2001), *Protocol of Accession of the People's Republic of China* WT/L/432 (01-S996), 23 November, Part I, Art. 7.
22. 'Learning and studying successful experiences of developed countries and neighboring regions in developing an integrated circuits industry and summing up our country's experiences and lessons in developing an integrated circuits industry has become undoubtedly and extremely vital to our country's development for the future,' Qu Weichi, Vice Minister of Information Industry, in 'How to develop integrated circuits industry', *Renmin Ribao*, 15 May 2000.

23. China has enacted various measures to protect against trademark, patent and copyright infringement, and has established a large administrative bureaucracy to enforce IPR. However the foreign perspective is that China's enforcement of IPR is wholly inadequate. See, generally, Office of the US Trade Representative, (*2005 Special 301 Report*), www.ustr.gov/assets/Document_Library/Reports_Publications/2005/2005_Special_301/asset_upload_file195_7636.pdf (accessed 27 August 2007); Office of the US Trade Representative (2005), *2004 National Trade Estimate Report on Foreign Trade Barriers*, Washington, DC: Office of the US Trade Representative, pp. 72–5; see also 'Watching for Chinese knock-offs', *Electronic Business Asia*, January 2003.

24. WTO Director-General Pascal Lamy commented in 2006 that 'In June the WTO conducted the first review of China's trade policy. The overall appreciation is a positive one. Even if there are still areas that need some improvements, the political commitments and determination shown by the Chinese government is serious and responsible and all members have acknowledged it,' P. Lamy, 'China in the multilateral trading system: its role and implication', *WTO News: Speeches – DG Pascal Lamy*, 6 September 2006.

25. 'Overview of the semiconductor market in China', *Tokyo Semiconductor FDP World*, November 2000.

26. 'China's latest chip plan adds help from Taiwan', *Semiconductor Business News*, 30 March 2001.

27. The preferential VAT policy was established by State Council Circular, 'Some policies for encouraging the development of the software industry and the integrated circuit industry', 18 June 2000.

28. 'Interview with Richard Chang, President and CEO of SMIC', *Nikkei Microdevices*, February 2002.

29. 'Interview with Tsuyashi Kawanishi', *Nikkei Sangyo Shimbun*, 28 March 2002. SMIC President Richard Chang made the same point in 'Interview with SMIC President Richard Chang', *Nikkei Microdevices*, February 2002. TSMC Chairman Morris Chang explained his company's decision to build a fab in China as follows: 'To try to serve the Chinese market from Taiwan does not make sense. There are things like VAT [value-added tax], local content [and other tariff related] barriers that will make it rather ineffective for a foundry to try to serve the Chinese market from outside,' 'China's fabless appeal', *Business Week Online*, 23 September 2002.

30. 'Chaos and resentment everywhere in Taiwan', *Jiefangjunbao*, 21 May 2001.

31. 'Taipei's talent exodus', *Time Asia*, 21 May 2001.

32. During the last six months of 2001 nearly 3000 Taiwanese reportedly migrated to China to take positions in the mainland semiconductor industry, drawn by incentives, such as higher salaries, and perks that included housing and cars.

33. 'New global player in IC market: China pushes chipmaking', *Solid State Technology*, February 2002, accessed at http://sst.pennet.com/articles/print_toc.dfm?p.= 5ev=45ei2.

34. In mid 2000 Taiwan's government and semiconductor industry were planning a massive investment drive, envisioning a total of 30 new Taiwanese wafer fabrication lines by the year 2010. No fabs were planned on the Chinese mainland. At the time of writing (August 2007) it appears that Taiwan will fall short of its 30-line goal while Taiwanese fabs on the mainland are proliferating. Source: interviews with Taiwan Ministry of Economic Affairs, Taipei, July 2000 and Electronics Research and Service organization, ERSO, Hsinchu, July 2000.

35. Taipei Central News Agency (10:30 GMT, 17 April 2002). Under regulations drafted by the National Science Council Taiwanese enterprises would be required to report to the government the names of their skilled employees. These employees would be required to obtain a licence from the government as a prerequisite for working on the mainland. The total number of licences would be limited and under a revolving door clause, personnel would still be subject to controls for two years after leaving their jobs. 'High tech employees must get license before working in the mainland', *Lien-Ho Pao*, 6 April 2002.

36. 'High tech personnel control narrowed down to one category', Taipei Central News Agency, 13:57 GMT, 24 April 2002.

37. Andrew Young, Secretary General of the Chinese Centre for Advanced Policy Studies, in 'Restrictions on workers seem futile', *Taipei Times*, 19 April 2002.
38. 'Report on "myth reality" of Taiwan chip makers investing in China', *Taipei Times*, 7 January 2001.
39. See T. R. Howell, B. L. Bartlett, W. A. Noellert and R. Howe (2003), *China's Emerging Semiconductor Industry: The Impact of China's Preferential Value-Added Tax as Current Investment Trends*, published by Dewey Ballantine for the Semiconductor Industry Association, Washington, DC, October, and Appendix 2. The cost comparisons were based on operating data from the US semiconductor companies that were aggregated. All subsidies were excluded from the calculations. Differences in operating rates and yield were not considered.
40. Direct and indirect labour accounted for about 14 per cent of the operating cost for a 200 mm fab based in Taiwan and about 6 per cent for a similar fab operating in China. The differential is narrowed by the cost of expatriate packages and facilities for Taiwanese companies shifting operations to China. Ibid., p. 14, n. 44. Richard Chong, the Taiwanese founder of SMIC, conceded in a 2001 interview that his operation had only a slight operating cost advantage over Taiwanese foundries, and was compelled to 'import pricey talent from Taiwan'. However, he said, there was 'one pressing reason for being based in China if you want to sell to the Chinese market: tax benefits . . ... Most importantly, the new foundries expect to pay less than 5 percent of China's 17 percent value-added tax'. 'Pioneering SMIC leads chip exodus to China', *Financial Times*, 13 November 2001.
41. Tseng Jin-hau, in 'Report on "myth, reality" of Taiwan chipmakers', *Taipei Times*, January. 2001.
42. J. Cassel, 'Why China is unlikely to abandon tax breaks', *Semiconductor Business News*, 19 December 2002.
43. In the early 1980s, in automobiles, the US government used the pendency of quota legislation in the Congress to pressure Japan into accepting a 'voluntary' quantitative ceiling on its exports to the US, an action that arguably was inconsistent with the GATT Article XI prohibition on quantitative restrictions. Japanese automakers were unofficially encouraged to participate in the US market by investing in US-based manufacturing operations, which they subsequently did (USITC, 1983, p. 182). During the Single Market Initiative, the EU raised the prospect that anti-dumping and other border measures would be used to deter operation of so-called 'screwdriver plants' (onshore assembly firms) and that foreign firms could avoid being shut out of the Single Market by investing in manufacturing plants in the EU and increasing the 'European Content' of their output. The result was a wave of foreign investment in the EU which might have occurred elsewhere in the absence of such measures. 'EC announces new chip rules to gain plants', *Journal of Commerce*, 7 February 1989; 'Car makers drive into Europe', *Financial Times*, 19 April 1989; 'Local chip production key to European mart', *Japan Economic Journal*, 30 September 1989.
44. 'U.S., China settle dispute over semiconductor tax refunds', http://usinfo.state.gov/ei/ Archive/2004/Jul/09-900696.html (accessed 27 August 2007).
45. Semiconductor technological level is also denoted by the line widths employed in the circuits in semiconductor devices. In 2006 the standard world semiconductor fabrication dimensions involved design rules of circuits 0.18 and 0.131 microns wide. Some Chinese wafer fabs were producing memory devices with these line widths. The US state of the art was 0.09 microns, and one Chinese fab was reportedly installing a 0.09 micron production line. Testimony of John H. Tracik, Heritage Foundation, before the U.S.–China Economic and Security Review Commission Hearing on Chinese Military Modernization and Export Control Regimes, 17 March 2006.
46. 'New wafer fab construction soars in June quarter; 2007 global capacity expected to increase 17 percent', *Semiseek News*, 31 July 2006, 'China will be greatest equipment market', *III-Vs Review*, 19 March 2005.
47. Q2 2006 SMIC earnings conference call – Final, FD Wire, 28 July 2006; 'Chinese Government builds 300 mm fab', *Semiconductor Fubtech*, 28 June 2006; 'SMIC gets $3B

nod from China's Wuhan government', *Electronic News*, 22 May 2006. SMIC describes its participation as a management contract under which SMIC 'will not invest any money to construct or equip the wafer manufacturing facilities but will manage the operations, including the wafer loading of the facilities', SMIC Form 20-F for period ending 31 December 2006, p. 23.

48. A ProMOS spokesman said 'It's a good incentive for us to build the fab there. You want to spend your money on equipment, not the shell, so that you can quickly ramp up the fab', 'ProMOS strikes deal for "leased" fab in Chongqing', *Electronic Engineering Times*, 21 January 2007.

49. These include the Ministry of Science and Technology's *Long Term S&T Plan to 2020*; the State Council's *National IPR Strategy*; the Ministry of Information Industry's *11th Five Year Plan for Information Industry 2006–2010*; the *State Plan on Science and Technology in the 11th Five Year Plan for National Economic and Social Development 2006–2010*; and the *State Medium and Long Term Development Program Regarding Science and Technology*.

50. See, for example, Peoples' Government of Shanghai Municipality, *Shanghai Intellectual Property Strategy (2004–2010)*, 14 September 2004; Peoples' Government of Shandong Province, *Outline of Shandong's Intellectual Property Strategy*, 14 July 2005; Shenzhen Municipal Government, *Notice of the Shenzhen Municipal Government on Distributing the Outline of Shenzhen IPR Strategy (2006–2010)*, *Shen Fu*, **214**, 26 December 2005.

51. The *Long Term S&T Plan to 2010* calls for China to 'formulate and perfect the policy of promoting re-innovation on imported technologies after digesting and assimilating them'. 'Chinese Premier Wen Jiabao vows increased spending on science, technology', *BBC Monitoring*, 24 January 2006.

52. The *Long Term S&T Plan to 2010* states that 'We must . . . develop a large number of important equipment sets and high tech equipment so that we can act as quickly as possible to change the situation where we basically have to depend on importing complete sets of key equipment because we do not have the core technologies for manufacturing them. . . . We should strengthen the management of importation of major technologies and equipment to stop unscrupulous and redundant imports', *BBC Monitoring*, 24 January 2006.

53. 'Chinese Premier Wen Jibao vows increased spending', *BBC Monitoring*, 24 January 2006.

54. Ministry of Science and Technology (MOST), Ministry of Finance and National Development and Reform Commission (NDRC).

55. *Accreditation Measures*, Art. 1 (draft, undated).

56. *Accreditation Measures*, Art. 4, Sect. 2. An applicant must 'possess the intellectual propety rights of the product in accordance with Chinese law by virtue of the applicants leading technical innovation activities, or through procurement of ownership or by assignment of rights by Chinese enterprises, public institutions, or citizens which own their own intellectual property in accordance with Chinese law'.

57. *Accreditation Measures*, Art. 4, Sect. 7.

58. The *Accreditation Measures* are being promulgated under the *Long Term Science and Technology Plan 2010* and its accompanying regulations released by the State Council in February 2006. *A Declaration of Instructions of National Indigenous Innovation Products* will be issued specifying the application procedures and qualifying requirements. *A Product Catalogue of National Indigenous Innovation Products* will also be issued itemizing categories of products eligible for benefits under the programme. Each ministry responsible for a given industry will draw up a list of appropriate products.

59. China committed in its protocol accession to the WTO to join the GPA 'as soon as possible'. China introduced the Government Procurement Law in 2003 in order to follow the 'spirit' of the WTO GPA, but this law entitles 'local' goods and services to preferential treatment with respect to procurement. The *10th Five year Plan (2001–05)*, which governed the period immediately following WTO accession, stated that the government would 'devise a national purchasing policy [in which] IT products sold to the government should be primarily produced locally', *10th Five Year Plan (2001–05)*, Sect. 3.6.4.

Promotional measures promulgated for the software and semiconductor industries in 2000 which remain in effect provide for procurement preferences for domestic products. Circular 18, *Several Policies for Encouraging the Development of the Software Industry and Integrated Circuit Industry*, 24 June 2000, Arts. 25, 50, 51.

60. WTO, *Report to the Working Party on Accession of China*, WT/MIN(01)/31, 10 November 2001.
61. TRIPS Code Art. 31.
62. TRIPS Code Art. 31(b).
63. TRIPS Code Art. 31(f).
64. TRIPS Code Art. 31(k).
65. TRIPS Code Art. 31(h).
66. TRIPS Code Art. 31(k).
67. Anti-Monopoly Law of the People's Republic of China, adopted at the 29th Session of the Standing Committee of the 10th National Peoples' Congress and promulgated on 30 August 2007, effective from 1 August 2008 ('AML'). See, generally, Wang (2004) and Jingzhou (2004).
68. AML Arts. 2–3, 17.
69. A rebuttable inference of dominance may be drawn if one undertaking has a share of half or above in a relevant market, the joint share of two undertakings accounts for two-thirds or more, or the joint share of three undertakings is three-quarters or above. AML Art. 19.
70. AML Art. 18.
71. AML Art. 17(i).
72. AML Art. 17(iii).
73. Chen Ziyun, an NPC delegate, commented with respect to Article 55 that 'We should have a definition or concept of "IPR abuse" in a bid to clarify the term due to its absence in IPR-related laws. While [this term] hasn't been defined, I hope a clear definition can be provided.' Debate of the NPC, 27 June 2006, 22nd session of the Standing Committee of the National Peoples' Congress.
74. Some Chinese media reports indicated that the AML drafting process was primarily motivated to counter a few specific multinationals in China and to secure proprietary technology from them. 'Antimonopoly laws planned to fight Microsoft', *Business Daily Update*, 13 April 2004.
75. Office of Anti-Monopoly, Fair Trade Bureau, SAIC, 'Anticompetitive practices of multi-national companies in China and countermeasures', *Administration of Industry and Commerce*, May 2004, pp. 42–3.
76. Lu Wei, Director General, Technical Economic Department, Development Research Center of the State Council, *Caijing Magazine*, 17 October 2005.
77. 'Beijing antitrust plans worry foreign firms', *Asian Wall Street Journal*, A1 and A2, 11 June 2004.
78. Wang was a Professor of Law, Institute of Law, Chinese Academy of Social Science. See, generally, Wang (2004, pp. 285–96).
79. The *State Medium-and-Long-Term Development Program regarding Science and Technology* provides that '[we shall] prevent the abuse of intellectual property which may unfairly restrict the market mechanism for fair competition and may prevent scientific-technological innovations and the expansion and application of scientific-technological achievements'.
80. China has begun to complain to the WTO Committee on Technical Barriers to Trade (TBT) that 'IPR issues in preparing and adopting international standards have become an obstacle for Members to adopt international standards and facilitate international trade' and has asked the TBT Committee to study this issue. Communication from the People's Republic of China, 'Intellectual Property Rights (IPR) issues in standardization', G/TBT/W/251, 25 May 2005. A number of ministries have been encouraging standards-setting working groups to compel patent holders to license on a royalty-free basis or via 'low royalty' patent pools. Article 14 of the IPR Policy of the Ministry of Information Industries (MII)'s Audio Video Coding Standard Workgroup requires

contributors either to issue royalty-free licences or join a patent pool for their essential Chinese patents, www.avs.org.cn/en/doc/AVS%20IPR%20Policy%20(Sep 122004-Dual%20Languages).doc (accessed 30 August 2007).

81. For example, in discussing China's 'National IPR Strategy' in 2005, Lu Wei, Director General of the Technical Economic Department, Development Research Center of the State Council, stated that 'the objective of formulating the National IPR Strategy is to improve national competitiveness and China's comprehensive national power. To adapt the strategy to China's development situation . . . [we shall] abide by international principles and *meet the lowest standards of the WTO*' (emphasis added), *Caijing Magazine*, 17 October 2005.

82. Office of the US Trade Representative, 'United States files WTO cases against China over deficiencies in China's IPR laws and market access barriers to copyright-based industries', 9 April 2007.

83. Soon after the US initiated WTO proceedings against China's export subsidies, China announced that it had terminated one of the subsidy programmes that had been the subject of the US challenge. Office of the US Trade Representative, 'Schwab lauds China's move to halt subsidized loans challenged by the United States in WTO Case', 9 March 2007.

REFERENCES

Aspray, W., F. Mayudas and M. Vardi (eds) (2006), *Globalization and Offshoring of Software: A Report of the ACM Job Migration Task Force*, New York and Beijing: Association for Computing Machinery.

Bayard, T. O. and K. A. Elliott (1994), *Reciprocity and Retaliation in US Trade Policy*, Washington, DC: Institute for International Economics.

Cassel, J. (2002), 'Why China is unlikely to abandon tax breaks', *Semiconductor Business News*, 19 December.

D'Andrea Tyson, L. (1992), *Who's Bashing Whom: Trade Conflict in High Technology Industries*, Washington, DC: Institute for International Economics.

Howell, T. R. (1998), 'The trade remedies: a US perspective', in G. Feketakuty (ed.), *Trade Strategies for a New Era: Ensuring US Leadership in a Global Economy*, New York: Council on Foreign Relations with the Monterrey Institute of International Studies, pp. 299–323.

Howell, T. R. (2003), 'Competing programs: government support for microelectronics', in C. W. Wessner (ed.), *Securing the Future: Regional and National Programs to Support the Semiconductor Industry*, Washington, DC: National Academies Press, pp. 221–3.

Hu, G. J. (2003), 'Government industry partnernships in Taiwan', in C. W. Wessner (ed.), *Securing the Future: Regional and National Programs to Support the Semiconductor Industry*, Washington, DC: National Academies Press, p. 154.

Hudec, R. (1975), *The GATT Legal System and World Trade Diplomacy*, New York: Praeger.

Jackson, J. H. (1969), *World Trade and the Law of GATT*, Charlottesville, VA: The Michie Company, p. 179.

Jingzhou, T. (2004), 'China's emerging antitrust regime', *China Business Review*, 1, May.

Mathews, J. A. (1997), 'A Silicon Valley of the East: creating Taiwan's semiconductor industry', *California Management Review*, State Administration of Industry and Commerce (*SAIC*) Summer, 26–54.

Mathews, J. (2000), *Tiger Technology: The Creation of a Semiconductor Industry in East Asia*, Cambridge: Cambridge University Press.

Office of Anti-Monopoly, Fair Trade Bureau, (2004), *Anticompetitive Practices of Multinational Companies in China and Countermeasures*, Administration of Industry and Commerce, pp. 42–3.

Office of the US Trade Representative (USTR) (2006), *US–China Trade Relations: Entering a New Phase of Greater Accountability and Enforcement*, February, p. 7, Washington, DC: USTR.

Ostry, S. (1997), 'Technology issues in the international trading system', in C. W. Wessner (ed.), *International Function and Cooperation in High-Technology Development and Trade*, Washington, DC: National Academies Press, p. 316.

Squires Meaney, C. (1994), 'State policy and the development of Taiwan's semiconductor industry', in J. D. Auerbach, D. Dollar and K. L. Sokoloff (eds), *The Role of the State in Taiwan's Economic Development*, Armonk, NY: M. E. Sharpe, Inc., pp. 170–92.

United States International Trade Commission (USITC) (1983), *Operation of the Trade Agreements Program, 34th Report*, publication no. 1414, Washington, DC: USITC, p. 182.

Wang, X. (2004), 'Issues surrounding the drafting of China's Antimonopoly Law', *Washington University Global Studies Law Review*, **3** (2), 185–96.

Wolf, A. W. (1994), 'The problems of market access in a global economy: trade and competition policy', in OECD (ed.), *New Dimensions of Market Access in a Globalizing World Economy*, Paris: OECD, accessed at www.tradewinsllc.net/publi/Lost-Leverage–Legal%20Times-89.pdf.

Wolff, A. M. and J. R. Magnus (1998), 'America's lost leverage', *Legal Times*, August, 24–31.

World Trade Organization (WTO) (1994), Agreement on Subsidies and Countervailing Measures, accessed at www.wto.org/english/docs_e/legal_e/24-scm.pdf.

5. From knowledge to innovation: resolving the 'European Paradox'

David B. Audretsch

5.1 INTRODUCTION[1]

A quiet and virtually unnoticed revolution is transforming public policy for economic growth, international competitiveness and employment generation. Where policy to ensure economic growth and job creation once looked to fiscal and monetary stimulation, on the one hand, and the large corporation, on the other, a new approach has emerged focusing on entrepreneurship. What was once anathema to economic efficiency and prosperity in the post-war era – new and small firms – has apparently become the engine of economic growth and job creation, not just in one economy, but spanning a broad spectrum of national, regional and local contexts.

Following the decade of Europe's worst economic performance since World War II, including record unemployment, it was perhaps not surprising when a bold new strategy to spur economic growth was unveiled. However, the focus of this new European growth policy would have seemed unimaginable only a few years earlier. With the 2000 Lisbon Proclamation, Romano Prodi, the then President of the European Commission (EC) committed Europe to becoming the entrepreneurship leader of the world by 2020 in order to ensure prosperity and a high standard of living throughout the continent.

Romano Prodi and the European Union (EU) were not alone in turning to entrepreneurship to provide the engine of economic growth. The entrepreneurial policy mandate mirrored similar efforts throughout the developed world. Public policy spanning a broad spectrum of national, regional and local contexts was turning to entrepreneurship to replace old jobs which were being lost to outsourcing and globalization, while at the same time trying to harness the potential that remained largely dormant from significant long-term investments in knowledge, such as universities and education and research institutions.

For example, at the 2006 Spring Summit of the European Government Leaders, igniting economic growth and reducing unemployment in Europe

was the main focus of the summit. The main policy strategy identified at
the summit was entrepreneurship. According to the then Chancellor of
Austria and President of the European Council, Wolfgang Schlüssel, 'The
member countries of the European Union must finally realize that they
have to undertake everything possible to facilitate the creation of new jobs
and economic growth. There would be ten million new jobs created in the
European Union by 2010, if the member countries were prepared to implement the necessary reforms, and especially reduce bureaucracy in order to
promote entrepreneurship.'[2]

By the 1980s and into the 1990s a new policy approach began to appear
with a greater focus on a very different set of instruments, such as research
and development (R&D), university research and investments in human
capital (Siegel et al., 2003). While these instruments were certainly not new,
the attention and concern they attracted in public policy debates to foster
growth and employment were certainly a contrast to the more macroeconomic focus of an earlier generation.

More recently, public policy has again refocused, this time towards entrepreneurship as an engine of growth. Trying to promote entrepreneurship in
order to foster economic growth might have seemed unfathomable just a
few years earlier. The purpose of this chapter is to explain how and why
public policy is turning towards entrepreneurship as a mechanism for generating economic growth and employment.

The chapter concludes by suggesting that entrepreneurship policy is the
purposeful attempt to create an entrepreneurial economy. Thus, this
chapter does not advocate any particular policies and certainly no specific
policy instruments to promote entrepreneurship. As Gordon Moore, who
is 'widely regarded as one of Silicon Valley's founding fathers' (Bresnahan
and Gambardella, 2004, p. 7) and Kevin Davis warn, the policy rush to
emulate the Silicon Valley's success is somewhat misguided, 'The potential
disaster lies in the fact that these static, descriptive efforts culminate in
policy recommendations and analytical tomes that resemble recipes or
magic potions such as combine liberal amounts of technology, entrepreneurs, capital, and sunshine; add one university; stir vigorously' (Moore
and Davis, 2004, p. 9). Apparently, creating the next Silicon Valley is not so
simple. Still, the purpose of this chapter is not to reveal the recipe, but
rather to suggest that the framework provided by the knowledge spillover
theory of entrepreneurship explains why the public policy community is
looking for the recipe to create an entrepreneurial economy.

5.2 PROMOTING INVESTMENT IN PHYSICAL CAPITAL IN THE SOLOW MODEL

In the post-World War II era the policy debate focusing on growth and employment looked to the macroeconomic instruments of fiscal and monetary policy, on the one hand, and the size and scale economies yielded by the large corporation, on the other. Writing in the post-war era, Robert Solow (1956, 1957) was awarded the Nobel Prize for his model of economic growth based on what came to be termed the neoclassical production function. In the Solow model two key factors of production – physical capital and (unskilled) labour – were econometrically linked to explain economic growth. The sources of economic growth depicted by the Solow model corresponded to the sources of growth in the actual post-World War II economy. The focus on physical capital as the key factor generating economic growth certainly corresponded to the post-war abundance of physical capital in the US. Several years after World War II, Robert Payne, the renowned historian from England, reflected:

> There never was a country more fabulous than America. She sits bestride the world like a Colossus; no other power at any time in the world's history has possessed so varied or so great an influence on other nations. Half of the wealth of the world, more than half of the productivity, nearly two-thirds of the world machines are concentrated in American hands; the rest of the world lies in the shadow of American industry. (cited in Halberstam, 1993, p. 116)

As a result of the unprecedented prosperity fuelled by the capital-driven, managed economy, *Fortune* magazine reported a vast rush of families moving up into the middle class – at the astonishing rate of 1.1 million per year. In 1956 there were 16.6 million middle-class families, and by 1959 there were 20 million (Halberstam, 1993, p. 586). *Life Magazine*, the stalwart magazine of the post-World War II era declared, 'Never before so much for so few' (Halberstam, 1993, p. 496). David Halberstam (1993, p. 116) reflects in *The Fifties*, 'It was to be a new, even easier age, the good life without sweat' (Halberstam, 1993, p. 496). He also observed that in *The Fifties* that:

> Life in America, it appeared, was in all ways going to get better. A new car could replace an old one, and a large, more modern refrigerator would take the place of one bought three years earlier, just as a new car had replaced an old one ... The market was saturated, but people kept on buying – newer, improved products that were easier to handle, that produced cleaner laundry, washed more dishes and glasses, and housed more frozen steaks. (Halberstam, 1993, p. 116)

Growth policy, or economic policy for growth, if not shaped by the Solow theoretical growth model, certainly corresponded to the view that inducing investments in physical capital in particular was the key to generating economic growth and advances in worker productivity. The view of the economy characterized by the Solow model framed the policy debate focusing on economic growth. The main mechanism for inducing higher growth rates was almost universally viewed as investments in physical capital. After all, the economy characterized by the Solow model was capital-driven. Increasing labour could increase the level of economic output, but not the rate of economic growth.

Both the economics literature and the corresponding public policy discourse were decidedly focused on which instruments, such as monetary policy versus fiscal policy, or interest rates versus capital depreciation allowances, were best suited to induce investment in physical capital and ultimately promote growth. While these debates may never have been satisfactorily resolved, their tenacity reflects the deep seated belief about the primacy of capital investment as the fundamental source of economic growth. Solow, of course, did acknowledge that technical change contributed to economic growth, but in terms of his formal model, it was considered to be an unexplained residual, which 'falls like manna from heaven'.

While technical change was acknowledged to shift the production function, in the Solow model it was considered to be exogenous, and therefore beyond the reach of policy. Thus, the policy debate during the post-war era, which may best be reflected by the Solow model, did not dispute the mechanism, physical capital, but rather the instruments. Something of a ferocious and vigorous dispute emerged both in the economics literature, as well as among the public policy community about which particular instruments were more conducive to inducing investments in physical capital.

On the one hand, were the advocates of monetary policy, who focused mainly on the instrument of interest rates as inducing capital investment. On the other hand, were the advocates of fiscal policy instruments, such as taxes and government expenditures, as the means of generating short-term growth to induce investments into new physical capital, thereby ensuring long-term growth. The choice of the particular instrument remained at the centre of an intellectual and public policy storm, but a near consensus left the actual policy mechanism to achieve economic growth virtually unchallenged.

While the context was considerably different, the choice of policy mechanisms to foster economic growth was no different for developing countries. The intellectual and policy focus on how to foster growth and prosperity in developing countries revolved around instruments to foster inward foreign direct investment (Kindleberger and Audretsch, 1983). The context of developing countries may have suggested the selection of different instruments uniquely suited to the development context, but the mechanism used to attain the policy goal of economic growth remained the same – investment in physical capital.

The policy focus on capital as the driving input for economic growth during the post-World War II era, generated a concomitant concern about the organization of that capital, at both industry and firm levels. The emerging field of industrial organization, in particular, was charged with the task of identifying how the organization of capital, or structure of an industry, influenced economic performance. A generation of scholars produced theoretical and empirical evidence suggesting that physical capital in many, but certainly not all, industries dictated a concentration of production resulting in an oligopolisitic market structure characterized by a concentration of ownership in relatively few producers (Scherer, 1970).

The large corporation was the source of jobs – good paying jobs – and security. No wonder when the Chairman of General Motors, Charlie 'Engine' Wilson was attributed with saying 'What's good for General Motors is good for America'[3] America believed. William H. Whyte called the men required to man the factories and corporations of this post-war economy, 'The Corporation Man'. This economy, driven by the efficiencies and power of large corporations such as General Motors, required massive interventions, regulations, fine-tuning and support, not just from government, but from virtually all facets of society, spanning a broad array of institutions ranging from schools to, as Betty Friedan (1972) was quick to point out in *The Feminine Mystique*, marriage and the family. It took what Audretsch and Thurik (2001) termed 'The Managed Economy' to provide the right institutions and policies to create a workforce and external conditions that could make an economy based on the efficiency of large-scale production in the form of the large corporation work the best.

Scholars spanning a broad spectrum of academic fields and disciplines generated a massive literature that attempted to sort out the perceived trade-off between economic efficiency, on the one hand, and political and economic decentralization, on the other. The large corporation was thought not only to have superior productive efficiency, but was also assumed to be the engine of technological innovation. Ironically, the literature's obsession with oligopoly was combined with an analysis that was essentially static. There was considerable concern over what to do about the existing industrial structure, but little attention was paid to where it came from and where it was going. Oliver Williamson's classic 1968 article 'Economies as an antitrust defense: the welfare tradeoffs', published in the *American Economic Review*, became something of a final statement demonstrating that gains in productive efficiency could be obtained through increased concentration and that gains in terms of competition, and implicitly democracy, could be achieved through decentralizing policies. But it did not seem possible to have both, certainly not in Williamson's completely static model.

Public policy towards business in this period revolved around finding solutions to the perceived trade-off between scale and efficiency, on the one hand, and decentralization and inefficiency, on the other hand. The three main policy instruments deployed to achieve the required balance in the industrialized countries were anti-trust (or competition policy, as it was called in Europe), regulation and public ownership of business.

The fundamental policy issue confronting Western Europe and North America during the post-war era, characterized by the Solow model, was how to live with this apparent trade-off between concentration and efficiency, and decentralization and democracy. The public policy question of the day was: how can society reap the benefits of the large corporation in an oligopolistic setting while avoiding or at least minimizing the costs imposed by a concentration of economic power? The policy response was to constrain the freedom of firms to contract. Such policy restraints typically took the form of instruments involving public ownership, regulation and competition policy or anti-trust. At the time, considerable attention was devoted to what seemed like glaring differences in policy approaches to this apparent trade-off by different countries. France and Sweden resorted to government ownership of private business. Other countries, such as the Netherlands and Germany, tended to emphasize regulation. Still other countries, such as the US, put a greater emphasis on anti-trust. In fact, most countries relied upon elements of all three policy instruments. While the particular instruments may have varied across countries, they were, in fact, manifestations of a singular policy approach – how to restrict and restrain the power of the large corporation. What may have been perceived as a disparate set of policies at the time appears in retrospect to comprise a remarkably singular policy approach. Of course, each country adapted its own particular mix of policy instruments to try to obtain the benefits of large-scale production and concentrated ownership while, at the same time, restricting and constraining those firms in an attempt to avoid political and economic abuse.

While a heated debate emerged about which approach best promoted large-scale production while simultaneously constraining the ability of large corporations to exert market power, there was much less debate about public policy towards small business and entrepreneurship. The only issue was whether public policy makers should simply allow small firms to disappear as a result of their inefficiency or intervene to preserve them on social and political grounds. Those who perceived small firms to contribute significantly to growth, employment generation and competitiveness were few and far between.

Thus, in the post-war era, small firms and entrepreneurship were viewed as a luxury, perhaps needed by the West to ensure a decentralization of decision making, but in any case obtained only at a cost to efficiency. Certainly the systematic empirical evidence, gathered from both Europe and North America, documented a sharp trend towards a decreased role of small firms during the post-war period. Public policy towards small firms generally reflected the view of economists and other scholars that they were a drag on economic efficiency and growth, generated lower quality jobs in terms of direct and indirect compensation, and were on the way to becoming less important to the economy, if not threatened by long-term extinction. Some countries, such as the former Soviet Union, but also Sweden and France, adapted the policy stance of allowing small firms to gradually disappear and account for a smaller share of economic activity.

The public policy stance of the US reflected long-term political and social valuation of small firms that seemed to reach back to the Jeffersonian traditions of the country. After all, in the 1890 debate in Congress, Senator Sherman vowed:

> If we will not endure a King as a political power we should not endure a King over the production, transportation, and sale of the necessaries of life. If we would not submit to an emperor we should not submit to an autocrat of trade with power to prevent competition and to fix the price of any commodity. (Scherer, 1977, p. 980)

Preservationist policies were clearly at work in the creation of the US Small Business Administration. In the Small Business Act of 10 July 1953 Congress authorized the creation of the Small Business Administration, with an explicit mandate to 'aid, counsel, assist and protect . . . the interests of small business concerns'.[4] The Small Business Act was clearly an attempt by Congress to halt the continued disappearance of small businesses and to preserve their role in the US economy.

5.3 KNOWLEDGE AS THE RESPONSE TO GLOBALIZATION

Globalization has shaken the comparative advantage of the Western developed OECD countries in manufactured goods based on physical capital. What has been the response of not just corporate America, but corporations throughout Europe and the developed world, at least in the traditional manufacturing industries? Outsource, offshore and downsize,

downsize and downsize. What production does remain is increasingly manufactured by high-technology and sophisticated machinery that requires only a minimal of (expensive) labour. The corporate response to globalization has been prevalent throughout the developed economies. As the headline story 'Deutschland: export weltmeister (von arbeitsplätzen)' or 'Germany: export world leader (of jobs)' in the most prestigious weekly German magazine, *Der Spiegel*, reports 'Bye-bye "Made in Germany"'.[5] Employment in manufacturing rose throughout the era of the managed economy, increasing from 12.5 million in 1970 to 14.1 million in 1991. Then, as globalization hit home in Germany, manufacturing jobs crashed to a low of 10.2 million by 2004. Between 1991 and 2004 the number of jobs in the German textile industry fell by 65 per cent, from 274 658 to 94 432. In the construction industry there was a 58 per cent decrease in employment in Germany, from 1.9 million jobs to 778 000. In the metalworking industries employment decreased from 476 299 to 250 024, or 47.5 per cent. And in the heart and pride of German manufacturing, the machine tool industry, the number of jobs fell from 1.6 million to 947 448 or by 39.1 per cent.

When the high-cost manufacturing plants of Germany are compared to the more moderate factories located not so far away, in Central and Eastern Europe, it is hard to imagine that German manufacturing will ever regain its prowess and pervasiveness in the German economy and society. Comparing typical workers at the Opel plant in Bochum and at the Opel plant in Gliwice in Poland, the worker in Germany spends 35 hours in the plant compared to 40 hours by his Polish counterpart, earns 2 900 euros monthly compared to 700 euros monthly, and receives 31 days of vacation compared to 26 for his Polish counterpart.

The devastation of the jobs and production in the traditional manufacturing industries could hardly be claimed to be better on the other side of the Atlantic. Substituting capital and technology for labour, along with shifting production to lower-cost locations has resulted in waves of corporate downsizing in the US. At the same time, it has generally preserved the viability of many of the large corporations. The *Financial Times* reports, 'French and German businesses have competed well on global markets' (Stephens, 2006, p. 11).

The workers of Europe, however, have not fared so well. As Figure 5.1 shows, based on statistics gathered in a careful study undertaken by the Germany Ministry of Economics and Technology, Siemens increased the amount of employment outside Germany by 50 per cent, from 108 000 in the mid-1980s to 162 000 in the mid-1990s. Over the same period, it decreased the amount of employment in Germany by 12 per cent, from 240 000 to 211 000. Volkswagen (VW) increased the level of employment in foreign countries by 24 per cent, from 78 000 in the mid-1980s to 97 000 in

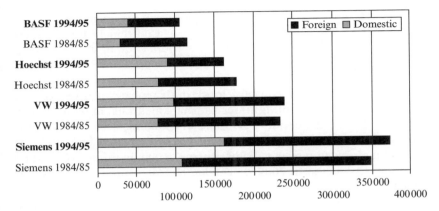

Figure 5.1 Employment in large German corporations

the mid-1990s. Over the same time period, it decreased employment in Germany by 10 per cent, from 156 000 to 141 000. Similarly, Hoechst increased the number of jobs outside Germany by 9 per cent, from 78 925 in the mid-1980s to 92 333 in the mid-1990s. The number of Hoechst employees in Germany fell over that same period by 26 per cent, from 99 015 to 73 338. And BASF increased employment in foreign countries from 29 966 in the mid-1980s to 40 297 in the mid-1990s. Domestic employment by BASF fell by 17 per cent over that same time period, from 85 850 to 65 969.

As *Der Spiegel* observes, 'Globalization is bursting at the seams, it seems. Long-established companies are muting into supranational conglomerates. But is there anything still German about Metro, Siemens or Deutsche Bank?' (Jung, 2005; p. 103). For example, the flagship German bank actually employs 66 per cent of its workforce abroad. Similarly, by 2005, well over half of VW's 305 695 workers were employed outside of Germany (Hofmann, 2005, p. 15). Only 158 570 VW employees actually worked in Germany. The reason? According to one of the leading German business newspapers, the *Handelsblatt*, 'Production in West German VW factories is much too expensive. Costs have to be reduced, primarily through downsizing and layoffs' (Hofmann, 2005, p. 15). By contrast, employment has continued to increase in VW establishments outside Germany. As of 2005 there were 23 456 VW employees in the Czech Republic, 23 240 in Spain, 21 860 in Brazil, 21 190 in China, 15 110 in Mexico, 8 150 in the Slovak Republic and 6 940 in Poland (Hofmann, 2005, p. 15).

These examples are not isolated, but are rather typical of the wave of German downsizing in the 1990s that resulted in levels of unemployment not seen since World War II. As *Der Spiegel* points out:[6]

> Worldwide competition has its dark sides: globalization is putting more pressure on German workers. Every week companies are announcing plans to relocate operations and jobs. Organizations such as Siemens, Schering and Deutsche Post – which are reporting strong, even record earnings – are laying off thousands of domestic employees.

The pervasiveness of job displacements due to job downsizing triggered by outsourcing and offshoring in German manufacturing subsequent to the fall of the Berlin Wall is evident. As Table 5.1 shows, between 1991 and 1995 manufacturing employment in German plants decreased by 1 307 000, while it increased in foreign subsidiaries by 189 000. In the chemical sector the decrease in domestic employment was 80 000, while 14 000 jobs were added by German chemical companies in plants located outside of Germany. In electrical engineering employment in German plants decreased by 198 000. In automobiles employment in Germany decreased by 161 000, while 30 000 jobs were added outside of Germany. The reaction of the German public was to accuse German firms of not fulfilling their social contract. As one of the leading newspapers, *Die Zeit*, accused German industry, 'When profits lead to ruin – more profits and more unemployment: where is the social responsibility of the firms?' (*Die Zeit*, 1996, p. 1).

Thus, one of the most profound consequences of globalization has been to trigger a shift in the working experience of most people, away from being directly or indirectly involved with manufacturing and towards some type of non-manufacturing activity, such as services or retailing. This shift has in no way been restricted to the US. For example, in 1970 about 50 per cent of German employment was in manufacturing. By 2005 the share of manufacturing employment had fallen to 27 per cent, or just one in four workers. As, *Der Spiegel*, comments, 'A sad record: In this land of engineers and automakers, the industrial core is melting away. With jobs being relocated to low-wage countries and processes performed by computers and robots, in the long term manufacturing jobs in Germany will not be created.'[7]

Writing from Germany, Karl Marx had warned the Western world of a spectre that was haunting capitalism and would ultimately pull it down – the increased consolidation and power resulting from ever greater control in the hands of fewer people, whom he called capitalists. Perhaps one day Marx will be proven right. But, in the meantime, the spectre haunting the West came from an entirely different direction – the East, but also the South – in the guise of Thomas Friedman's globalization. Unprecedented success in mastering the economics of economy, particularly in terms of production, management and distribution, resulted in unprecedented prosperity, growth and employment in the West during the post-war era. The

Table 5.1 Change in employment figures in Germany and at foreign subsidiaries (1991–95, in thousands)

Employment Sector	Manufacturing	Chemicals	Electrical engineering	Automotive	Mechanical engineering	Textiles	Banking and insurance
Foreign	189	14	–17	30	16	–6	21
Domestic	–1.307	–80	–198	–161	–217	–68	28

Source: Bundesministerium für Wirtschafts und Technologie (2000) (German Federal Ministry of Economics and Technology).

fall of the Berlin Wall, which was supposed to extend this post-war prosperity by facilitating access to new and previously untapped markets, resulted in a shock to the system – the system focused on and organized around the factor of capital, which had thrived so long and served the West so well. But, even as the Europeans were beginning to realize that their social market economies, which had been adapted and evolved perhaps even better to nurture and tend the capital-based economy, also were not immune to the very forces that had undermined the American post-war version of the managed economy, a new strategy for prosperity in the era of globalization was emerging. This new strategy was based on a shift in the comparative advantage of the advanced economies away from the factor of physical capital and towards ideas and knowledge.

If physical capital was at the heart of the economic model that won Robert Solow the Nobel Prize in economics, knowledge capital replaced it in the model of endogenous growth introduced by Paul Romer (1986). While the policy goals remained relatively unchanged, economic growth, the Romer model reflected the emergence of a new emphasis on a strikingly different policy mechanism, knowledge capital, involving very different policy instruments.

The new policy instruments corresponding to the knowledge-driven economy, or the Romer model, generally involved inducing investments not necessarily in physical capital, but rather in knowledge capital. While the concept of knowledge capital seemed to be vaguer and less conducive to measurement than did the traditional factor of physical capital, it clearly involved knowledge augmenting investments in human capital and research and development (R&D). Such instruments were strikingly diFerent from their counterparts corresponding to the Solow economy. These instruments included, but were not limited to, education at all levels, but certainly at university level, public research support, and tax and subsidy incentives to encourage private R&D. For example, investment in universities was not necessarily viewed as an instrument promoting economic growth in the capital-driven economy. After all, it was not at all clear how the output of universities, students and research would contribute to augmenting investments in capital. While there was an important case to be made for investing in universities for political, social and even moral reasons, the case was less compelling for economic reasons, and particularly for economic growth. It was indeed possible to view investments in universities as actually detracting from economic growth in that they diverted resources away from physical capital. But no one can dispute the primacy of investment in universities in the Romer economy. Investments in new knowledge were expected to be particularly potent because of the assumption that knowledge spills over from the firm or research organization creating that knowledge to other firms for commercialization, thus resulting in increasing returns in terms of economic growth.

Thus, just as the enormous investment in physical plant and equipment propelled Europe and North America to unprecedented post-war prosperity in the Solow economy, both scholars and policy makers have been looking towards the unrivalled investment in research and knowledge to generate economic growth, employment and competitiveness in the era of globalization.

5.4 THE KNOWLEDGE FILTER

How does this knowledge created at universities spill over for commercialization in the market? Does it perhaps blow over or simply fall, like Robert Solow's famous manna from heaven, ripe for commercialization by the private sector? There are compelling reasons to think that it is not so easy or automatic. Certainly there is a long tradition of a wall between the university and the community. A barrier divided the university from the rest of society. This wall may have been invisible, but it was keenly felt by those on each side. Professors and students were proudly, and certainly gladly, cut off from society and isolated in the ivory tower afforded by the gates of the university. Those on the outside peered at a distance, typically with disdain and curiosity, if not hostility towards this ivory tower.

Thus, it is now recognized that investment in scientific knowledge and research alone will not automatically generate growth and prosperity. Rather, such knowledge investments must penetrate what Acs et al. (2004) and Audretsch et al. (2006) term the knowledge filter, in order to contribute to innovation, competitiveness and ultimately economic growth. In fact, the knowledge filter impeding the commercializing of investments in research and knowledge can be formidable. As the American Senator Birch Bayh warned, 'A wealth of scientific talent at American colleges and universities – talent responsible for the development of numerous innovative scientific breakthroughs each year – is going to waste as a result of bureaucratic red tape and illogical government regulations . . .'.[8] It is the knowledge filter that stands between investment in research, on the one hand, and its commercialization through innovation, leading ultimately to economic growth, on the other. Certainly seen through the eyes of Senator Bayh, the magnitude of the knowledge filter is daunting, 'What sense does it make to spend billions of dollars each year on government-supported research and then prevent new developments from benefiting the American people because of dumb bureaucratic red tape?'[9]

This is just as true for Europe. According to Garching Innovation, GmbH: Would you build a car without wheels? Presumably not. But something similar happens every day in Germany, at least when R&D is involved. We are investing around 17.5 billion euros in publicly supported science and research. About half of that investment, around 9 billion euros is in basic research, which, even though it could of course be improved, is still at the cutting edge by global standards. However, we lack the 3–4 per cent of this investment required to transform these investments into new and innovative products. It is as if you would invest a huge sum of money to develop a new automobile, but in the end realize there are not sufficient funds to purchase tyres.[10]

In each of these examples from Europe and America there will be no or at least only restricted knowledge spillovers. Investments were made in creating new knowledge, both privately from the firm, but also publicly, if generation of the new knowledge utilized any type of public knowledge emanating from research at universities or publicly provided investments in human capital. However, in the absence of knowledge spillover, such investments will not be appropriated either by the firm or by society. It must not be forgotten that the social investments of education and research are also expected to generate a return in terms of growth and employment.

Thus, the spillover of knowledge that exists by assumption in the Romer (1986), Lucas (1993) and Krugman (1991) models, in fact, may not be so automatic, but may be impeded by a knowledge filter (Acs et al., 2004; Audretsch et al., 2006). The knowledge filter serves to impede, if not preempt, the spillover and commercialization of knowledge.

If all of the existing, status quo organizations could effectively move society into the future, there would be no particularly interesting or important role for entrepreneurship, at least the version that is restricted to the creation of a new organization. That would mean that sufficient innovation was being generated by the status quo. If there were a deficiency of new, viable ideas, the problem area would lie in terms of people.

However, the last decade or so has seen an explosion in concern about the investment society makes in what enables people to think up new ideas – education at all levels, R&D and universities. In some places there is indeed a severe deficiency in human capital and education. In other places the constraint may be less in terms of the formal education and more in terms of creativity.

But in many contexts the problem may lie less in the education, human capital, experience or creativity of people and be more attributable to the knowledge filter. People have ideas, aspirations, insights and visions about how to do things differently or better. That is, how to lead into a future that is better and better equipped to compete globally. But in the actual doing of it, putting the idea into action, the implementation gets hung up in the knowledge filter.

5.5   ENTREPRENEURSHIP AS THE MISSING LINK

New knowledge that generates innovation is the key to moving into the future in a proactive way that, rather than being defeated by globalization, harnesses the new opportunities offered by globalization. The way into the future is through doing something new, different and better, at least as defined by the (global) market, that is, by innovating. Sticking to the same old 'same old' may be familiar and comfortable. But, thanks to globalization, it will be becoming increasingly familiar in other and cheaper parts of the world. If the same old 'same old' can be done in Mexico or South America, not to mention Romania or Poland, or even China and India, it will continue to be done, but not in the same old place. Innovation is a way of taking advantage of globalization's opportunities rather than being victimized by its liabilities. But what about entrepreneurship, what is it and why is it needed?

Entrepreneurship is about two things. First, it is about starting a new organization or firm. For those that cannot pursue their ideas, dreams and insights in the context of an incumbent organization, it is about moving to a context where they can. And, second, it is about moving into the future. Lots of people have ideas about how to do something differently. About how some aspect of the future, however small or big, could look different from today. But simply having a vision is not entrepreneurship. As the German writer, Johann Wolfgang von Goethe observed some two centuries ago, 'Es ist nicht genug zu wissen, man muss es auch anwenden; es ist nicht genug zu wollen, man muss es auch tun' (Knowledge alone does not suffice, it must also be applied: wanting is not enough, one has to actually do it).

By endogenously facilitating the spillover of knowledge created in a different organization and perhaps for a different application, entrepreneurship may provide what Acs et al. (2004) and Audretsch et al. (2006) describe as the missing link in economic growth. Confronted with a formidable knowledge filter, public policy instruments emerging from new growth theory, such as investments in human capital, R&D and university research may not result in adequate economic growth. One interpretation of the European Paradox, where such investments in new knowledge have certainly been vigorous and sustained, is that the presence of such an imposing knowledge filter chokes off the commercialization of those new investments, resulting in diminished innovative activity and, ultimately, stagnant growth.

By serving as a conduit for knowledge spillovers, entrepreneurship is the missing link between investments in new knowledge and economic growth. Thus, the spillover theory of knowledge entrepreneurship provides not just an explanation of why entrepreneurship has become more prevalent as the factor of knowledge has emerged as a crucial source for comparative advantage, but also why entrepreneurship plays a vital role in generating economic growth. Entrepreneurship is an important mechanism permeating the knowledge filter to facilitate the spillover of knowledge and ultimately generate economic growth.

Entrepreneurship policy to ignite economic growth is spreading throughout the developed countries. For example, in the Lisbon Accord of 2002, the EC made a formal commitment to becoming the entrepreneurship and knowledge leader in the world by 2020 in order to foster economic growth and prosperity on the continent. As Bresnahan and Gambardella (2004, p. 1) observe:

> Clusters of high-tech industry, such as Silicon Valley, have received a great deal of attention from scholars and in the public policy arena. National economic growth can be fuelled by development of such clusters. In the United States the long boom of the 1980s and 1990s was largely driven by growth in the information technology industries in a few regional clusters. Innovation and entrepreneurship can be supported by a number of mechanisms operating within a cluster, such as easy access to capital, knowledge about technology and markets, and collaborators.

Similarly, Wallsten (2004, p. 229) remarked that, 'Policy makers around the world are anxious to find tools that will help their regions emulate the success of Silicon Valley and create new centers of innovation and high technology.'

The mandate for entrepreneurship policy has emerged from what would superficially appear to be two opposite directions. One direction emanates from the failure of the traditional policy instruments corresponding to the Solow model, or those based on instruments promoting investment in physical capital, to adequately maintain economic growth and employment in globally linked markets. The second push for the entrepreneurship policy mandate is from the other direction – the failure of the so-called new economy policy instruments, corresponding to the Romer model, or those promoting investment into knowledge capital, to adequately generate economic growth and employment. Although coming from opposite directions, both have in common unacceptable economic performance. Which is to say that the mandate for entrepreneurship policy is rooted in dissatisfaction – dissatisfaction with the status quo and, in particular, with the status quo economic performance.[11]

The first direction underlying the mandate for entrepreneurship policy emanates from regions and even countries, which had prospered during the post-war economy, characterized by the Solow model, but which more recently have been adversely affected by globalization and loss of competitiveness in traditional industries, resulting in a poor economic performance. The loss of competitiveness by large-scale producers in high-cost locations is manifested by the fact that, confronted with lower-cost competition in foreign locations, producers in the high-cost countries have four options apart from doing nothing and losing global market share: (1) to reduce wages and other production costs sufficiently to compete with the low-cost foreign producers; (2) to substitute equipment and technology for labour to increase productivity; (3) to shift production out of the high-cost location and into the low-cost location; or (4) to outsource the production of inputs to third-party firms, typically located in lower cost locations.

The second push for the entrepreneurship policy mandate is from the opposite direction – the inability of investments in knowledge to foster economic performance. Much has been made of the so-called European Paradox, where high levels of investment in new knowledge stem from both private firms as well as public research institutes and universities. Countries such as Sweden rank among the highest in terms of investment in research, at least as measured by the ratio of R&D to GDP. Similarly, levels of human capital and education in Sweden as well as throughout many parts of Europe, rank among the highest in the world. Yet, growth rates remained stagnant and employment creation sluggish throughout the 1990s and into the new century.

In this case there were no knowledge spillovers. Investments were made to create new knowledge, both privately by firms, and also publicly. However, in the absence of knowledge spillovers, such investments will not be appropriated by either firms or society. It must not be forgotten that social investments in education and research are also expected to generate a return in terms of growth and employment.

Entrepreneurship can contribute to economic growth by serving as a mechanism that permeates the knowledge filter. There is a virtual consensus that entrepreneurship revolves around the recognition of opportunities combined with the cognitive decision to commercialize those opportunities by starting a new firm. If investments in new knowledge create opportunities that are asymmetric in that they are more apparent or valued more highly by economic agents (potential entrepreneurs) than by the incumbent firms themselves, the only organizational context for commercializing that new idea will be a new firm. Audretsch et al. (2006) show that those regions in Germany with the highest levels of entrepreneurial activity also exhibit the highest growth rates. Similarly, Acs et al. (2004) show that those countries exhibiting the highest rates of entrepreneurship also tend to experience the highest rates of economic growth.

Confronted with a non-trivial knowledge filter, investments in labour, physical capital and knowledge capital may not result in adequate levels of economic growth and employment creation. Entrepreneurship makes a unique contribution to economic growth by permeating the knowledge filter and commercializing ideas that would otherwise remain uncommercalized.

Shifting to a policy focus on knowledge capital, involving instruments to induce investments in knowledge capital has clearly been successful in generating economic growth in many regions. However, investments in knowledge capital may be a necessary, but not a sufficient condition to ensure that such investments are actually commercialized and generate economic growth. The existence of a severe knowledge filter will impede the spillover and commercialization of investments in new knowledge, thereby choking off the potential for economic growth. There is no patent recipe for public policy to create an entrepreneurial economy. But the effort to do so has resulted in the emergence of a distinct new public policy approach to generate economic growth – entrepreneurship policy. While the goals remain the same, economic growth and employment creation or at least maintenance, the mechanism used, entrepreneurship and accompanying instruments are strikingly different. For example, in an effort to penetrate such a formidable knowledge filter, the US Congress enacted the Bayh-Dole Act in 1980 to spur the transfer of technology from university research to commercialization.[12] The goal of the Bayh-Dole Act was to encourage the commercialization of university science. Assessments of the impact of the Bayh-Dole Act on penetrating the knowledge filter and facilitating the commercialization of university research have bordered on the euphoric:[13]

Possibly the most inspired piece of legislation to be enacted in America over the past half-century was the Bayh-Dole Act of 1980. Together with amendments in 1984 and augmentation in 1986, this unlocked all the inventions and discoveries that had been made in laboratories through the United States with the help of taxpayers' money. More than anything, this single policy measure helped to reverse America's precipitous slide into industrial irrelevance. Before Bayh-Dole, the fruits of research supported by government agencies had gone strictly to the federal government. Nobody could exploit such research without tedious negotiations with a federal agency concerned. Worse, companies found it nigh impossible to acquire exclusive rights to a government owned patent. And without that, few firms were willing to invest millions more of their own money to turn a basic research idea into a marketable product.[14]

An even more enthusiastic assessment suggested that:

> The Bayh-Dole Act turned out to be the Viagra for campus innovation. Universities that would previously have let their intellectual property lie fallow began filing for – and getting patents at unprecedented rates. Coupled with other legal, economic and political developments that also spurred patenting and licensing, the results seems nothing less than a major boom to national economic growth (Mowery, 2005, p. 2).

The Bayh-Dole Act is only one example of the new American entrepreneurship policy. The policy shift to enabling the creation and viability of knowledge-based entrepreneurial firms is evidenced by the passage in the US Congress of the Small Business Innovation Research (SBIR) programme in the early 1980s. Enactment of the SBIR was a response to the loss of American competitiveness in global markets. Congress mandated each federal agency with allocating around 4 per cent of its annual budget to funding innovative small firms as a mechanism for restoring American international competitiveness (Wessner, 2000). The SBIR provides a mandate to the major R&D agencies in the US to allocate a share of the research budget to innovative small firms.

The SBIR represents about 60 per cent of all public entrepreneurial finance programmes. Taken together, public small-business finance is about two-thirds bigger than private venture capital. In 1995 the sum of equity financing provided through and guaranteed by public programmes financing small and medium-sized enterprises was $US2.4 billion, which amounted to more than 60 per cent of the total funding disbursed by traditional venture funds in that year. Equally important is the emphasis in SBIR and most public funds on early stage finance, which is generally ignored by private venture capital. Some of the most innovative American companies received early stage finance from SBIR, including Apple Computer, Chiron, Compaq and Intel.

There is compelling evidence that the SBIR programme has had a positive impact on economic performance in the US (Wessner, 2000). The benefits have been documented as:

- The survival and growth rates of SBIR recipients have exceeded those of firms not receiving SBIR funding.
- The SBIR induces scientists involved in biomedical research to change their career paths. By applying the scientific knowledge to commercialization, these scientists shift their career trajectories away from basic research towards entrepreneurship.
- The SBIR awards provide a source of funding for scientists to launch

start-up firms that otherwise would not have had access to alternative sources of funding.
- SBIR awards have a powerful demonstration effect. Scientists commercializing research results by starting companies induce colleagues to consider applications and the commercial potential of their own research.

University entrepreneurship can contribute to economic growth by serving as a mechanism that permeates the knowledge filter (Lohr, 2006, p. 7). It is a virtual consensus that entrepreneurship revolves around the recognition of opportunities along with the cognitive decision to commercialize those opportunities by starting a new firm. If investments in new knowledge create opportunities that are asymmetric in that they are more apparent or valued more highly by economic agents (potential entrepreneurs) than by the incumbent firms themselves, the only organizational context for commercializing that new idea will be a new firm.

From the perspective of the singular or effectively closed economy at the turn of the last century Schumpeter (1911) may have been led to conclude that the contribution of entrepreneurship is through the destruction of the status quo by displacement by new firms, or creative construction. However, in the globalized economy of the twenty-first century, the destruction comes from global competition. Creative construction of new possibilities and sources of growth comes from sources such as university entrepreneurship (Audretsch et al., 2006).

As first, the capital-driven Solow model, and more recently the knowledge-driven Romer model have not delivered the expected levels of economic performance, a mandate for entrepreneurship policy has emerged and begun to diffuse throughout the entire globe. Whether or not specific policy instruments will work in their particular contexts is not the point of this chapter. What is striking, however, is the emergence and diffusion of an entirely new public policy approach to generating economic growth – entrepreneurship policy. It is becoming increasingly the case that it is upon this new mantel of entrepreneurship that economic policy, ranging from communities to cities, states and even entire nations hangs its hopes, dreams and aspirations for prosperity and security.

5.6 CONCLUSIONS

Globalization has rendered the post-war growth strategies of the leading developed countries, which were based on promoting investments in physical capital, as no longer viable. As a response to globalization, the growth and employment strategies of the developed countries have increasingly shifted to investments in new knowledge and ideas. Policy instruments, such as the promotion of university research, human capital and R&D, have become increasingly important. However, such knowledge investments do not automatically spill over to result in innovative activity. Rather, the existence of a knowledge filter impedes the spillover of knowledge and constrains subsequent innovative activity by private firms. Entrepreneurship provides one important mechanism, penetrating the knowledge filter and facilitating the spillover and commercialization of knowledge. Thus, growth and employment policies are increasingly reshifting their focus to promoting entrepreneurship as a vital vehicle to ensure economic growth, employment generation and competitiveness in a globalizing economy.

NOTES

1. The author is grateful for suggestions and comments on an earlier draft of this chapter from participants at the April 2006 VINNOVA Conference on Knowledge and Innovation held in Stockholm, Sweden.
2. 'Schlüssel: Zehn millionen arbeitsplätze bis 2010: der Ratspräsident ruft die EU-Staaten zu reformoffensive auf – mittelstand fördern, Entbürokratisierung vorantreiben', *Die Welt*, 18 March 2006, p. 1.
3. Halberstam (1993, p. 118) corrects this conventional wisdom. What Wilson actually said was, 'We at General Motors have always felt that what was good for the country was good for General Motors as well.'
4. www.sba.gov/aboutsba/history/index.html.
5. 'Bye-Bye "Made in Germany" ', *Der Spiegel* (2004), **44**, pp. 94–99.
6. Ibid.
7. Ibid., pp. 94–9, 101.
8. Introductory statement by Birch Bayh, 13 September 1978, cited from AUTUM (2004, p. 5).
9. Statement by Birch Bayh, 13 April 1980, on the approval of S. 414 (Bayh-Dole) by the US Senate on a 91–4 vote, cited from AUTUM (2004, p. 16).
10. 'Konzeption eines Innovationsfonds der Deutschen Forschung (IFDF) zur stärkung des technologietransfers', *Garching Information*, January 2006.
11. A third direction contributing to the mandate for entrepreneurship policy may be in the context of less developed regions and developing countries. Such regions have had endowments of neither physical capital nor knowledge capital, but still look to entrepreneurship capital to serve as an engine of economic growth.
12. Public Law 98–620.
13. Mowery (2005, p. 2) argues that such a euphemistic assessment of the impact on Bayh-Dole is exaggerated, 'Although it seems clear that the criticism of high-technology startups that was widespread during the period of pessimism over U.S. competitiveness was overstated, the recent focus on patenting and licensing as the essential ingredient in university-industry collaboration and knowledge transfer may be no less exaggerated. The emphasis on the Bayh-Dole Act as a catalyst to these interactions also seems somewhat misplaced.'
14. 'Innovation's golden goose', *The Economist*, 12 December 2002.

REFERENCES

Acs, Z., D. Audretsch, P. Braunerhjelm and B. Carlsson (2004), 'The missing link: the knowledge filter and endogenous growth', Center for Business and Policy Studies, discussion paper, Stockholm.

Association of University Technology Managers (AUTM) (2004), Recollections: Celebrating the History of AUTM and the Legacy of Bayh-Dole, Northbrook, IL: AUTM.

Audretsch, D. (2007), *The Entrepreneurial Society*, New York: Oxford University Press.

Audretsch, D. and R. Thurik (2001), 'What's new about the new economy? Sources of growth in the managed and entrepreneurial economies', *Industrial and Corporate Change*, **19**, 795–821.

Audretsch, D. B., M. Keilbach and E. Lehmann (2006), *Entrepreneurship and Economic Growth*, New York: Oxford University Press.

Bresnahan, T. and A. Gambardella (2004), *Building High-Tech Clusters: Silicon Valley and Beyond*, Cambridge: Cambridge University Press.

Bundesministerium für Wirtschaft und Technologie (BMWi) (German Federal Ministry of Economics and Technology) (2000), *Annual Report 2000*, Berlin: BMWi.

Die Zeit (1996), 'Wenn der profit zur pleite fuehrt: mehr gewinne und mehr arbeitslose – wo bleibt die soziale verantwortung der unternehmer?' [When profits lead to ruin: more profits and more unemployed – where is the social responsibility of the firms?], 2 February, p. 1.

Friedan, B. (1972), *The Feminine Mystique*, New York: Penguin.

Halberstam, D. (1993), *The Fifties*, New York: Villard.

Hofmann, J. (2005), 'VW greift nur im Ausland durch', *Handesblatt*, **87**(5–7), May: 15.

Jung, A. (2005), 'A new economic age', *The Spiegel Special International Edition*, **4**, 103.

Kindleberger, C. and D. Audretsch (1983), *The Multinational Corporation in the 1980s*, London: MIT Press.

Krugman, P. (1991), *Geography and Trade*, Cambridge, MA: MIT Press.

Lohr, S. (2006), 'US research funds often lead to start-ups, study says', *New York Times*, 10 April, accessed 2 July 2008 at www.nytimes.com/2006/04/10/business/10cancer.html.

Lucas, R. (1993), 'Making a miracle', *Econometrica*, **61**, 251–72.

Moore, G. and K. Davis (2004), 'Learning the Silicon Valley way', in T. Bresnahan and A. Gambardella (eds), *Building High-Tech Clusters: Silicon Valley and Beyond*, Cambridge: Cambridge University Press, pp. 7–39.

Mowery, D. (2005), 'The Bayh-Dole Act and high technology entrepreneurship in US universities: chicken, egg, or something else?', paper presented at the Eller Center Conference on Entrepreneurship Education and Technology Transfer, University of Arizona, 21–22 January.

Romer, P. (1986), 'Increasing returns and long-run growth', *Journal of Political Economy*, **94**, 1002–37.

Scherer, F. (1970), *Industrial Market Structure and Economic Performance*, Chicago: Rand McNally.

Scherer, F. M. (1977), 'The Posnerian harvest: separating wheat from chaff', *Yale Law Journal*, **86**, 974–1002.

Schumpeter, J. (1911), *Theorie der Wirtschaftlichen Entwicklung. Eine Untersuchung über Unternehmergewinn, Kapital, Kredit, Zins und den Konjunkturzyklus*, Berlin: Duncker und Humblot.

Siegel, D. R., C. Wessner, M. Binks and A. Lockett (2003), 'Policies promoting innovation in small firms: evidence from the US and UK, *Small Business Economics*, **20**, 121–7.

Solow, R. (1956), 'A contribution to theory of economic growth', *Quarterly Journal of Economics*, **70**, 65–94.

Solow, R. (1957), 'Technical change and the aggregate production function', *Review of Economics and Statistics*, **39**, 312–20.

Stephens, P. (2006), 'A future for Europe shaped by museums and modernity', *Financial Times*, 28 April, p. 11.

Wallsten, S. (2004), 'The role of government in regional technology development: the effects of public venture capital and science parks', in T. Bresnahan and A. Gambardella, *Building High-Tech Clusters. Silicon Valley and Beyond*, Cambridge: Cambridge University Press, pp. 229–79.

Wessner, C. (2000), *The Small Business Innovation Research Program (SBIR)*, Washington, DC: National Academy Press.

Williamson, O. (1968), 'Economies as an antitrust defense: the welfare tradeoffs', *American Economic Review*, **51**(1), 18–36.

6. Innovative entrepreneurship: commercialization by linking ideas and people

Åsa Lindholm Dahlstrand

6.1 INTRODUCTION[1]

Entrepreneurship and innovation rank high on policy agendas. Both are considered vital for economic growth and industrial renewal. Also their combination, that is, innovation-based entrepreneurship, is a phenomenon that has become increasingly important during the last decades. While many traditional industrial sectors have witnessed declining importance, new emerging sectors have been expanding rapidly. Such sectors are often based on technology and innovation, exploited in either the manufacturing or the service industries. The change from heavy industry to creative and knowledge-based activities is sometimes argued to be as great a transformation as the industrial revolution.

While innovation policy and entrepreneurship policy share certain common strategic outcomes, such as economic growth and creation of wealth, they often differ in their policy objectives. On the one hand, entrepreneurship policy has emerged primarily from small and medium enterprise (SME) policy, becoming particularly evident as a policy area in the late 1990s and early 2000s (European Commission, 1998, 2004; OECD, 1998, 2001; Stevenson and Lundström, 2001, 2002; Hart, 2003). Whereas the main objective of SME policy is to protect and strengthen existing SMEs, entrepreneurship policy emphasizes the individual person or entrepreneur. Thus, entrepreneurship policy encompasses a broader range of policy issues geared to creating a favourable environment for the emergence of entrepreneurial individuals and the start-up and growth of new firms. A critical issue for entrepreneurship policy is how to get more new growing firms. Since the majority of new firms are born small, it is natural that SMEs and entrepreneurial firms have a lot in common, and that SME policy and entrepreneurship policy have some similarities. However, it is important to remember that there are also differences, not all entrepreneurial firms stay small. Sometimes, SME policy and entrepreneurship policy are contradictory. One example of this is bankruptcy regulations and laws. An SME policy focusing on the protection of existing SMEs would try to help small firms to avoid bankruptcy. An entrepreneurship policy could very well have the opposite focus: high frequency of bankruptcies and exits is known to be related to high frequency of new start-ups.

Innovation policy, on the other hand, has largely evolved from science and technology (S&T) policy (OECD, 2006). The first generation of innovation policy, based on the 'science push' or 'linear model', focused primarily on funding science-based research in universities and government laboratories. Since then, innovation policy has shifted towards having more of an innovation systems perspective, including 'demand pull' and interaction between users and producers of innovation. The 'innovation system' concept can be understood in a narrow as well as a broad sense (Lundvall, 1992). The narrow approach concentrates on those institutions that deliberately promote the acquisition and dissemination of knowledge and are the main sources of innovation. The broad approach recognizes that these 'narrow' institutions are embedded in a much wider socio-economic system. Much of this literature insists on the central importance of national systems, but a number of authors have argued that globalization has greatly diminished or even eliminated the importance of the nation state (Freeman, 2002). As a result, there have been several new concepts emphasizing the systemic characteristics of innovation, but related to other levels than the nation state. Sometimes the focus is on a particular country or region, which then determines the spatial boundaries of the system. The literature on 'regional systems of innovation' has grown rapidly since the mid 1990s (cf., e.g., Cooke, 1996; Maskell and Malmberg, 1999). In other cases the main dimension of interest is a sector or a technology. Carlsson and Jacobsson (1997) developed the concept 'technological systems' while Malerba uses the notion of 'sectoral systems of innovation' (Breschi and Malerba, 1997). Usually these different concepts and dimensions reinforce each other and are not in conflict. However, despite this growing interest in systems of innovation, there have been few attempts to include entrepreneurship as a central component. For example, Arundel and Hollanders (2006, p. 3) are critical of the fact that both the European policy community and academics interested in innovation have failed to adopt modern innovation theory, which places more emphasis on the process of innovation for diffusing new technologies and knowledge.

This chapter examines the creation and subsequent development of innovative entrepreneurial firms. A main question is whether innovation entrepreneurship policy should encourage innovation or entrepreneurship, or if it is possible for it to do both at the same time.

Empirical data on innovative new Swedish firms are used to illustrate how a country can balance highly innovative activities with low levels of entrepreneurship. The data show that Swedish innovative entrepreneurship is more successful than the country's entrepreneurial activities would suggest, but also that there are different categories of innovative new firms where the linking of the idea/innovation with the person/entrepreneur seems to create different conditions for the commercialization of an innovation and the subsequent development of a new firm. In Section 6.2 indicators of and earlier research on innovation and entrepreneurship are discussed. Section 6.3 analyses and compares different categories of Swedish innovative firms. The chapter ends with discussion of some policy implications and some conclusions.

6.2 INNOVATIVE ACTIVITIES AND ENTREPRENEURIAL FIRMS

It is now well established that entrepreneurship is important for economic growth and job creation. Both the creation and the expansion of new firms affect growth. Among the first to arrive at this conclusion was David Birch (1981). He conducted an extensive analysis of all American firms in the period 1969 and 1976, and found that small firms were responsible for 81 per cent of net new job creation. His finding was confirmed by studies of firms in many other countries. It is also well known that there is a relationship between innovation and economic welfare. Exactly how and why is not always clear. Not all new firms create jobs, and not all innovations create economic growth. For example, using the European Innovation Scoreboard (EIS), Arundel and Hollanders (2005) were unable to demonstrate a direct link between innovation and economic growth, even though such a relationship could be found in some sectors. Moreover, the majority of business start-ups are set up by 'lifestyle entrepreneurs' whose businesses will not grow beyond a very small size; and it is generally not typical that new firms generate more employment than do larger firms. It is rather the case that small firms that exhibit fast and large growth pull the average up (e.g. Storey, 1994; Schreyer, 2000; Hölzl, 2006). This suggests that it is not only the high frequency of entrepreneurial firms, but also the high quality of these new firms that has relevance for employment generation. What causes this high quality is largely unclear. It is often assumed that innovative new firms are more likely to encompass high quality and, thus, to become high-growth firms or 'gazelles'. For example, Kirchhoff (1994) empirically demonstrated this to be true for a cohort of American firms, but at the same time he also found more high growth new firms among low innovative companies. One reason for this, of course, is that there are many more low innovative new firms than there are high innovative firms. Thus, a relatively high share of high innovative new firms appears to have high growth rates. Also, innovative entrepreneurship is more likely to lead to higher value-added jobs and wealth creation, new firm founders perhaps being more compelled by the opportunity of the venture and its innovativeness (Stevenson, 2002). This, in many instances, leads to the targeting of government support for higher growth potential, technology-oriented sectors. Many governments want greater entrepreneurial activity of the 'innovative', high-growth potential kind, and it has been argued that encouraging the effective combination of entrepreneurship and technology capability needed to create high-technology SMEs, 'fostering appropriate sources of finance, and enabling the market access and business transformations needed for their subsequent development and rapid growth would seem to present innovation policy makers with their biggest challenge' (OECD, 2004, p. 17).

The *Global Entrepreneurship Monitor* 2004 report (Acs et al., 2004) concluded that changing the entrepreneurial mindset was one of the most important challenges in the European Union (EU). A less positive attitude towards entrepreneurship (i.e. compared to other Organisation for Economic Co-operation and Development (OECD) countries) was found to be linked to relatively high employment security and an ageing population. The report also argued that complex regulations hinder the creation, growth and expansion of new businesses in the EU; and that the pervading culture and reward system penalizes the commercialization of knowledge created in research institutions. Repeated measurements in the *Global Entrepreneurship Monitor* (e.g. Minniti et al., 2006; Acs et al., 2004; Reynolds et al., 2002; Delmar and Aronsson, 2000) show that, among the countries in the world, Sweden has one of the lowest levels of entrepreneurial activity in its adult population (Figure 6.1). Despite this low figure, it has been concluded that the major share of net new jobs in Sweden (approx 70 per cent in the 1980s) was in firms with less than 200 employees (Davidsson et al., 1994). Around a third of these were created by the establishment of new firms, and two-thirds by the expansion of small firms. Moreover, it seems that the growth patterns of many new and/or small firms in Sweden differ from growth patterns in other countries. For example, Storey (1994) found for the UK that relatively few new firms expand, but that these few are responsible for a substantial part of overall growth. It has become common to refer to such firms as 'gazelles'. Sweden has few gazelles, but in Sweden it seems to be the large number of slowly growing new/small firms rather than the gazelles that are responsible for the majority of net new job creation (Davidsson et al., 1996; Blixt, 1997; Delmar et al., 2001).

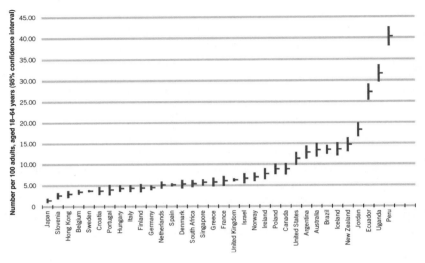

Source: Acs et al. (2004).

Figure 6.1 Total Entrepreneurial Activity (TEA)

In an international comparison of so-called 'High-Expectation Entrepreneurial Activity' (HEA) Autio (2005) found that only between 3 per cent and 17 per cent of all entrepreneurial activity consists of entrepreneurs (nascent or baby business) that expected to have more than 20 employees within five years. This corresponds to only some 0.2–1.6 per cent of the adult-age population actively participating in HEA. In general, countries with a high Total Entrepreneurial Activity (TEA) (Figure 6.1) also have a high HEA. But, interestingly, Sweden, which has a low TEA, performs relatively well in measurements of HEA (12.4 per cent). Nevertheless, the share of adults participating in entrepreneurial activities in Sweden, in general as well as in HEA, is low in international comparisons. The explanation seems to be that high-income countries with a low TEA (such as Sweden and Japan) often have a relatively high share of high-growth expectation new firms. High-expectation entrepreneurship is relatively most prevalent in manufacturing and business services, and high-growth expectation businesses are often created by entrepreneurs that already have a job, for example, by the creation of new spin-offs. In addition, Autio (2005) found that high-expectation firms are responsible for up to 80 per cent (Sweden and US 77 per cent) of total expected jobs in new firms. He argues that this pattern is consistent with empirical studies on actual job creation and that it underlines the importance of high-growth potential entrepreneurial activity for job creation. For Sweden, this implies

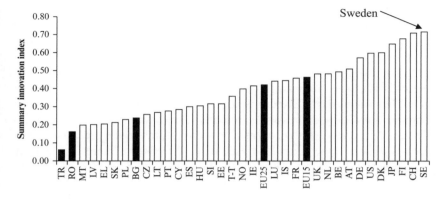

Source: EU (2005).

Figure 6.2 The 2005 Summary Innovation Index

that a very small share of the adult population (0.5 per cent) are entrepreneurs creating the bulk of future jobs.

There has been much recent debate in Sweden on how to improve the growth of new firms, which has led to policy initiatives as well as research. A major concern seems to be creating more Swedish gazelles. In a bid to achieve this objective research-based new firms and seed financing have been prioritized by the Swedish government. This focus on research- and technology-based entrepreneurship is shared by many other countries and regions. In Europe all EU member states and candidate countries have committed to the Lisbon Agenda and increased public research and development (R&D) expenditure. Thus, in the 2000s, European innovation policy has become somewhat biased towards a science push or linear model, in which R&D is supposed to lead to increased innovation and entrepreneurship. An example of this can be found in the EU's *Annual Digest of Industrial Research* (2006), where it is recommended that R&D policies targeting SMEs and low intensive R&D firms should be emphasized, but this is not accompanied by any analysis of the role played by SMEs/entrepreneurial firms. Without this knowledge policy makers will find it difficult to create a functioning innovative entrepreneurship policy.

As illustrated by the EIS (Figure 6.2), based on innovation indicators, Sweden in many respects is a high performer. Also, a study by Florida and Tinagli (2004) on 'Europe in the creative age' shows that Sweden is ranked top in the EuroCreativity index, outperforming not only all the European countries, but also the USA. According to this index, the other Nordic countries and some Northern European countries (Ireland, the Netherlands and Belgium) are also performing well. This is confirmed by the ranking in the growth competitiveness index of the World Economic Forum (WEF), which shows Finland to be the most competitive country followed by the USA and Sweden, and which ranks the five Nordic countries among the top ten ranked nations.

In the Swedish debate, however, it is often claimed that the high investments in R&D are not resulting in correspondingly high economic growth. It has been argued that Sweden is not able to benefit economically from the commercialization of academic research (less than 1 per cent of gross domestic product (GDP) goes on academic research, while private industry spends almost three times that amount). In addition, there is a lack of entrepreneurial culture, or what Venkataraman (2004) calls 'vicious cycles' in which talent is attracted to successful and existing corporations.

The Swedish government's innovation strategy in 2004 highlights the importance of increasing the commercialization of research results (Regeringskansliet, 2004, pp. 31–2). It is claimed that efforts are needed to:

- transform research results and ideas more effectively into businesses and enterprises.
- increase financing at early stages of business and company development.
- design workable ground rules and promote the use of intellectual property protection
- create sound conditions for competition that favour the growth of new enterprises.

This focus was confirmed in the Science Policy Proposition (Regeringen, 2005), which gave much attention to incentives for academics to become entrepreneurs, to the role of holding companies in supporting commercialization efforts and to the provision of risk capital: 'The investments in research give, however, insufficient results in the form of economic growth . . . knowledge transfer to industry and commercialization of research results need to be increased' (Regeringen, 2005, p. 140). One of the main funders of academic research, VINNOVA, also suggests that 'the knowledge and results from research are not efficiently transformed into firm formation and growth' (VINNOVA, 2003b, p. 1).

Particular attention has been paid to academic entrepreneurship as a central, but underutilized mechanism for exploiting the results of academic research. In the Swedish context this mechanism began to receive attention in the early 1990s (VINNOVA, 2003a). Much concern was expressed over the alleged low propensity to spin-off firms from academia, and to poor growth and associated small direct impact on the economy of firms that were spun off (e.g., Jacobsson and Rickne, 1997; Goldfarb and Henrekson,

2003; Delmar and Wiklund, 2003). Consequently, many policy initiatives have centred on promoting academic entrepreneurship, an example of which is the 'Innovationsbron' (innovation bridge), which was set up in March 2005. The stated ambition of Innovationsbron is to 'help researchers, innovators and entrepreneurs with business development and commercialization, and to increase knowledge transfer and sharing between industry and university'.[2] In announcing this new organization, the Swedish Minister of Industry wrote that 'During a ten year period, Innovationsbron AB will spend SEK1.8 billion to enhance the conditions for commercializing research results and ideas in industry' (DN, 2005). Hence, the focus of Teknikbroarna, the predecessor of Innovationsbron, and the focus of Innovationsbron are firmly on academic entrepreneurship and seed funding.

To sum up, it has been argued that both entrepreneurship and innovation are linked to economic growth and industrial renewal. But it is not always clear exactly how. Often the relationships between growth, entrepreneurship and innovation tend to be indirect rather than direct. The combination of entrepreneurship and innovation results in innovative entrepreneurship: new firms based on new (inventive) ideas, sometimes, but not always, research-based. Such firms often have relatively high growth potential and may become future gazelles. Unfortunately, the research on and knowledge about innovative entrepreneurship is limited. The next section, however, provides some examples based on Swedish data.

6.3 THE ORIGIN AND DEVELOPMENT OF NEW INNOVATIVE SWEDISH FIRMS: SOME EMPIRICAL DATA

In order to assess the importance of innovation-based entrepreneurship there is a need to know how frequent the phenomenon is, and to what extent – and which – innovative entrepreneurial firms tend to grow. In this section some earlier studies on Swedish new innovative technology-based firms are summarized.

There are approximately 30 000 to 40 000 new firms established each year in Sweden. Unfortunately, there are no reliable statistics on how many of these can be considered innovative and/or technology-based. International estimations in the *Global Entrepreneurship Monitor* suggest that less than 10 per cent of new firms can be classified as 'Science, Technology and High Potential' (Reynolds et al., 2002). Data from Statistics Sweden and ITPS[3] (2003) show that approximately 35 per cent of new Swedish firms are in the knowledge-intensive industries, and another 15 per cent in manufacturing.

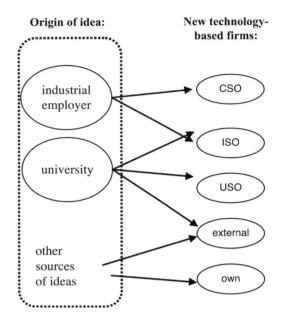

Note: CSO: corporate spin-off (49%), ISO: indirect university spin-off (12%), USO: university spin-off (5%), external idea (15%), own idea (19%)

Source: Lindholm Dahlstrand (2004).

Figure 6.3   Innovation-based entrepreneurship – requires both ideas and people

Not all of these can be considered technology-based, although it is likely that a substantial share will depend on technology for their development and survival.

In a study of some 350 Swedish New Technology Based Firms[4] (NTBF), Lindholm Dahlstrand (2001, 2004) analysed the origins of the ideas and the entrepreneurs. She found that two-thirds of new firms were established as entrepreneurial spin-offs from some other organization;[5] almost half of these were spin-offs from established private firms, that is, corporate spin-offs (CSO), and an additional sixth were either directly or indirectly spun off from universities (Figure 6.3). The remaining third were based on the founders' own ideas or externally acquired ideas.

Thus, if around 10 per cent to 15 per cent of all new firms are technology-based, this means that approximately 5 per cent to 8 per cent are CSO, and a corresponding 0.5 per cent to 0.75 per cent are direct university spin offs (USO). Slightly over 1 per cent to 1.5 per cent can be considered indi-

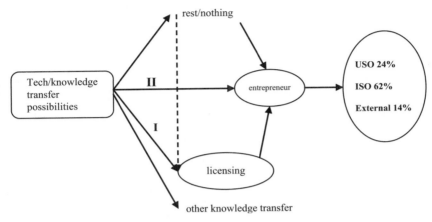

Source: Lindholm Dahlstrand (2005).

Figure 6.4 Academic spin-offs and spin-outs in the Swedish case

rect USO (ISO), that is, they are based on an idea originating in a university, which did not materialize until the founder(s) had been working for some time in the private sector. In addition, among the start-ups based on an external idea, approximately a fifth of these ideas had been developed in a university (Lindholm Dahlstrand, 2005). That is, 3 per cent of the NTBF (and less than 0.5 per cent to 0.7 per cent of all new firms) had been set up by external entrepreneurs acquiring the rights to university research.

Figure 6.4 depicts Swedish academic spin-offs. Here, 24 per cent are direct USO in which the new firm is established by a faculty member. The major proportion of academic spin-offs, 62 per cent, are ISO, in which the intellectual property or ideas have 'rested' while the entrepreneur was working in private industry. The third category, 14 per cent of the academic spin-offs, consists of cases where university research has been acquired (with or without a licence) by an external entrepreneur, that is, not a faculty member.

Thus, taken together, the share of academic spin-offs in Sweden is some 2 per cent to 3 per cent of all new firms. This figure is in line with the findings reported for several other well performing OECD countries (Callan, 2001).

In an earlier paper on Swedish NTBF, Lindholm Dahlstrand (2001) found that CSO outperformed other spin-offs in terms of economic growth. At approximately age ten, the ISO grow faster than the USO, but they do not show such high growth as CSO. Thus, there is no support for the hypothesis that ISO are able to take advantage of a mixed entrepreneurial origin in order to create a high-growth, highly innovative firm. However, ISO are able

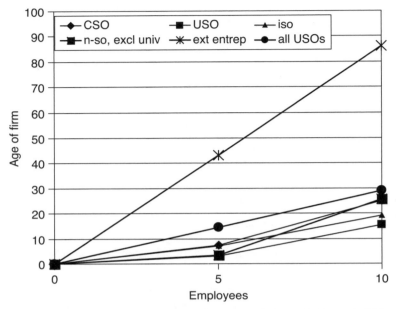

Source: The data for CSO, USO and ISO are taken from Lindholm Dahlstrand (2001). Data on growth for the category of firms based on university ideas, but established by an external entrepreneur (ext entrep) and data for all USO are new and include external entrepreneurs. Finally, data for the ext entrep group were excluded from the data illustrating growth of non-spin-offs (i.e. n-so, excl univ).

Figure 6.5   Growth (employees) in different categories of spin-offs

to generate higher growth than USO. Perhaps the founders of ISO were able to complement their knowledge to compensate for some of the growth disadvantages of USO. The same study found that, relative to their size, USO had significantly higher degrees of innovativeness. NTBF often network and contribute knowledge to other corporations, which can enable innovations from USO to be exploited outside the firm, and this economic potential may indirectly benefit the economy. In addition, USO may be important for radical innovations/industrial change, but this is a question that needs further study and in-depth exploration.

Lindholm Dahlstrand (2001) does not include firms established by external entrepreneurs because these firms were not considered to be spin-offs from an earlier employer. However, if the origin of the idea/innovation is taken as the focus rather than the earlier employment of the entrepreneur, the resulting growth patterns show that ideas spun off from universities are showing good performance (Figure 6.5).

Figure 6.5 shows that new firms set up by external entrepreneurs commercializing university ideas are demonstrating the highest growth of all Swedish NTBF, and are growing faster than ISO and CSO. These firms were not set up by entrepreneurs previously employed as university researchers and it might be that these founders are able to combine the best of both the commercial knowledge and advanced technical research worlds. It is possible that these European firms will demonstrate high-growth rates similar to those found in American studies. It might be that this category of academic spin-offs is more common in the USA than Europe. The available data do not lend themselves to answering these questions, but they would be an important focus for future studies.

One final comment on the growth of Swedish academic spin-offs is that it requires considerable time for these firms to begin to grow. As mentioned above, the size and growth of academic spin-offs varies with the age of the firm. While the USO show very limited growth during their first ten years of operations, the situation improves considerably after this time. At ten years, the average size of the direct spin-offs was 15.5 employees. Five years later the mean increases to 33, that is, an annual increase of 16.3 per cent. This means that at 15 years, half of the firms had over 25 employees. However, the corresponding figure for ISO is about the same, that is, an annual increase of 17.6 per cent. At age 15, the average number of employees in ISO was 44. Thus, growth rates increase after the initial ten years of operation for both direct and indirect university spin-offs. This suggests that innovation and product development are complex and time consuming for academic spin-offs.

Therefore, general entrepreneurial activities, gazelles and the expansion of newly established firms all seem to contribute to economic growth. It is not only the number of new firms, but also the quality of their entrepreneurial activities that matter, and it seems likely that there are many high-expectation new businesses, as well as gazelles, among innovative and technology-based new firms.

6.4 CONCLUSION AND IMPLICATIONS FOR POLICY MAKERS

In this chapter it has been argued that innovative entrepreneurship is becoming increasingly important. The establishment and expansion of new firms are creating a high share of net new jobs. Gazelles and high-expectation entrepreneurial firms are often found among innovative and technology-based new businesses, but for them to play a key role in economic growth it is also essential that their numbers are large enough.

That is, encouraging general entrepreneurial activities is not only likely to result in increased entrepreneurship, but also in a higher number of innovative high-growth firms. A country such as Sweden, with high innovation activity, should be encouraged to increase its entrepreneurial activities.

Summarizing what has been said above about innovative and technology-based entrepreneurship, a key point is that around 10 per cent to 15 per cent of newly created firms are technology-based (the higher share is knowledge-based). These firms are generally located where the entrepreneur lives and/or previously worked, that is, it is a regional phenomenon in which innovative firms are most often spin-offs from other organizations. Also, the majority of the spin-offs are from private industry, and these firms in general are able to demonstrate higher growth than other innovative new firms. However, in certain knowledge fields USO are more frequent and contribute to radical change and transformation. Different sorts of USO tend to show different growth patterns. The slowest growth occurs in firms created by entrepreneurs that formerly were university researchers. If former academics who have had a period of private employment go on to establish entrepreneurial firms, these firms show higher growth. However, the technology-based new firms that exhibit the highest growth are those that are set up by external entrepreneurs who have not been involved in this university research.

Sweden has a relatively high share of innovative entrepreneurship, spin-offs from both private industry and from universities. However, it is not clear whether this innovative entrepreneurship is of sufficient magnitude to make an important contribution to economic growth. To achieve this, the entrepreneurial activity must be sufficiently large and sufficiently innovatively entrepreneurial. Sweden, similar to several other European countries, is not a highly entrepreneurial country (see, e.g., the GEM reports, Acs et al., 2004; Minniti et al., 2006). This low level of entrepreneurial activity might not be sufficient to produce a high share of innovative and/or technology-based entrepreneurship. Designing a policy to encourage innovative and/or technology-based entrepreneurship, and the creation of new high-growth firms (a 'picking-the-winners' SME policy) might prove problematic if the intention is to encourage economic development and growth. International research suggests that huge amounts of resources are needed to enable research-based firms to become gazelles (Mustar, 2001; Clarysse et al., 2005). To secure resources and create high-growth research-based firms often requires substantial amounts of venture capital. Very few firms are able to find this, and if they do the result can be surrender of the firm's ownership, frequently to international investors. Thus, shifting from general encouragement for a high number of new start-ups to a policy targeting future high-growth firms might be rather expensive if it is to succeed (Lindholm Dahlstrand, 2005).

What is called for from a policy perspective are 'platform policies' that include and integrate key components from several policy domains. Improving innovative entrepreneurship will – at the least – require a combination of entrepreneurship, SME, innovation, S&T, university and regional policies. For example, SME policies are often developed to help existing small firms, while entrepreneurship policies often focus on individuals and their entrepreneurial capacity (e.g. skills and motivation). A university policy is important since universities are responsible both for the education of a large part of future key personnel, and for a substantial part of the advancement of science, technology and innovation. Thus, the technological/knowledge profile and responsiveness of a (strong) university will influence the innovative entrepreneurship and profile of a dynamic region. In turn, innovation policy must, of course, include aspects linked to universities.

Finally, Callan (2001, p. 37) asked 'Are there policies that can accelerate firm growth? Should policies distinguish between spin-offs which are essentially consulting firms or research boutiques, and spin-offs which aspire to rapid growth and product development?' These are still very important questions. A key aspect for governments and policy makers must be whether a policy should focus on encouraging the formation of a high number of new firms, or helping the formation of high-growing new firms, research-based or not. These policies, and the programmes necessary to accomplish this, ought to be quite different. If policies focus solely on the gazelles, this risks losing sight of the importance of the phenomenon (Mustar, 2001). Policies and programmes effective for creating both a high number of new firms and, at the same time, a high number of high-growth firms are not very likely. At least not without high costs. There is a need to know more about the role played by innovative entrepreneurship in society and about the direct and the indirect effects of these firms. As argued earlier, indirect effects or the importance of having academic spin-offs acting as research boutiques might be of high importance for economic renewal and growth. Until there is a better understanding of these mechanisms there is little point in designing programmes for spin-off financing, support services, business networks and so on.

Swedish policy makers seem to have concluded that academic spin-offs are not very successful. The basis for this conclusion, however, is weak. For example, there are no studies analysing the indirect effects of the mechanism, and no systematic international comparisons. Shifting away from general encouragement of a high number of academic spin-offs towards a policy targeting future high-growth firms might be expensive if it is to be successful. Earlier research suggests that a well functioning spin-off policy should encourage either: (1) entrepreneurship in general or (2) a comprehensive and costly system focusing on the creation of high-growth firms. For example, Clarysse et al. (2005) found that incubators that purported to support academic spin-offs, but did not have the required resources, were the most unsuccessful policies; those with a – less costly – entrepreneurial enhancing focus were much more successful. Thus, a spin-off policy should be very clear about whether it tries to encourage the creation of a high number of small entrepreneurial academic spin-offs, or if it is designed to facilitate the creation of a smaller number of fast growing firms.

It might be that the indirect effects of academic spin-offs are of greater importance for economic growth. One important aspect is their role as mediators between universities and private industry. Another, and perhaps even more important aspect, is the behaviour of some spin-offs as research boutiques. Many academic spin-offs do not focus on commercializing innovations; instead they sell their innovations to other firms, which might be better equipped to commercialize them. Thus, the role of research consultant and/or research boutique might be the most important aspect of academic spin-offs. To my knowledge, however, there has been no serious attempt to analyse this aspect, and future studies would be welcome and highly recommended.

NOTES

1. Parts of this chapter appeared in a paper commissioned by the OECD (Lindholm Dahlstrand 2005). I am grateful for support from the OECD, and for permission to publish the material in this paper. The study on which this chapter is based is linked to a larger research programme at the RIDE centre, at IMIT and Chalmers University of Technology, Sweden. The research was funded by the Swedish Strategic Science Foundation, with contributions from VINNOVA through its financing of the RIDE centre.
2. See www.innovationsbron.se (accessed 23 July 2007).
3. Swedish Institute for Growth Policy Studies, see www.itps.se (accessed 11 September 2007).
4. As many as 84 per cent of NTBFs are innovative entrepreneurial firms with their own developed products. On average, the firms had generated 5.6 innovations during their first ten years.
5. The classification of spin-offs is based on where the idea and the intellectual property were developed. To be defined as a spin-off the new firm has to be based on an idea developed by a former employer. (In one case an academic spin-off was set up by a student.)

REFERENCES

Acs, Z., P. Arenius, M. Hay and M. Minitti (2004), *Global Entrepreneurship Monitor: 2004 Executive Report*, Babson Park, MA, USA and London: Babson College and London Business School.

Arundel, A. and H. Hollanders (2005), *Policy, Indicators and Targets: Measuring the Impacts of Innovation Policies*, European trend chart on innovation, December, Brussels: Enterprises Directorate-General, European Commission.

Arundel A. and H. Hollanders (2006), 'Searching the forest for the trees: "missing" indicators of innovation', 2006 trend chart methodology report for the Maastricht Economic Research Institute on Innovation and Technology (MERIT), July, accessed 11 September 2007 at http://trendchart.cordis.lu/scoreboards/scoreboard2006/pdf/eis_2006_methodology_report_missing_indicators.pdf.

Autio, E. (2005), *Global Entrepreneurship Monitor 2005, Report on High-Expectation Entrepreneurship*, London and Babson Park, MA, USA, London Business School: Mazars and Babson College.

Birch, D. (1981) 'Who creates jobs?' *The Public Interest*, **65**, 3–14.

Blixt, L. (1997), 'Tillväxtföretagen i Sverige stora som små och från norr till söder', NUTEK, Stockholm (in Swedish).

Breschi, S. and F. Malerba (1997), 'Sectoral innovation systems', in C. Edquist (ed.), *Systems of Innovation: Technologies, Institutions and Organisations*, London: Pinter, pp. 30–56.

Callan, B. (2001), 'Generating spin-offs: evidence from across the OECD', *STI Review*, **26**, 14–54.

Carlsson, B. and S. Jacobsson (1997), 'Diversity creation and technological systems: a technology policy perspective', in C. Edquist (ed.), *Systems of Innovation: Technologies, Institutions and Organisations*, London: Pinter, pp. 266–94.

Clarysse, B., M. Wright, A. Lockett, E. Van de Vele and A. Vohora (2005), 'Spinning out new ventures: a typology of incubation strategies from European research institutions', *Journal of Business Venturing*, **20**, 183–216.

Cooke, P. (1996), 'The new wave of regional innovation networks: analysis, characteristics and strategy', *Small Business Economics*, **8**, 159–71.

Davidsson, P., L. Lindmark and C. Olofsson (1994), *Dynamiken i Svenskt Näringsliv*, Lund: Studentlitteratur (in Swedish).

Davidsson, P., L. Lindmark and C. Olofsson (1996), *Näringslivsdynamiken under 90-talet*, Stockholm: NUTEK (in Swedish).

Delmar, F. and M. Aronsson (2000), *Entreprenörskap i Sverige, Global Entrepreneurship Monitor 2000*, Stockholm: ESBRI.

Delmar, F., P. Davidsson and J. Wiklund (eds) (2001), *Tillväxtföretagen i Sverige*, Stockholm: SNS Förlag (in Swedish).

Delmar, F. and J. Wiklund. (2003), 'The involvement in self-employment among the Swedish science and technology labor force between 1990 and 2000', ITPS, A2003, p. 17.

DN (2005), 'Två miljarder kronor satsas för att stärka innovationer', *Dagens Nyheter*, 18 February (in Swedish).

European Commission (EC) (1998), 'Fostering entrepreneurship in Europe: priorities for the future', Communication from the Commission to the Council, Brussels: European Commission, 7 April.

European Commission (EC) (2004), 'Action plan: the European agenda for entrepreneurship', COM(2004) 70 final, communication from the Commission to the

Council of the European Parliament, the European Economic and Social Committee and the Committee of the Regions, Brussels: European Commission, 11 February.

European Union (EU) (2005), *European Innovation Scoreboard 2005: Comparative Analysis of Innovation Performance, TrendChart Innovation Policy in Europe*, Brussels: European Commission.

EU (2006), *Annual Digest of Industrial Research*, Brussels: IPTS JRC of the European Commission.

Florida, R. and I. Tinagli (2004), *Europe in the Creative Age*, Pittsburgh, PA and London: Carnegie Mellon Software Industry Center and Demos.

Freeman, C. (2002), 'Continental, national and sub-national innovation systems', *Research Policy*, **31**,191–211.

Goldfarb, B. and M. Henrekson (2003), 'Bottom-up versus top-down policies towards the commercialization of university intellectual property', *Research Policy*, **32**, 639–58.

Hart, D. M. (2003), 'Entrepreneurship policy: what is it and where it came from', in D. M. Hart (ed.), *The Emergence of Entrepreneurship Policy*, Cambridge, MA: Cambridge University Press, pp. 3–19.

Hölzl, W. (2006), 'Gazelles', Innovation Watch, Europe Innova, scoping paper, Brussels, EU, 31 May 2006.

Jacobsson, S. and A. Rickne (1997), 'New technology based firms in Sweden – a study of their direct impact on industrial renewal', *Economics of Innovation and New Technology*, **8**: 197–223.

Kirchhoff, B. (1994), *Entrepreneurship and Dynamic Capitalism: The Economics of Firm Formation and Growth*, Westport, CT: Praeger.

Lindholm Dahlstrand, Å. (2001), 'Entrepreneurial origin and spin-off performance: a comparison between corporate and university spin-offs', in P. Moncada-Paternò-Castello, A. Tübke, R. Miège and T.B. Yaquero (eds), *Corporate and Research-Based Spin-offs: Drivers for Knowledge-Based Innovation and Entrepreneurship*, European Commission, IPTS Technical Report Series, EUR 19903 EN, pp. 43–66.

Lindholm Dahlstrand, Å. (2004), *Teknikbaserat Nyföretagande, Tillväxt och Affärsutveckling*, Lund: Studentliotteratur (in Swedish).

Lindholm Dahlstrand, Å. (2005), 'University knowledge transfer and the role of academic spin-offs', commissioned paper for the OECD Conference on Fostering Entrepreneurship: The Role of Higher Education, Trento, Italy, June.

Lundvall, B.-Å. (1992), *National Systems of Innovation: Towards a Theory of Innovation and Interactive Learning*, London: Pinter.

Maskell, P. and A. Malmberg (1999), 'Localised learning and industrial competitiveness', *Cambridge Journal of Economics*, **23** (2), 167–86.

Minniti, M., W. Bygrave and E. Autio (2006), *Global Entrepreneurship Global Entrepreneurship Monitor: 2005 Executive Report*, Babson Park, MA, USA and London: Babson College and London Business School.

Mustar, P. (2001), 'Spin-offs from public research: trends and outlook', *STI Review*, **26**, 165–72.

Organisation for Economic Co-operation and Development (OECD) (1998), *Fostering Entrepreneurship*, Paris: OECD.

OECD (2001), *Entrepreneurship, Growth and Policy*, Paris: OECD.

OECD (2004), 'Innovation policy and performance: introduction and synthesis', paper by the Directorate for Science, Technology and Industry, Committee for Scientific and Technological Policy, DSTI/STP(2004)19, Paris.

OECD (2006), *Governance of Innovation Systems Volume 3: Case Studies in Cross-Sectoral Policy*, Paris: OECD.

Regeringen (2005), *Regeringens Proposition 2004/05:80 Forskning för ett Bättre liv*, Stockholm: Utbildnings och Kulturdepartementet (in Swedish).

Regeringskansliet (2004), *Innovative Sweden: A Strategy for Growth Through Renewal*, Ds 2004, p. 36.

Reynolds, P., W. Bygrave, E. Autio, L. Cox and M. Hay (2002), *Global Entrepreneurship Global Entrepreneurship Monitor 2002 Executive Report*, Babson Park, MA, USA and London: Babson College, Ewing Marion Kauffman Foundation and London Business School.

Schreyer, P. (2000), 'High-growth firms and employment', Organisation for Economic Co-operation and Development STI working paper, March 2000.

Stevenson, L. (2002), 'Innovation and entrepreneurship: a Dutch policy perspective in an international context', in *Innovative Entrepreneurship: New policy challenges!* Zoetermeer: EIM Business and Policy Research, February, pp. 43–66.

Stevenson, L. and A. Lundström (2001), *Patterns and Trends in Entrepreneurship/SME Policy and Practice in Ten Countries*, Stockholm: Swedish Foundation for Small Business Research, FSF.

Stevenson, L. and A. Lundström (2002), *Beyond the Rhetoric: Defining Entrepreneurship Policy and its Best Practice Components,* Stockholm: Swedish Foundation for Small Business Research, FSF.

Storey, D. J. (1994), *Understanding the Small Business Sector*, London: Routledge.

Venkataraman, S. (2004), 'Regional transformation through technological entrepreneurship', *Journal of Business Venturing*, **19**, 153–67.

VINNOVA (2003a), 'VINNFORSK, VINNOVAS förslag till förbättrad kommersialisering och ökad avkastning i tillväxt på forskningsinvesteringar vid högskolor', VINNOVA Policy VP 2003, p. 1 (in Swedish).

VINNOVA (2003b), 'Behovsmotiverad forskning och effektiva innovationssystem för hållbar tillväxt: VINNOVAS verksamhetsplanering 2003–07, VINNOVA POLICY, VP 2003:2, Stockholm, Sweden.

7. The role of innovation award programmes in the US and Sweden

Charles W. Wessner

7.1 INTRODUCTION

Policy makers in both the US and Sweden recognize that innovation remains the key to international competitiveness in the twenty-first century. Moreover, policy makers in both countries increasingly recognize that equity-financed small firms are an effective means of capitalizing on new ideas and bringing them to the market. Small firms, however, face a variety of obstacles as they seek to bring new products and processes to market. In this context public policies that reduce the structural and financial hurdles facing such innovative small firms can play a useful role in enhancing a nation's innovative capacity.

In the US innovation awards, such as the Small Business Innovation Research (SBIR) programme and the Advanced Technology Program (ATP)[1] have proven effective in helping small innovative firms overcome these hurdles while also enhancing networking among US universities, large firms and small innovative companies. Innovation award programmes, such as SBIR and ATP, could also help Sweden realize higher returns to its substantial investments in research and development (R&D).

7.2 THE NEW INNOVATION IMPERATIVE

This imperative to innovate more rapidly comes as new entrants from China and India expand their presence in the global economy. While this expansion provides opportunities for businesses around the world to lower costs, develop new ideas and business processes, and develop new markets, it also poses new challenges to countries, such as Sweden and the US, to maintain their competitiveness and preserve their standards of living by accelerating their innovative potential.

China brings not only scale advantages, but also a remarkable high-level focus to the challenge of competitiveness. The clear goal of China's leaders is the acquisition of technological capabilities and control of the national market as a means of maintaining national autonomy and generating political and military strength. As Jiang Zemin (23 August 1999) stated, 'In today's world, the core of each country's competitive strength is intellectual innovation, technological innovation and high-tech industrialization' (Wolff, 2007). This high-level commitment is evident in the rapid rise in Chinese R&D expenditure. In 1999 China's R&D spending accounted for 6 per cent of total world expenditure on R&D ($618 billion). By 2004, China accounted for 12 per cent of the world total of $836 billion spent on R&D.

India is also another increasingly important locus of innovation.[2] Gaining momentum from a decade of economic liberalization, India is changing rapidly from a locus for business process outsourcing to a global centre for advanced R&D. Even as US and other multinational companies are increasingly locating their advanced R&D operations in India, Indian companies – drawing on their nation's vibrant entrepreneurial class and a critical mass of capable, highly trained scientists and engineers – are seeking to become globally competitive, with active international partnering and acquisition strategies now underway.[3]

The rise of new competitors and new markets alerts us to the need to invest in our nations' innovation potential. Growing our capacity for rapid and productive innovation is essential for our future security and economic well-being.[4] A key element in enhancing a nation's innovation capacity is its small firms. They play a catalytic role in capitalizing on existing public investments in research to bring new ideas to the market (Acs and Audretsch, 1990).

7.3   THE IMPORTANCE OF SMALL BUSINESS INNOVATION

It is now widely recognized that small firms are a leading source of employment growth in the US, generating 60 per cent to 80 per cent of net new jobs annually over the past decade. What is less widely recognized is that these small businesses also employ nearly 40 per cent of the US science and engineering workforce (SBA, 2004). What is more, scientists and engineers working in small businesses in the US, produce 14 times more patents than their counterparts in large patenting firms – and these patents tend to be of higher quality and are twice as likely to be cited (SBA, 2004).

In the US firms such as Microsoft, Intel, AMD, FedEx, Qualcomm and Adobe, all of which grew rapidly in scale from small beginnings, continue to transform how people everywhere work, transact and communicate. The resulting economic growth and social benefits underscore the need to encourage new equity-based high-technology firms in both the US and Sweden in the hope that some may develop into larger, more successful firms that create the technological base for future competitiveness.

7.4   US STRENGTH IN INNOVATION

This capacity to renew the economy by developing numerous large firms from small beginnings is a significant comparative advantage for the US. It draws on the nation's large and integrated domestic market, and an economic and institutional infrastructure that is able to redeploy resources rapidly to maximize their efficient use. A strong and highly developed higher education infrastructure with important public and private entities is another key advantage. Deep and flexible capital and labour markets permit the rapid reallocation of the resources mentioned above. These competitive strengths are buttressed by highly distributed and highly developed science and technology (S&T) institutions that are endowed with significant resources and charged with applications-oriented missions ranging from space exploration to health to national security. Flexible managerial and organizational structures and a willingness to adopt innovative management practices and products are further distinguishing features of the US economy.

The US also benefits from an entrepreneurial culture that accepts failure as a byproduct of new entrepreneurial initiatives and a willingness by investors to provide second chances to experienced, but initially unsuccessful managers. Bankruptcy laws that limit the liability that an entrepreneur can incur from an initial bankruptcy further support this 'second-chance' cultural and business perspective on entrepreneurial failure and success.

Yet, despite these many strengths, there is great diversity in the innovative capacity of the various regions of the US. Much of the innovative activity in the US is geographically concentrated in areas in states, such as California and Massachusetts, reflecting in part the polycentric nature of the American federal system of government (Figure 7.1).

This diversity, decentralization and willingness to tolerate initial failure is not new. Alexis de Tocqueville noted in *Democracy in America* 1835 [2000] that:

> In America, the social force behind the state is much less well regulated, less enlightened, and less wise, but it is a hundred times more powerful than in Europe. Without doubt, there is no other country on earth where people take such great efforts to achieve social prosperity. ... So it is no good looking in the United States for perfection of administrative procedures; what one does find is

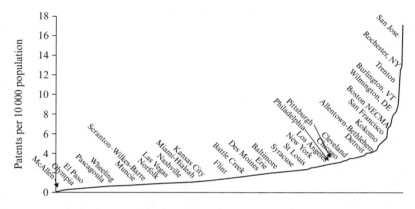

Source: Gerald Carlino, Satyajit Chatterjee and Robert Hunt, Ferrara OECD Conference on IAVC, October 2005 Ferrara, Italy.

Figure 7.1   Urban density and the rate of innovation

a picture of power, somewhat wild perhaps, but robust, and a life liable to mishaps but full of striving and animation. (Book I. Chapter 5)

7.5   GROWING CONCERNS ABOUT US COMPETITIVENESS

These underlying strengths in the US system suggest that the overall economic prospects in the US will remain healthy. Nonetheless, there are clouds on the horizon. Many US business leaders, senior academics and experienced policy makers believe that the country is now facing major challenges to its technological leadership. They point, for example, to inadequacies in the education system, especially at secondary level where US students score below their peers abroad in science and mathematics. These concerns have spawned recent studies that highlight troubling trends in publications, foreign student retention, high-technology exports and the production of information technology products. It is also true that fewer American students are pursuing science careers, and that the US may be losing some of its attraction as a destination for the best students from around the world.[5]

Responding to this and other concerns about the nation's innovation capacity, the US Congress recently requested the National Academies to assess the nation's competitive situation and identify concrete steps to ensure US economic leadership. The resulting National Academies report,

Rising Above the Gathering Storm (National Academy of Science, 2005) notes that weakening federal commitments to S&T places the future growth and prosperity of the US in jeopardy:

> Although many people assume that the US will always be a world leader in science and technology, this may not continue to be the case, inasmuch as great minds exist throughout the world. We fear the abruptness with which a lead in science and technology can be lost – and the difficulty of recovering a lead once lost, if indeed it can be regained at all. (National Academy of Sciences, 2005, p. 3)

To overcome this growing vulnerability, the report calls for (among other measures) an increase in America's talent pool through the provision of greater incentives for science and mathematics teachers. The report also calls for an increase of 10 per cent per annum in federal investments in long-term basic research to 2012. In addition, it recommends a number of steps to make the US a more attractive place to study and perform research for foreign students, including actions to increase the number of visas that permit US trained foreign students to remain and work in the US after their studies are completed (National Academy of Sciences, 2005, ES2).

The Academies report has helped to advance the policy debate. In his 2006 State of the Union Speech President Bush called for a competitiveness initiative that would, inter alia, double the federal commitment to basic research programmes in physics and engineering over ten years, improve K-12 education in mathematics and science, reform and expand workforce training programmes, and support immigration reform to compete for the world's best and brightest high-skilled workers. Despite the President's endorsement and Congressional interest, the new legislation, 'Protecting America's Competitive Edge Act', is pending in the US Congress, having not become law in the last Congress.

7.6   POLICY MYTHS AND INNOVATION REALITIES

While these new measures are welcome, commonly held myths about the innovation process remain an obstacle to developing and maintaining policies that encourage small business innovation. Many American policy makers have ideological convictions about the primacy of the market and a corresponding reluctance to recognize its limitations despite ample evidence concerning the close interactions between markets and public policy initiatives to encourage innovation.

In the case of early-stage finance, a common American myth, at least among Washington policy makers, is that 'if it's a good idea, the market will fund it'. In reality, there is no such thing as 'the market'. Unlike the market model found in introductory economics texts, real world markets always operate within specific rules and conventions that lend unique characteristics to particular markets, and nearly all markets suffer from seriously imperfect information.

Indeed, the problem of imperfect capital markets is particularly challenging for fledgling entrepreneurs. The knowledge that an entrepreneur has about their product is normally not fully appreciated by potential customers – a phenomenon that economists call asymmetric information. This asymmetry can make it hard for small firms to obtain funding for new ideas; as Michael Spence, a recent winner of the Nobel Prize points out, market noise often obscures the significance of promising new ideas[6] (see Spence, 1974).

Market entry is thus a challenge for new entrepreneurs, especially those with new ideas for potentially disruptive products. Access to government procurement markets can be particularly difficult for new, small entrepreneurial firms. These entrepreneurs tend to be unfamiliar with arcane government regulations and complex procurement procedures that are often referred to as a 'procurement thicket'. In addition, academic researchers and entrepreneurs may be unacquainted with government commercial accounting and business practices, a more prosaic, but important obstacle. Many small firms are therefore at a severe disadvantage vis-à-vis incumbents in the defence procurement process, and face especially high challenges with regard to market access and finance (see Branscomb and Auerswald, 2001; Lerner, 1999).

Innovators in large firms face similar problems in that multiple options, established hurdle rates for financing new initiatives, and technological and market uncertainties militate against even promising technologies. As Dr Bruce Griffing, the laboratory manager responsible for developing mammography diagnostic technology for General Electric, noted, 'there is a valley of death for new technologies, even in the largest companies' (Griffing, 2001).

Another hurdle for entrepreneurs is the leakage of new knowledge that escapes the boundaries of firms and intellectual property protection. The creator of new knowledge can seldom fully capture the economic value of that knowledge for their own firm. This spillover can inhibit investment in promising technologies for large and small firms – though it is especially important for small firms focused on a particularly promising product or process (Mansfield, 1985).

The challenge of incomplete and insufficient information for investors and the problem for entrepreneurs of moving quickly enough to capture a sufficient return on 'leaky' investments pose substantial obstacles for new

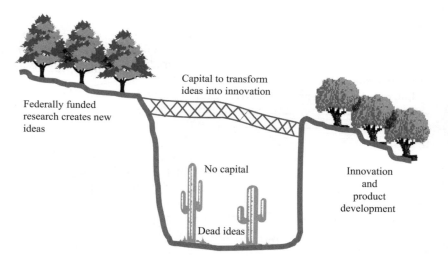

Federally funded
research creates new
ideas

Capital to transform
ideas into innovation

No capital

Innovation
and
product
development

Dead ideas

Figure 7.2   The Valley of Death

firms seeking private capital. The difficulty of attracting investors to support an imperfectly understood, yet-to-be-developed innovation is especially daunting. Indeed, the term, 'Valley of Death' has come to describe the period of transition when a developing technology is deemed promising, but too new to validate its commercial potential and thereby attract the capital necessary for its development (Figure 7.2)

This simple image of the Valley of Death captures two important points. The first is that while there are substantial national R&D investments in the US, Sweden and elsewhere, the transition from investments in research to creation of valuable products is not self-evident, given the informational and financial constraints noted above. A second, related point is that technological value does not lead inevitably to commercialization. Many good ideas perish on the way to the market. The challenge for policy makers is to help firms create additional, market relevant information by supporting the development of promising ideas through this difficult early phase.

7.7   DOES VENTURE CAPITAL PROVIDE THE BRIDGE?

Notwithstanding the reality of these early-stage financing hurdles, many policy makers in the US believe that the US venture capital markets are so broad and deep that entrepreneurs can readily access the capital needed to

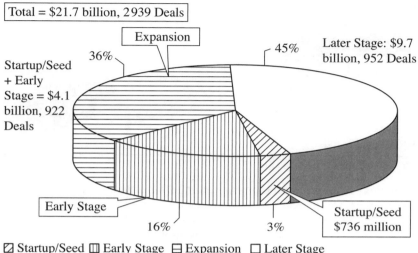

Total = $21.7 billion, 2939 Deals

Source: National Venture Capital Association (2005).

Figure 7.3   Breakdown of US venture capital by stage of development (2005)

cross the Valley of Death. In actual fact, venture capitalists not only have limited information on new firms, but are also prone to herding tendencies, as witnessed in the recent dot-com boom and bust (Jacobs, 2002). Venture capitalists are also, quite naturally, risk averse. Their primary goal, after all, is not to develop the nation's economy but to earn significant returns for their investors.[7] Accordingly, as Figure 7.3 shows, most funds tend to focus on later stages of technology development because there is more information at this stage in the process about the commercial prospects of the innovation (and hence less risk to their investment). As Figure 7.3 and Table 7.1 show, the result is that the US venture capital market, although large, is not focused on early-stage firms: in 2005 startups in the US received only $736 million or about 3 per cent of the $21.7 billion of available venture capital.

7.8   BRIDGING THE FUNDING GAP

The limitations of the market for venture capital mean that small innovative firms seek funding from a variety of sources (Branscomb and Auerswald, 2002). In addition to business angels and venture capital firms, early-stage

Table 7.1   Sources of startup funds

Multiple Sources of Early-Stage Finances	
VCs	~$0.3 billion
(PWC MoneyTreeTM data)	(< 200 companies)
State Funds	<$0.5 billion
(estimate by S. Weiss)	
Angel investors	$20 billion
(Center for Venture Research)	
SBIR/STTR Funds	$2.2 billion

technology firms seek development funding from industry, federal and state governments and universities. Indeed the diversity of these sources for early-stage funding represents one of the strengths of the US system.

As Table 7.1 shows, venture funding is a small proportion of early-stage finance. State funds play a larger role than many realize. By far the most important contributor to early-stage funding are angel investors, at more than 20 times the contribution of state and venture funding combined.

The significant size and importance of federal government's role is interesting here. Research by Branscomb and Auerswald (2002) estimates that the federal government provides between 20 per cent and 25 per cent of all funds for early-stage technology development – a substantial role by any measure and one that often surprises Americans in its dimensions. (Figure 7.4). This federal contribution is rendered more significant in that competitive government awards address segments of the innovation cycle that private institutional investors often (quite rightly) find too risky for investment.

The availability of early-stage financing and its interaction with other elements of the US innovation process are the focus of growing analytical efforts.[8] Below we examine the SBIR and the ATP, which are the most important examples of the government's efforts to draw on the inventiveness of small, high-technology firms through competitive innovation awards. The potential of SBIR and ATP in this regard underscores the need to understand how they strengthen the nation's innovative capacity.

7.9   SBIR

Created in 1982 through the Small Business Innovation Development Act, SBIR is designed to stimulate technological innovation among small private sector businesses while providing the government with new, cost-effective, technical and scientific solutions to challenging mission problems.

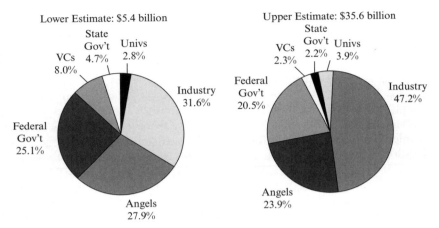

Figure 7.4   Estimated distribution of funding sources for early-stage technology development[9]

SBIR is also designed to encourage a role for small businesses in federal R&D and facilitate the development of innovative technologies in the private sector, helping to stimulate the US economy.[10]

The SBIR concept has several significant advantages.

- Entrepreneurship: SBIR focuses on helping small companies bring their ingenuity to focus on government and societal needs in domains as diverse as health, security, the environment and energy efficiency and alternative energy sources.
- Bottom-up proposal: needs are articulated by government agencies; proposals are initiated by individual companies, often with no previous experience in government R&D programmes.
- Highly selective: a two-phase filter is employed with less than 15 per cent of applicants being accepted in the first phase and approximately half or less in the second phase.
- No new funds: SBIR has no budget line, requires no new funds, and is therefore both politically viable and relatively impervious to the whims of the budget process. This provides the continuity and predictability that encourages small firm participation and, over time, allows for portfolio effects.
- Decentralized: the programme is decentralized across government. Programme ownership rests with many agencies, quite different in size and with dramatically different missions. SBIR does not come under the responsibility of a single 'innovation agency'.

Since its establishment in 1982, the SBIR programme has grown to some $2 billion per year and now includes 11 federal agencies that are currently required to set aside 2.5 per cent of their extramural R&D budgets exclusively for SBIR contracts for small companies, defined in the US as less than 500 employees.[11] Each year these agencies identify various R&D topics for pursuit by small businesses under the SBIR programme, representing scientific and technical problems requiring innovative solutions.

Features that make SBIR grants attractive from the perspective of the entrepreneur, aside from the funding itself, include the fact that there is no dilution of ownership or repayment required. Importantly, grant recipients retain the rights to intellectual property developed using the SBIR award, with no royalties owing to the government. The government retains royalty-free use for a period, but this is very rarely exercised. Selection to receive an SBIR grant also tends to confer a certification effect – a signal to private investors of the technical and commercial promise of the technology.[12] The awards usually provide a faster route to new technology than traditional procurement processes allow. Importantly, firms with successful SBIR awards add to the diversity and competitiveness of the supplier base for US companies.

From the perspective of the government, the SBIR programme helps officials draw on private sector ingenuity to achieve their respective agency missions (National Research Council, 2004). By providing a bridge between small companies and the federal agencies, especially for procurement, SBIR serves as a catalyst for the development of new ideas and new technologies to meet federal missions in health, transport, the environment and defence.

SBIR also provides a bridge between universities and the marketplace. Nearly one-third of SBIR awards involve university researchers either as firm founders or as participants in the research, in the latter case as principal investigators or subcontractors. Thanks to the commercialization-sensitive environment created by the Bayh Dole Act, SBIR awards are increasingly seen by researchers and university administrators as a source of early-stage financial support for university researchers with promising ideas.[13]

7.10   THE ATP

Along with the SBIR programme, the Advanced Technology Program (ATP) is a key example of programmes designed to help bring high-risk, enabling and innovative civilian technologies to market. Founded in 1989, ATP's mission is to provide funds for the development of generic technologies that are often too risky for individual firms but, if successful, can offer high payoffs for society as a whole.

Proposals for ATP funding are first vetted by technical and business experts – a distinguishing feature of the programme. Another key feature is the requirement for matching resources from the firms themselves. This requirement serves as a constant reality check and ensures public funds are used effectively. Moreover, the requirement for significant risk and broad-based economic benefits means that ATP awards complement private capital, since venture capitalists normally search for projects with lower risks that will provide an exit strategy in a relatively short timeframe.

One of the strongest features of the ATP approach is its support for joint ventures. ATP encourages cooperation between large and small companies to develop technologies with broad applications that would be beyond the resources or interests of an individual firm. Small firms benefit from ATP because it provides them with access to the skills, management expertise and marketing reach of larger firms. It also helps them become suppliers to larger firms and, over time, shift to a fuller partnership in an ongoing relationship. Large firms like ATP because the cooperation it facilitates helps them compete in rapidly changing markets by providing access to niche expertise and unique talents often found in small firms.

The ATP and SBIR programmes complement each other. The larger award sums offered by ATP, its focus on next-stage commercialization and the synergies it creates between small and large firms make ATP, in effect, an SBIR Phase III – helping to commercialize successful prototypes funded by the SBIR programme.

7.11   KEY FEATURES OF THE US INNOVATION AWARD PROGRAMMES

Both the SBIR and ATP innovation award programmes exemplify the 'best practice' principles behind successful US public-private partnerships.

- Competitiveness: first and foremost, the programmes are intensely competitive, with multiple stage reviews and a limited number of successful applicants. Although quite different in absolute scale – SBIR at \$2 billion and ATP at \$160 million – both programmes make awards to some 12–15 per cent of applicants. They are, perhaps aptly, compared to leading scholarship programmes for outstanding students, not only in terms of their success rate, but more profoundly in terms of the social investment in private individuals based on the rationale of long-term public gain.

- Limits: a distinguishing characteristic of the American innovation awards is that they are limited in time and amount. It is important that innovation award programmes remain open to new entrants and remain competitive for each round of funding. This does not mean that companies cannot re-apply for additional work in the case of SBIR, or for a new project in the case of ATP. It does mean that there are no 'politically favoured firms' able to draw regularly on government support.
- Cost share: more formally with ATP, but equally with SBIR, the programmes require industry to take ownership through risk and cost sharing. An explicit and distinctive feature of ATP is the focus on collaboration among small companies, large companies and (increasingly) universities. SBIR provides an avenue to cooperative contracts and has a major de facto cooperative feature with university-based founders, consultants and principal investigators.
- No recoupment: for both the SBIR and ATP programmes, the federal authorities do not seek to recoup the funds that they grant to the companies that are successful in the competition. This is sound practice because it is often difficult to distinguish the relative contribution of an award to a particular project (paradoxically, unsuccessful projects can prove valuable in that they illuminate technological dead ends while imparting knowledge that can be useful on a related technological path). The cost of determining the contribution of an award can be both a poor use of public funds and a deterrent to would-be participants. The US system relies, very simply, on the tax system to obtain funds from salaries paid to workers and managers and on firm earnings.
- Evaluation: another characteristic of the US innovation awards is their increasing reliance on internal and external evaluation. The ATP has probably the best evaluation programme in the US, and perhaps the world. The agencies responsible for the SBIR programme were required to undertake a major evaluation at the last reauthorization. The mandate (to the National Academies) to review the achievements, operations and challenges of the SBIR programme has contributed to the development of a 'culture of evaluation' among the agencies responsible for managing the SBIR programme. Additional studies have been commissioned by the agencies and more extensive programme experimentation has occurred.
- Networking benefits: the broader competitive benefits of the networking activities created by these award programmes are not insignificant. The dissemination of enabling technologies made pos-

sible by these programmes makes both small and large firms more competitive. Indeed, large firms increasingly must rely on the niche technological strengths of small companies.[14]

- Opportunities for growth: small companies, of course, are the source of tomorrow's large companies. One of the distinguishing features of the US economy is its ability not only to create large numbers of small high-technology companies, but also to provide the conditions that enable an exceedingly small number of these new firms to grow into the Intels, Microsofts and Googles of tomorrow. Companies such as ATMI (environmentally safe manufacturing), Martek (microalgae products that promote infant health), Luna (nanotechnologies and sensors) and, by some accounts, Qualcomm (cell phones) all benefited from SBIR awards at a critical phase. Similarly, companies such as Affymetrix (first DNA GeneChips) and Plug Power (fuel cells) benefited from ATP awards. These companies focus on highly promising technologies that will offer significant benefits in health, energy and the environment.

Even without the growth of these exceptional firms, a vibrant and regularly renewed stock of innovative small- and medium-sized companies can play a critical role in helping the government to accomplish its many missions at lower costs and with improved efficiency, thereby contributing to the nation's productivity and, more fundamentally, enabling all citizens to enjoy the fruits of technological advances and economic growth.

7.12 SWEDEN'S INNOVATION CHALLENGE

Although already one of the world's most innovative countries, Swedish policy makers recognize the need to spur innovation to sustain their nation's economic growth and standard of living. In this regard innovation award programmes, similar to the SBIR and ATP concepts, may provide Sweden with higher returns on its significant investments in R&D.

Sweden ranks first among the EU countries in innovation, according to the European Commission.[15] Indeed, the Swedish national innovation system shows major strengths in the education level of the workforce and in the high level of R&D conducted by its business sector. Stable macroeconomic conditions and a reliable institutional framework further enable Swedish enterprises to integrate and compete successfully in global markets.

Yet, as the 2005 European Trend-Chart on Innovation reports, 'There is however, a general lack of incentives for radical innovation and also an inadequate use of scientific achievements, which might hamper future economic growth and prosperity' (EC, 2005). This analysis is also reflected in the fact that few new major firms have been created in Sweden since 1970 (Davis and Henrekson, 2003). Sweden's challenge, therefore, is one of creating the incentives for research commercialization and small business formation.

In the US the SBIR and ATP innovation award programmes serve as catalysts for innovation by motivating entrepreneurs and by generating new information for the capital markets about the commercial potential of new ideas. They encourage networking by bringing together university researchers and the small and big business communities. Lastly, they introduce better solutions to government missions – thereby keeping down the cost of government services.

Recognizing its potential in Sweden, VINNOVA is experimenting with an SBIR-type programme. Already, this pilot has demonstrated real demand for early-stage finance in Sweden. This is a good start, but Sweden needs to meet the demand for funding innovation by increasing the scale of its programme. If carefully adapted to the Swedish context, innovation awards have the potential to help Sweden develop innovative technologies, create new dynamic companies and jobs, and compete in the new global economy.

7.13 OUR COMMON CHALLENGES

While national innovation systems differ in scale and flexibility, both Sweden and the US face similar challenges in innovation. We have to address the new competition from low-wage, high-skill countries by becoming more innovative and productive and we have to justify R&D expenditures by creating new jobs and new wealth.

To do this, our countries have to reform existing institutions and create new ones. Recognizing the need for change, we need to craft new mechanisms that shift incentives in a positive way. As the SBIR and ATP cases reveal, effective partnerships require that entrepreneurs, firms, government agencies and other organizations be able to work towards a common goal. For this cooperation to be successful, effective industry-led leadership, shared costs and stakes in a positive outcome as well as regular evaluation and learning are necessary.

NOTES

1. Editor's note: The ATP was considered one of the most effective US public private partnerships. Yet it was also one of the most controversial. It had three flaws. It was not large, except perhaps in the initial years of the Clinton administration, and therefore did not have a correspondingly large constituency. It was highly selective and completely objective. These otherwise exemplary attributes became liabilities in the constituency–driven US Congress. Some members of the Congress argued that the programme's awards constituted a form of 'corporate welfare'. This often strident, indeed disproportionate, opposition led to the third disadvantage, which was the uncertainty associated with the programme. Its budget was never secure, nor was the funding amount known until, often, late in the legislative process. This impeded planning and applications by R&D managers. Notwithstanding these drawbacks, the programme was evaluated by the National Academy of Science Committee on Government-Industry Partnerships chaired by Intel's Gordon Moore. The Moore Committee published a report praising the programme's concept, operation and exceptional evaluation programme. (See C. Wessner (ed.), (2001) *National Research Council, The Advanced Technology Program, Assessing Outcomes*, Washington, DC: National Academy Press.)

   To address these essentially political concerns, and build a bi-partisan constituency for a new innovation programme, a new mechanism called the Technology Innovation Program designed to address 'critical national needs' with no federal funding for large corporations but more involvement of universities was passed by Congress and signed into law on 6 August 2007. (See The America COMPETES Act (PL 110–69, Section 3012).) While now in existence, many key features of this programme are yet to be defined.

2. For an analysis of India's economic potential compared to China, see Yasheng Huang and Tarun Khanna, 'Can India overtake China?' *Foreign Policy*, July–August 2003. The authors argue that India's development strategy, while initiated later than China's and thus lagging China, is more sustainable because it is more strongly based on fostering bottom-up entrepreneurial capacity.

3. Tata's recent takeover of Corus Steel is the latest in a series of global acquisitions by Indian firms. Other Indian firms recently acquiring assets overseas include Bharat Forge, Ranbaxy, Wipro and Nicholas Piramal. According to *The Economist*, Indian companies announced 115 foreign acquisitions, with a total value of $7.4 billion in the first three quarters of 2006. See *The Economist*, 'India's acquisition spree', 12 October 2006.

4. France, for example, has allocated €1 billion for a new Industrial Innovation Agency, following the release of the Beffa Report. Similarly, Japan is restructuring and making significant investments in its innovation system.

5. The drop off in foreign students was largely self-inflicted. Following the 9/11 attacks, the US government imposed much tighter controls on foreign students without having the necessary procedures or enough staff in place to implement them. The result was long delays, lengthy travel and often arbitrary rulings. In the last few years procedures have been relatively stabilized and the US share of foreign students is rising again. See, for example, recent reports by the President's Council of Advisors on Science and Technology, 'Sustaining the nation's innovation ecosystems' (January 2004) and the Council on Competitiveness (2005), *Innovate America: Thriving in a World of Challenge and Change*, Washington, DC: Council on Competitiveness. See also National Academy of Sciences (2005).

6. The Nobel Committee cited Spence's contribution in highlighting the importance of market signals in the presence of information asymmetries.

7. 'The goal of venture capitalists is to make money for our investors – not to develop the economy', personal communication from David Morgenthaler, founder of Morgenthaler Ventures and past President of the National Venture Capital Association.

8. The growth and subsequent contribution of venture capital have begun to attract the serious study needed to illuminate the dynamics of high-technology firm evolution. See,

for example, the work of Jeffrey Sohl and colleagues and the University of New Hampshire's Center for Venture Research, described at www.unh.edu/cvr (accessed 23 July 2007).

9. It is important to remember that these are estimates. The authors stress the 'limitations inherent in the data and the magnitude of the extrapolations' and urge caution in interpreting the findings. They note further that while the funding range presented for each category is wide, these approximate estimates, nonetheless, provide 'valuable insight into the overall scale and composition of early-stage technology development funding patterns and allow at least a preliminary comparison of the relative level of federal, state, and private investments'. For further discussion of the approach and its limitations, see Branscomb and Auerswald (2002, pp. 20–4).

10. The evolution of the SBIR legislation was influenced by an accumulation of evidence beginning with David Birch in the late 1970s suggesting that small businesses were assuming an increasingly important role in both innovation and job creation. This trend gained greater credibility in the 1980s and was confirmed by empirical analysis, notably by Zoltan Acs and David Audretsch of the US Small Business Innovation Data Base, which confirmed the increased importance of small firms in generating technological innovations and their growing contribution to the US economy. See Acs and Audretsch (1990).

11. These include the Department of Defense, the Department of Health and Human Services, the National Aeronautics and Space Administration, the Department of Energy, the National Science Foundation, the Department of Agriculture, the Department of Commerce, the Department of Education, the Department of Transportation, the Environmental Protection Agency and, most recently, the Department of Homeland Security.

12. This certification effect was initially identified by Lerner (1999). For a similar concept from the Advanced Technology Program, see M. Feldman and M. Kelly (2001), 'Leveraging research and development: the impact of the Advanced Technology Program', in C. Wessner (ed.), *The Advanced Technology Program, Assessing Outcomes*, Washington, DC: National Academy Press, pp. 189–210.

13. The Bayh-Dole Act of 1980 is designed to encourage the utilization of inventions produced under federal funding by permitting universities and small businesses to elect to retain the title to inventions made in performance of federally-funded programmes.

14. As Acs and Audretsch (1990) argued in their seminal study of small companies, small firms show unparalleled capacity to focus on and develop new innovative products and processes.

15. European Commission Press Release, 16 January 2006.

REFERENCES

Acs, S. J. and D. B. Audretsch (1990), *Innovation and Small Firms,* Cambridge, MA: MIT Press.

Branscomb, L. M. and P. E. Auerswald (2002), *Between Invention and Innovation; An Analysis of Funding for Early-Stage Technology Development*, Gaithersburg, MD: National Institute of Standards and Technology.

Branscomb, L. M. and P. E. Auerswald (2001), *Taking Technical Risks: How Innovators, Managers and Investors Manage Risk in High Tech Innovations*, Cambridge, MA and London: MIT Press.

Davis, Steven J. and Maganus Henrekson (2006), 'Economic performance and work activity in Sweden after the crisis of the early 1990s', NBER working paper no. 12768, December.

de Tocqueville, Alexis (1835), Democracy in America, reprinted 2000, Chicago: University of Chicago Press.

Griffing, B. (2001), 'Between invention and innovation, mapping the funding for early stage technologies', Carnegie Conference Center, Washington, DC, 25 January, accessed 23 July 2007 at www.access.gpo.gov/congress/house/science/cp105-b/science105b.pdf.

Jacobs, T. (2002), 'Biotech follows dot.com boom and bust', *Nature* **20**(10), 973.

Lerner, J. (1999), 'Public venture capital', in C. Wessner (ed.), *National Research Council, The Small Business Innovation Program: Challenges and Opportunities*, Washington, DC: National Academies Press, pp. 115–28.

Mansfield, E. (1985), 'How fast does new industrial technology leak out?' *Journal of Industrial Economics,* **34**(2), 217–24.

National Academy of Sciences (2005), *Rising Above the Gathering Storm: Energizing and Employing America for a Brighter Economic Future*, Washington, DC: National Academies Press.

National Research Council (2004), *The Small Business Innovation Research Program, Program Diversity and Assessment Challenges,* Washington, DC: National Academies Press.

Small Business Administration (SBA) (2004), 'Small business by the numbers', SBA Office of Advocacy, June.

Spence, M. (1974), *Market Signaling: Informational Transfer in Hiring and Related Processes*, Cambridge, MA: Harvard University Press.

The European Trend Chart on Innovation (EC) (2005), *Country Report for Sweden*, Luxembourg: Office for Official Publications of the European Communities.

Wolff, A. W. (2007), China's national innovation system, presentation to the OECD Conference on the Review of China's Innovation System and Policy, Beijing, 27 August.

8. About the US Advanced Technology Program[1]

Marc G. Stanley and Christopher J. Currens

8.1 BACKGROUND TO THE ATP

The US Advanced Technology Program (ATP) bridges the gap between the research laboratory and the market place, stimulating prosperity through innovation. Through partnerships with the private sector, ATP's early-stage investment is accelerating the development of innovative technologies that promise significant commercial payoffs and widespread benefits for the nation. As part of the highly regarded National Institute of Standards and Technology (NIST), the ATP is changing the way industry approaches research and development (R&D), providing a mechanism for industry to extend its technological reach and push the boundaries of what can be attempted.

Technology research in the private sector is driven by today's global, economic realities. The pace of technological change is faster than ever before, and victory goes to the swift. These realities force companies to make narrower, shorter-term investments in R&D that maximize returns to the company quickly.

The ATP views R&D projects from a broader perspective – its bottom line is how the project can benefit the nation. In sharing the relatively high development risks of technologies that potentially make feasible a broad range of new commercial opportunities, the ATP fosters projects with a high payoff for the nation as a whole – in addition to a direct return to the innovators. The ATP has several critical features that set it apart from other US government R&D programmes:

- For-profit companies conceive, propose, co-fund and execute ATP projects and programmes in partnerships with academia, independent research organizations and federal laboratories.
- The ATP has strict cost-sharing rules. Joint ventures (JV) (two or more companies working together) must pay at least half of the project costs. Large, Fortune-500 companies participating as a single

firm must pay at least 60 per cent of total project costs. Small and medium-sized companies working on single firm ATP projects must pay a minimum of all indirect costs associated with the project.

- The ATP does not fund product development. Private industry bears the costs of product development, production, marketing, sales and distribution.
- ATP awards are made strictly on the basis of rigorous peer-reviewed competitions. Selection is based on the innovation, technical risk, demonstrated need, potential economic benefits to the nation and the strength of the commercialization plan of the project.
- The ATP's support does not become a perpetual subsidy or entitlement – each project has goals, specific funding allocations and completion dates established at the outset. Projects are monitored and can be terminated for cause before completion.
- The ATP partners companies of all sizes, universities and non-profit organizations, encouraging them to take on greater technical challenges with potentially large benefits that extend well beyond the innovators – challenges they could not or would not take up alone. For smaller, startup firms early support from the ATP can spell the difference between success and failure.
- Projects are evaluated from the outset on proper and clear metrics.

Universities and non-profit independent research organizations play a significant role as participants in ATP projects. Out of 768 projects selected by the ATP since its inception, well over half include one or more universities either as subcontractors or JV members. All told, there are more than 170 individual universities and over 30 national laboratories participating in ATP projects.

ATP awards are selected through open, peer-reviewed competitions. All industries and all fields of science and technology are eligible. Proposals are evaluated by one of several technology-specific boards that are staffed by experts in fields such as biotechnology, photonics, chemistry, manufacturing, information technology and materials. All proposals are assured an appropriate, technically competent review even when they involve a broad, multi-disciplinary mix of technologies.

The ATP accepts proposals only in response to specific, published solicitations. Notices of ATP competitions are published in *Commerce Business Daily*. The ATP Proposal Preparation Kit includes thorough discussion of the ATP goals and procedures as well as useful guidelines for preparation of a proposal. ATP also has a web site with extensive information about the programme and its awards.

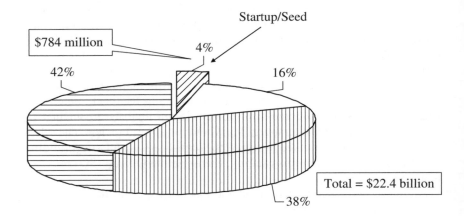

Startup/Seed
$784 million
4%
42%
16%
Total = $22.4 billion
38%

☒ Startup/Seed ☐ Early stage ⊞ Expansion ⊟ Later Stage

Source: National Venture Capital Association (2005).

Figure 8.1   Large US venture capital market is not focused on early-stage firms: breakdown of US venture capital by stage of development (2005)

Since 1990, ATP has received 6924 proposals submitted to 44 competitions, requesting a total of $US14.7 billion. ATP has awarded 768 projects (see Figure 8.1) involving 1511 participants and as many subcontractors (218 JV and 550 single companies). High-risk research to the value of $US4.4 billion has been funded (ATP share: $US2.3 billion; industry share: $US2.1 billion). Small businesses are thriving, with 66 per cent of projects led by small businesses. As part of its evaluation process, ATP has documented the filing of over 1,418 patents. In 2007 over 346 projects report new technologies under commercialization.

8.2   HOW ARE PROPOSALS EVALUATED?

The ATP uses a competitive, peer-reviewed process to evaluate both the technical and the business/economic aspects of the proposals we receive. The technical reviewers come almost exclusively from within the federal government – NIST is a rich source of reviewers. We also draw heavily on the National Institutes of Health (NIH), the Department of Defense (DOD) and the Department of Energy (DOE). For the business and economic reviews, we draw on industry consultants, who are often retired executives and business development experts. In all cases ATP checks for potential conflicts of interest and requires reviewers to sign non-disclosure agreements. The safeguarding of proprietary information is taken very seriously.

The technology-specific project selection boards manage the multiple peer reviews and, through informed discussions and feedback, determine which proposals will become semi-finalists. Semi-finalists are invited to come to the ATP in Gaithersburg, Maryland for an oral review. The selection board develops a ranked listing of the semi-finalists and offers funding recommendations. From this ranking, the Selecting Official (SO) makes a final funding decision.

All unsuccessful proposers are offered a debriefing. This debriefing provides feedback that points out the strengths and weaknesses of the proposal as measured against the ATP criteria. Using what they have learned from debriefings, many unsuccessful proposers have submitted new proposals that have resulted in awards.

8.3 TRANSFER GAP: WHY IS THE PROGRAMME NEEDED?

Very simply, although we recognize that innovative technologies have the potential to bring enormous benefits to society as a whole, private investors often cannot adequately support their developments because profits are often too uncertain or too distant. ATP complements rather than displaces private capital.

The capital markets are shifting away from basic R&D. After Internet and communications company stocks collapsed in mid-2000, a long winter of technology finance followed. The market for initial public offerings (IPO) of all technology companies closed too. Without an 'exit' strategy, venture capitalists could not, or would not, invest in startups. Still uncertain following the bursting of the technology bubble, financiers remain disinclined to invest in emerging technologies. While the valuations for later-stage startups increased in 2004, money for younger startups did not. Venture capitalists are funding technologies much closer to commercialization, in established companies, especially those whose work is relevant to Internet security, national security and biodefence.

Business angels continue to be the largest source of seed and startup capital, with 55 per cent of 2005 angel investments in the seed and startup stage. This preference for seed and startup investing is followed closely by post-seed/startup investment at 43 per cent. The increase in post-seed/startup investing is continuing a trend that began in 2004 and represents a 10 per cent increase on historical levels.

According to Jeffrey Sohl, Director of the University of New Hampshire Center for Venture Research and Professor of Entrepreneurship and Decisions Sciences:

> While angels are not abandoning seed and startup investing, it appears that market conditions, and the preferences of large formal angel alliances, are resulting in angels engaging in more later-stage investments. New, first sequence, investments represent 70% of 2005 angel activity, indicating that some of this post seed investing is in new deals. This shift in investment strategies toward post seed investments reduces the proportional amount of seed and start-up capital. This restructuring of the angel market has in turn resulted in fewer dollars available for seed investments, thus exacerbating the capital gap for seed and start-up capital in the United States, Sohl (2005).

This would matter less if public companies were investing in emerging technologies, but they are not. Over the last four years, corporations have focused their attention on heightened global competition and less and less on basic R&D.

The dearth of VC for early-stage startups, the shifting of public companies away from basic R&D, and the emphasis on security by the government has created a 'transfer gap'. A transfer gap occurs when technologies emerging from basic research activities never enter the market. A transfer gap occurs because financiers demand more certainty about the future prospects of a given technology than technologist can supply. Clearly, early-stage technology development involves both high risks and large uncertainties. When financiers feel very cautious, as they do now, the gap widens.

Transfer gaps also result, in part, from the different levels of information that exist between entrepreneurs and potential investors and partners. Lacking full appreciation of the technology, investors hesitate to provide the funds that would permit the entrepreneur to demonstrate the concept. These funding gaps matter because equity-financed small businesses are one of the most effective mechanisms for capitalizing on new ideas and bringing them to market. Small businesses are also a leading source of growth and employment in the US.

8.4   ENCOURAGING PARTNERSHIPS

ATP catalyses companies, universities, research organizations and state and local entities to partner creatively to develop innovative technologies. ATP encourages teaming arrangements that bring research, development, manufacturing and commercialization partners together at an early stage of innovation.

There are specific examples of what works well in the general area of government-industry-university technology partnerships. Each is part of the overall complex of technology programmes that the US government supports. Examples include working with the Office of Naval Research, the Defense Advanced Research Projects Agency (DARPA) or the DOE. State governments provide a relatively small portion of total early-stage technology development, but establish regional environments that help bridge the gap from invention to innovation. They facilitate university-industry partnerships, leverage federal academic research funds, build a technically educated workforce and ease regulatory burdens. National laboratories (e.g. Sandia) also participate in ATP projects.

Although the ATP was designed to assist US businesses specifically, its defining legislation also directs that it 'aid industry-led US joint R&D ventures, which may include universities and independent research organizations'. Since the ATP began in 1990, about $US200 million in ATP funding has flowed to 172 different universities. In fact, universities have been involved in 377 of the 768 ATP projects that are either still active or that went to completion; and when non-profit organizations are involved in an ATP project, more than one usually participates.

Non-profit organizations may also participate in ATP by creating spin-off companies. A unique capability that non-profits bring, especially to small and medium-sized companies, is tremendous expertise in government contracting. This value cannot be overstated, especially when the R&D triggers complex government regulations, such as those concerning human and animal subjects. Non-profit involvement can also facilitate post-project equipment disposal to the non-profit.

These non-profit organizations have recognized that ATP can provide critical funding for state-of-the-art laboratory equipment and for the high-risk development of innovative technologies for commercial exploitation. An ATP JV is required to pay the majority of shared costs, both direct and indirect, on an ATP project. Although ATP does not require them to do so, the industry partners often cover a portion or all of the non-profit's share of the costs.

By virtue of its role as the catalyst and cement that creates and binds non-profit/industry partnerships, the ATP provides non-profits with other, more intangible rewards. For instance, it exposes faculty and students to how industry does cutting-edge R&D. It also provides faculty with opportunities for external consulting and exposes students to potential career opportunities. It may also provide graduate students with part-time or temporary employment opportunities at an ATP awardee/company. Working in an advanced technology project frequently gives non-profit researchers valuable leads for future research. Probably most importantly, collaborating in an ATP award broadens and deepens the relationships that non-profits have with companies, which often lead to future gifts and sponsored projects.

In order to facilitate the use of such partnerships in ATP awards, non-profits can use a variety of mechanisms that exist within ATP to:

- educate their scientific staff about collaborative R&D (companies view partnership-savvy partners as more desirable partners)
- convince companies to collaborate in an R&D proposal
- refer company partners to ATP regulations and forms
- post available technology on the ATP Collaboration Bulletin Board (can be used anonymously).

Companies, too, benefit significantly when non-profits participate in their ATP projects. There are the obvious benefits of access both to creative and eminent scientists, and to other resources found only in world-class R&D institutions, such as state-of-the-art equipment and libraries. In addition, close interaction with uniquely knowledgeable and capable faculty gives industrial scientists timely technical training, a recruiting tool for potential employees, and stimulates them to engage in the kind of 'out-of-the-box' thinking that is needed in high-risk R&D. Virtually all ATP awardees report that creative thinking was stimulated through the collaborative involvement of outside organizations. University R&D staff are uniquely capable of adding creativity, breadth and depth to the scientific activities of industry.

8.5   EVALUATION: HOW WELL DOES IT WORK?

An impartial National Academies assessment found ATP to be a proven programme, with a positive track record. The ATP has succeeded in evaluating retrospective impacts from some of its investments in high-risk technology, and the returns are significant. In fact, ATP over 15 years, has demonstrated that it works well. It achieves its goals of stimulating risky new, high-payoff technology development by funding small companies and bringing together universities, small firms, large companies, government laboratories and non-profits. It facilitates an orderly transition from invention to commercially viable innovation. ATP facilitates the allocation of risk capital to early-stage technology ventures. It plays a significant role in converting the nation's portfolio of science and engineering knowledge into innovations generating new markets and industries, aimed at sustaining long-term economic growth.

ATP initiated evaluation at the outset – several years prior to the passage of the Government Performance and Results Act. We put an evaluation effort into place (1) as a management tool to ensure that programme goals are met to improve the effectiveness of the programme, and (2) to meet the many external requests for ATP programme results. There are some basic principles to follow in setting up an evaluation programme. One basic principle is to measure against the mission. The key elements from the ATP Statute provide a guide as to what to measure, as follows:

- creation and application of high-risk, generic technology
- accelerated R&D commercialization
- refinement of manufacturing processes
- collaborative activities
- competitiveness of US businesses
- widespread applications and broad-based benefits.

ATP also tracks revenues and cost savings of participant companies. For instance, ATP recently assembled retrospective metrics for 36 ATP-funded projects. Metrics were derived from (1) ATP's Business Reporting System (BRS), which tracks the economic and financial status of ATP projects, and (2) telephone interviews conducted with many of the 36 projects to supplement and update the BRS data. Projects were selected because ATP had company-approved success stories showing early economic and financial success.

The metrics chosen for this retrospective summary include revenue and patents. Most of the companies chosen for this retrospective summary are small as defined by the Small Business Administration (i.e. fewer than 500 employees).

For the 36 projects that were reviewed, it was found that approximately $US1 billion in revenue is associated with $US80 million in ATP investment. In many instances significant cost savings accrued to companies and/or customers. Many noted employment growth. Substantial intellectual property was generated (102 patents issued or pending).

It should be noted that highlighting revenues or cost savings tells only part of the story. Traditionally, such metrics are indicative of 'private benefits'. In assessing the impact of any public programme, evaluators generally focus on the totality of benefits and costs for the nation. It has been demonstrated in the literature that social benefits are several times private benefits. Because ATP is a long-term programme that only funds up to prototype development, revenues and societal benefits are typically not realized until several years after the project has ended.

8.6 SUMMARY OF FINDINGS

ATP helps firms bridge the transfer gap enabling:

- increased rates of innovation
- broadly enabling technology platforms
- commercialization by US companies
- improved competitiveness of US industries
- broadly distributed economic benefits from large spillovers
- increased collaborations
- strong small business participation
- ATP a strong causal factor – leveraging, not substituting.

In summary, ATP:

- focuses on the civilian sector
- funds enabling technologies with high spillover potential
- focuses on overcoming difficult research challenges
- encourages company-university-laboratory collaboration, capitalizing on R&D investments
- requires commercialization plans and implementation to ensure societal outcomes
- measures against mission in its evaluation work.

8.7 ATP RESOURCES

'A toolkit for evaluating public R&D investment', www.atp.nist.gov/eao/gcr 03-857/contents.htm (accessed 27 July 2007).

'Between invention and innovation', www.atp.nist.gov/eao/gcr 02-841/gcr 02-841.pdf (accessed 27 July 2007).

ATP Factsheets, www.atp.nist.gov/factsheets/factsheets.htm (accessed 27 July 2007).

ATP Funded Projects Database, http://jazz.nist.gov/atpcf/prjbriefs/listmaker.cfm (accessed 27 July 2007).

'ATP Economic Studies', www.atp.nist.gov/eao/eao_pubs.htm (accessed 27 July 2007).

NOTES

1. Editor's note: The ATP was considered one of the most effective US public private partnerships. Yet it was also one of the most controversial. It had three flaws. It was not large, except perhaps in the initial years of the Clinton administration, and therefore did not have a correspondingly large constituency. It was highly selective and completely objective. These otherwise exemplary attributes became liabilities in the constituency-driven US Congress. Some members of the Congress argued that the programme's awards constituted a form of 'corporate welfare'. This often strident, indeed disproportionate, opposition led to the third disadvantage, which was the uncertainty associated with the programme. Its budget was never secure, nor was the funding amount known until, often, late in the legislative process. This impeded planning and applications by R&D managers. Notwithstanding these drawbacks, the programme was evaluated by the National Academy of Science Committee on Government-Industry Partnerships chaired by Intel's Gordon Moore. The Moore Committee published a report praising the programme's concept, operation and exceptional evaluation programme. (See National Research Council, *The Advanced Technology Program, Assessing Outcomes*, C. Wessner, ed., Washington, DC: National Academy Press, 2001.)

   To address these essentially political concerns, and build a bi-partisan constituency for a new innovation programme, a new mechanism called the Technology Innovation Program designed to address 'critical national needs' with no federal funding for large corporations but more involvement of universities was passed by Congress and signed into law on 6 August 2007. (See The America COMPETES Act (PL 110–69, Section 3012).) While now in existence, many key features of this programme are yet to be defined.

REFERENCE

Sohl, J. (2005), *The Angel Investor Market in 2005: The Angel Market Exhibits Modest Growth*, Durham, NH: University of New Hampshire Center for Venture Research, p. 2.

9. Globalization of converging nanotechnologies

Evan S. Michelson

9.1 INTRODUCTION: CONVERGENCE AT THE NANOSCALE[1]

While the hybridization of contemporary science and technology (S&T) innovation is occurring on a global level and is becoming evident across a range of industrial sectors, one of the best examples of this trend is in the nascent field of nanotechnology – the ability to see and manipulate matter at the nanoscale. Though the current, formative stage of nanotechnology research and development (R&D) has been compared to that of the computer industry of the 1960s or the biotechnology industry of the 1980s, the very fact that these technological advancements emerged beforehand has moved nanotechnology along a path that is more closely connected with such branches of technology. Because of its close relationship to multiple disciplines, a number of S&T forecasts have begun to identify nanotechnology as the leading edge of a new worldwide trend – termed converging technologies – that is meant to indicate the growing interaction and blurring of the lines between nanotechnology, biotechnology, information technology (IT) and neuroscience. The concept underlying converging technologies at the nanoscale is that as these and other scientific disciplines and their associated technologies have begun to emerge, progress and mature over the past few years, there has been an increasing tendency for such strands of thinking to intersect with and cross-pollinate one another, thereby creating the potential for great improvement in the quality of the human life around the world.

However, the impacts of this new technological fusion are not simply limited to the research enterprise itself. Revolutions in nanotechnology and other strands of emerging technologies are beginning to have impacts on the international policy-making process in particular, and also on national education systems, and the formation and management of firms and industries across sectors and national boundaries. As a major driver of this process, the development of nanotechnology has been affected, with hopes and fears about its potential benefits and risks becoming entangled in a range of political, social and economic issues that are also closely connected to developments in other strands of technology. This chapter describes the nature and characteristics of nanotechnology, how it is increasingly interacting with other technologies, and the nature of its impact on the international innovation landscape. In doing so, the chapter discusses some of the key metrics that indicate how this process of convergence at the nanoscale is affecting a wider sphere of influence beyond basic and applied R&D. Certainly, this attempt to measure the merger of technologies is not meant to categorize or codify every single instance of convergence worldwide. Rather, the point is to describe a series of variables that sketch an outline of where to look for and how to gauge the true nature of such convergence, using nanotechnology as a prime example. Moreover, the fact that the notion of converging technologies covers a wide intellectual space implies that our views on a variety of subjects must be broad in order to understand how these tendencies are taking hold in a multiplicity of domains.

First, a general description of what is meant by converging technologies at the nanoscale is provided. This discussion is based on three primary sources: the first is a foundational report, edited by Mihail Roco and William Sims Bainbridge of the National Science Foundation (NSF), entitled *Converging Technologies for Improving Human Performance* (Roco and Bainbridge, 2003); the second is a report released in 2004 by the European Union (EU) S&T Foresight Unit, entitled *Converging Technologies – Shaping the Future of European Societies* (Nordmann, 2004); the third is a more critical report, released by the Action Group on Erosion, Technology and Concentration (ETC) Group, entitled *The Big Down: From Genomes to Atoms* (ETC Group, 2003). Along with other related sources, these reports help to provide the context and background for the subsequent discussion. Second, having described the basic nature of converging technologies, the chapter goes on to discuss a number of indicators that detail how this process of nanotechnology convergence has already started to occur internationally and how it is impacting on broader policy and economic concerns beyond the research enterprise. The aim is to provide a series of useful categories of analysis, supported by a number of examples, that are robust enough to be repeatedly applied as this trend progresses over time.

Finally, a series of policy recommendations is presented, which could be implemented to fill the gaps that currently exist in our understanding of the broader trend of technological convergence and assist in providing additional measures capable of illuminating other facets of nanotechnology innovation. In short, this integrated plan of action is an attempt to identify ways of overcoming some of the major barriers that currently are hindering a more comprehensive and widespread understanding of converging technologies at the nanoscale. By depicting some of the main variables that are already demonstrating and indicating movement towards increased convergence – while, simultaneously, outlining some potential policy prospects that could help increase public awareness of this process – it is hoped that this analysis will move beyond mere presentation of an abstract conceptualization of converging technologies at the nanoscale, to a more concrete and practical appreciation of how this trend has, and will continue to, come to pass.

9.2   THE FUNDAMENTALS OF CONVERGENCE: NBIC, CTEKS AND BANG

In 2002 Roco and Bainbridge released an extensive report describing the potential of what they called convergent technologies, defined as 'the synergistic combination of four major "NBIC" (nano-bio-info-cogno) provinces of science and technology, each of which is progressing at a rapid rate' (Roco and Bainbridge, 2003, p. ix). In short, the report describes the merging and interplay between four key technologies – nanotechnology, biotechnology, IT and cognitive science – all of which have undergone significant changes, improvements and expansion over the last half-century. As the report highlights, the driving force behind this kind of unification is that new scientific and technological paradigms are being developed at the nanoscale, which, for the first time in human history, are allowing for 'a comprehensive understanding of the structure and behavior of matter from the nanoscale up to the most complex system yet discovered, the human brain' (Roco and Bainbridge, 2003, p. 1).

The report draws attention to the fact that these new technologies are no longer merely progressing towards their own ends and goals. Instead, both individually and in conjunction with one another, they are increasingly holding out the promise that 'both human performance and the nation's productivity' will be enhanced in ways previously unimagined (Ibid.). For example, this convergence has led to the hope that, one day, engineered nano-sized devices could be used not only as medical diagnostic and therapeutic tools, but as bio-computational processing structures, in which massively connected and distributed information systems are linked together and directed towards improving human cognition and memory. It is because of these and other inviting and enticing scenarios that Sonia Miller, lawyer and founder of the Converging Technologies Bar Association, and Roco, the NSF's Senior Advisor for Nanotechnology, concluded that 'NBIC represents the multidisciplinary blending of science, engineering, technology, and medicine with the human dimension' (Miller and Roco, 2003, p. 1). The idea, echoed in the underlying theme of the report edited by Roco and Bainbridge, is that these developments will not be limited or restricted simply to affecting S&T. In fact, as Miller and Roco astutely note, it is clear that 'the issues converging technologies will raise cuts across a wide swatch of important practice areas', from 'intellectual property law' to 'corporate formation and partnership' to 'technology transfer and commercialization' (Ibid.).

Though the interface between these four fields of S&T is growing ever more blurred and porous, the main driver underlying the transformational prospects of converging technologies is the 'N', or nanotechnology, aspect of the relationship. Roco and Bainbridge agree with this assertion, commenting that 'convergence of diverse technologies is based on material unity at the nanoscale and on technology integration from that scale' (Ibid., p. 2). The point is that without the potential capability of manufacturing and manipulating matter at the nanoscale – which is on the order of one billionth of a metre – none of the other disciplinary interplays would be nearly as enticing, inviting or appealing. A more recent analysis of the subject by the ETC Group, a civil society organization based in Canada, points out that part of the reason why nanotechnology is so fundamental to this process of convergence is that 'all matter – living and non-living – originates at the nano-scale. The impacts of technologies controlling this realm cannot be overestimated: control of nano-scale matter is control of nature's elements' (ETC Group, 2003, p. 6). Along these lines, a report analysing the risks and dangers of nanotechnology by the Risk Assessment Unit of the Health and Consumer Protection Directorate General of the European Commission (EC) supports this claim, stating that 'nanotechnologies enable other technologies' and because of their very ability to 'connect disciplines as diverse as physics, chemistry, genetics, information and communication technologies (ICTs), and cognitive sciences, they offer the foundation of the so-called nano-bio-info-cogni (NBIC) "convergence"' (Risk Assessment Unit, 2004, p. 13). Angella Hullman expands on this point in her recent monograph *The Economic Development of Nanotechnology*, noting that 'nanomaterials are expected to have . . . [a] major influence on virtually all fields', including nanoelectronics, nanobiotechnology and other nanotools (Hullman, 2006, p. 8).

A more recent analysis of converging technologies was undertaken by the EU in an attempt to take a first step beyond the initial conceptual investigation of convergence at the nanoscale, with a primary focus on providing a deeper understanding of how this phenomenon could be directed and implemented from a distinctly European perspective. Compared with the

Roco and Bainbridge's version, this report offers a somewhat complimentary definition of converging technologies as being 'enabling technologies and knowledge systems that enable each other in the pursuit of a common goal' (Nordmann, 2004, p. 14). However, the High Level Expert Group (HLEG), which was responsible for undertaking this examination on behalf of the EU, also makes a point of describing and defining a more restricted and particular agenda for Europe with regards to converging technologies under the heading of Converging Technologies for the European Knowledge Society (CTEKS). Unlike the more open-ended, and unabashedly optimistic conceptualization of NBIC in the Roco and Bainbridge report, CTEKS 'prioritizes the setting of a particular goal for CT research' but also calls for 'an awareness of their potential and limits' (Nordmann, 2004, p. 19). The notion of CTEKS was established to introduce critical analyses from the social sciences and the humanities as significant participants and players within the European approach, thereby allowing representatives from these fields a voice in setting the converging technology research agenda and determining the acceptable boundaries for enquiry. For this reason, the CTEKS version of converging technologies attempts to situate developments in nanotechnology, biotechnology, IT and cognitive science in explicit conjunction with the needs and requirements of other disciplines, such as ecology, anthropology, psychology, geography, economics and sociology.

It should also be noted that, unlike the Roco and Bainbridge and EU reports – which, as mentioned earlier, approach the subject of technological convergence with a mostly positive mindset – the ETC Group offers an alternative conception that warns of the consequences and dangers of allowing such technological developments to continue unfettered. For example, the ETC Group has adopted the acronym BANG to identify the main drivers of convergence – the bits associated with IT, the atoms associated with nanotechnology, the neurons associated with cognitive science and the genes associated with biotechnology – which they assert 'will profoundly affect national economies, trade and livelihoods . . . in countries of both the North and the South' (ETC Group, 2004, p. 5). While this cautionary attitude leads to the conclusion that the interaction of technologies has the potential to 'allow human security and health – even cultural and genetic diversity – to be firmly in the hands of a convergent technocracy', it does raise the very real worry that the emergence of converging technologies will further exacerbate the disparities and discrepancies between the haves and the have-nots of the world (Ibid.). As shall be discussed later, these concerns must be taken into account and addressed to ensure that the benefits of technological convergence come to outweigh its drawbacks.

Finally, it is clear that all three seminal reports offer suggestions and recommendations that are aimed at advancing their converging technology agendas, with the Roco and Bainbridge and EU reports focusing on how to institutionalize converging technologies R&D within their respective systems of innovation, and the ETC Group report calling for wider public participation and involvement in discussions over the role that converging technologies should play in society. Along these lines, the Roco and Bainbridge report recommends developing 'a national R&D priority area on converging technologies focused on enhancing human performance' (Roco and Bainbridge, 2003, p. 24). Similarly, the EU report calls for the implementation of the Widening the Circles of Convergence (WiCC) initiative, which would 'establish CTEKS within a limited time frame of three to five years as a thematic priority for European research primarily in the general areas of health, education, information and communication infrastructure, energy and the environment' (Nordmann, 2004, p. 44). Clearly, the Roco and Bainbridge and EU efforts to establish converging technologies as a central priority within government are still in the incubation stages and, as per the viewpoint of the ETC Group, will require a number of 'seed' workshops, planning committees and public outreach efforts to help marshal and garner support for any and all policy proposals. However, as will be demonstrated in the next section, even without these large-scale national or regional investments directly aimed at fostering the convergence of different technologies – particularly nanotechnology – there are a number of indicators, from a variety of sectors and sources, demonstrating that technological convergence has already begun and, most likely, will continue to expand in the future.

9.3 INDICATORS OF NANOTECHNOLOGY CONVERGENCE: EVIDENCE OF TECHNOLOGICAL INTERACTION

In order to appreciate, recognize and measure this growing trend towards convergence, outlined below are five different indicators or metrics that offer useful evidence that such movements have already started to occur: government spending, university programmes, inter-firm strategic alliances, intra-firm expansion and patent citations. As noted earlier, the following framework is meant only to provide a rough sketch of how technological convergence with respect to nanotechnology is affecting broad areas beyond S&T research and how these impacts can be identified and quantified. The aim here is to provide a starting point for thinking about how these indicators should be grouped and to offer suggestions to guide future enquiries into the subject. Over time, new types of examples will emerge with respect to other modes of convergence and, once they emerge, these instances will require attention in their own right. Moreover, as different technologies mature in interesting and novel ways, entirely new classes of indicators will arise, thereby depicting new kinds of phenomena, which, in turn, will invite and require further evaluation and assessment.

9.3.1 Government Spending

The first – and most significant – indicator of convergence is the spending and allocation of funds by governments, particularly in the US and Europe, for interdisciplinary nanotechnology programmes, multidisciplinary projects and inter-agency collaboration. Though worldwide estimates vary, it is believed that government funding for nanotechnology R&D exceeded $US2 billion in 2002 (NNI, n.d.) and reached over $US4.6 billion in 2005 (Lux Research, 2006) and may have reached a cumulative total of $US24 billion for all historical nanotechnology spending by the end of 2006 (Schenker, 2007). Furthermore, the market for nanotechnology-enabled products is expected to reach $US2.6 trillion by 2014 (Lux Research, 2006) and there are already over 600 nanotechnology consumer products available commercially from 20 different countries (Project on Emerging Nanotechnologies, 2008). These high levels of investment are not restricted to the developed world; nations in the developing world, including China, India, Russia and South Africa, are also beginning to invest heavily in nanotechnology. For example, in 2007 it was reported that the Russian government intended to establish a state council for nanotechnology and allocate the equivalent of $US7.7 billion to develop nanotechnology through 2015 (RIA Novosti, 2007). A three way nanotechnology partnership involving India, Brazil and South Africa has been established, to which each country has pledged an initial investment of $US1 million to fund joint research projects (Project on Emerging Nanotechnologies, 2007a). Also, China is focusing strongly on improving its nanotechnology innovation infrastructure employing multiple ways: making nanotechnology a central component of its medium and long-term strategic plans for science and technology (Michelson, 2006); establishing a joint nanotechnology research centre with Korea in 2007 (Chinese Academy of Sciences, 2007); and increasing its investment in nanotechnology above the estimated $US230 million it spent between 2000 and 2004 (Jia, 2005).

However, the US federal government remains the predominant source of nanotechnology funding around the world, so understanding how it allocates resources with respect to nanotechnology is paramount. Only a close analysis of its budget allocations can provide a deeper appreciation of the true nature and progression of converging technologies. For instance, one of the first major steps towards government support of converging technologies at the nanoscale occurred on 3 December 2003, when Congress passed the 21st Century Nanotechnology Research and Development Act, which stipulates that nanotechnology, and all associated interdisciplinary research, are a S&T priority for the nation. Along these lines, a supplementary budgetary account produced by the National Nanotechnology Initiative (NNI) – which coordinates all US government R&D on nanotechnology – points out that investments in nanotechnology have increased over the past six years, with the budget request for fiscal year 2007 totalling nearly $US1.3 billion, an increase of 21 per cent over the budget request for fiscal year 2006 (NSTC, 2006, p. 36). Moreover, the 2007 budget request for research into the environmental, health and safety impacts of nanotechnology exceeded $US44 million in total, an increase of 18 per cent on estimated investments in 2006, including a near doubling of the budget for such research at the Environmental Protection Agency.

Along with this rise in government funding with respect to the NNI budget over the past few years, there are additional funding schemes that demonstrate the increasing desire of the US government to harness and garner the benefits of nanotechnology convergence with other areas of research. The most illuminating example of the government's focus on converging technologies at the nanoscale is the decision of the National Cancer Institute (NCI) to support 'a new $144.3 million, five-year initiative to develop and apply nanotechnology to cancer' (NCI, 2004, n.p.). This project is the epitome of how different disciplines can profit mutually from the convergence of technologies, with research in nanotechnology being directly aimed at discovering and curing the underlying causes of cancer. In order to carry out this project, the NCI 'is forming the NCI Alliance for Nanotechnology in Cancer, a comprehensive, integrated initiative encompassing researchers, clinicians, and public and private organizations that have joined forces to develop and translate cancer-related nanotechnology research into clinical practice' (Ibid.). In order to accomplish this mission, the NCI released a thorough Cancer Nanotechnology Plan (NCI, 2004), which outlines a number of cancer-related nanotechnology activities that will be realized in the future, from the creation of numerous Centers of Cancer Nanotechnology Excellence to the founding of a Nanotechnology Characterization Laboratory to support the various multidisciplinary research teams, all of which have the common goal of applying insights from one scientific field to solve problems in another. In its triennial review of the NNI the National Academies highlighted the importance of this investment and work at the boundary of nanotechnology and biotechnology as one of the key collaborative, interagency funding and research mechanisms in the US (The National Academies, 2006, pp. 1–10).

A similarly significant, though perhaps somewhat unexpected, site of technology convergence is occurring under the auspices of the US Department of Agriculture (USDA). In a June 2003 special report, entitled *21st Century Agriculture: A Critical Role for Science and Technology*, USDA highlighted nanotechnology as one of the key drivers of research in agriculture and food safety, in an attempt to identify and exploit the potentials inherent in possible 'nano-agri' convergences. In particular, this report highlights the fact that the merging of technologies can 'increase agricultural productivity, enhance the nutrient content of foods, and offer new capabilities and options in food and agriculture production and marketing' (USDA, 2004, p. 1). Moreover, the report points out that developments in the field of nanotechnology and bioinformatics – which links biology and computer science in order to generate computer-based statistical models related to the investigation of food quality, pharmaceutical safety and the health impact of certain chemical compounds – should be acknowledged for their applicability in the agriculture sector, particularly in the facilitation of 'international databases' that will help scientists assess 'the quality of data on plants, animals, and microbes' (USDA, 2003, p. 24). In fact, it is this kind of 'nano-agro-info' convergence that led the ETC Group to conclude that 'in our molecular future, the farm will be a wide area biofactory that can be monitored and managed from a laptop and food will be crafted from designer substances delivering nutrients efficiently to the body' (ETC Group, 2004, p. 8). In other words, the improvements associated with the rise in technological convergence could provide biologists, farmers and policy makers with better opportunities to investigate the physiology and environment of plants and animals in an attempt to raise productivity, improve efficiency and ensure security.

In Europe the recently released 7th Framework Programme (FP7) of the EC has placed an even more explicit emphasis on interdisciplinary research related to nanotechnology, noting that the aim of these investigations is to generate '"step changes" in a wide range of sectors and implementing decisive knowledge for new applications between different technologies and disciplines' (Seventh Research Framework Programme, 2006, n.p.). It is anticipated that funding for nanotechnology-related research in FP7 will eventually be double the funding under FP6 for this area, with an anticipated €300–400 million to be spent on nanotechnology research in 2007 alone. In addition to funding under the nanotechnology research theme, FP7 is allocating money for nanoelectronics within the ICT theme, and for nanomedicine under the health theme. For both the nanomedicine and nanoelectronics modules, the EU has launched strategic research agendas to guide funding decisions that cross traditional disciplinary boundaries (European Nanoelectronics Initiative Advisory Council, 2005; European Technology Platform, 2006). Moreover, by including representatives from industry and academia in the initial research planning phase for converging nanotechnologies, the EU has established a strategic framework that responds to the interests of multiple stakeholders. Finally, by formally including funding components for social science research into the broader societal implications of nanotechnology's diverse applications in medicine, energy and electronics, the EU has taken the first steps to making the notion of converging technologies more concrete at the nanoscale.

9.3.2 University Programmes

A second significant indicator is the rise of new multidisciplinary academic programmes and departments that not only produce basic research, but also grant degrees and reward interdisciplinary collaboration. In particular, the rise in the number of interdisciplinary programmes throughout the US and in other countries over the past few years demonstrates that, at some level, convergence is beginning to become established in academic circles. While a number of these programmes focus on the 'nano-bio' interface, there are examples of institutions that have established more complex programmes to address and research in multiple points of the 'nano-bio-info-cogno' intersection.

Although there are a number of universities outside the US that support leading nanotechnology programmes, the US has placed particular emphasis on developing graduate and post-graduate programmes that focus specifically on furthering nanotechnology innovation in particular and converging technologies in general. Institutions such as Cornell University, Rice University, the University of South Carolina, the State University of New York-Albany and the University of Washington all support degree-granting programmes and research centres that link nanotechnology and biotechnology. One of the pioneers in this group is Cornell's Nanobiotechnology Center (NBTC), which was founded in 2000 in an attempt to create an institution that would highlight the 'interdisciplinary nature' of research and that would feature 'a close collaboration between life scientists, physical scientists, and engineers' (Cornell University, 2004, p. 1). NBTC has done just that, by supporting a 40 strong faculty comprising members from Cornell and other universities, and by sponsoring programmes with a focus on multidisciplinary subjects, such as biomolecular devices and analysis, biomolecular dynamics and nanoscale cell biology.

Also, Rice University's Center for Biological and Environmental Nanotechnology (CBEN) undertakes research that addresses not only the 'nano-bio' interface, but also the 'nano-enviro' interface, where nanotechnology begins to have either a positive or negative effect on the external environment. In short, CBEN explores 'the interaction between nanosystems and biosystems' through the design and examination of 'artificial, chemically prepared nano-biosystems', and, by doing so, 'CBEN's research program is oriented towards specific engineered systems that exemplify how nano-biosystems can be used to solve real world problems' (CBEN, 2004, p. 1). Along the same lines, both the University of South Carolina's Nanoscience and Technology Studies Program (NSTS) and the University of Washington's Center for Nanotechnology (CNT) have dedicated a significant portion of their programmes to the nascent field of bionanotechnology. For example, the NSTS programme offers graduate and undergraduate coursework in nano-medicine and holds conferences on the human and biological impact of nanotechnology. Washington's CNT supports a number of research groups that focus on 'bio-inspired materials', and the State University of New York-Albany has created a programme focusing on biologically compatible nanosystems, adopting 'nanobioscience' as one of its core research areas. In short, these programmes are at the forefront of a trend in academia that will continue to redefine the landscape of university research, as an increasing number of programmes are being designed to straddle the boundaries of different technologies and fields of scientific study.

Finally, two state funded research centres have been established to fund more extensive nanotechnology-related, interdisciplinary collaboration within universities. Established in 2000, the California NanoSystems Institute (CNSI) is a research centre based at the University of California-Los Angeles, in conjunction with collaborators at the University of California-Santa Barbara. Two of CNSI's three main 'thrust groups' are focused on, first, the investigation of nanobiotechnology and, second, the investigation of nanoelectronics (CNSI NanoSystems Institute, 2006). By fusing research teams and disciplinary approaches into a more cohesive 'nano-bio-info' understanding of phenomena at the nanoscale, the eventual aim of the institute is to develop new applications that are relevant to and that can spur new industries. Similarly, the Biodesign Institute at Arizona State University, funded in 2003 by a state research infrastructure bill, adopts a converging technologies view of R&D even more completely. The stated aim of the institute is to foster interdisciplinary research, noting that 'innovations of the future will spring from a purposeful convergence of diverse scientific disciplines' (The Biodesign Institute, n.d., p. 3). The Biodesign Institute has a research portfolio organized around four key 'systems' – biological, nanoscale, cognitive and sustainable – and supports a host of research centres that truly work at the 'nano-bio-info-cogno' interface. By adopting this 'bold new approach' to research, the Biodesign Institute is an experiment in both scientific reorganization and institutional design, aiming to move beyond traditional departmental structures and into the new paradigm of converging technologies investigation.

9.3.3   Inter-firm Strategic Alliances

A third strong indicator related to converging technologies is the creation of numerous inter-firm strategic alliances between companies that, traditionally, have worked in different sectors and generated different kinds of products. While such trends have increased on a global scale, it should not be surprising that as research centred on the different interfaces of technology becomes more prevalent and common within academia and government, private corporations will move to benefit from such convergence by investing in new products and creating new markets. In order to maximize the impacts of this convergence, corporations may decide to partner with one another so that they can share competencies, gain from each other's central capabilities and profit by aligning their interests in a like-minded manner.

Since the nanotechnology sector, in particular, is relatively young, it might seem somewhat surprising that there have been a number of inter-firm strategic alliances between companies that occupy a variety of different sectors of the market and that corporate partnerships related to nanotechnology have begun to flourish over recent years. Lux Research, a private technology consulting company, points out in *The Nanotech Report 2004* that 30 per cent of the companies comprising the Dow Jones Industrial Average have already announced partnerships related to nanotechnology. Not surprisingly, many of these companies are multinational corporations that work with researchers and suppliers around the world to develop new products. Moreover, this report notes that of the eight nanotechnology-related mergers and acquisitions that took place in 2003, 'three were in semiconductor capital equipment, and two were in chemicals', thereby denoting the start of a trend towards the convergence of nanotechnology with the electronics and chemical industries (Lux Research, 2004, p. xii). One such alliance included Nanosys Inc., a manufacturer of nano-sized particles, with Eastman Kodak Company and H. B. Fuller Company, both of which are interested in the chemical and reactive properties of these particles. Also, NeoPhotonics – a joint venture between companies in the US and China – aims to develop 'advance photonic integration technology' by applying advancements in nanotechnology to IT (Wolfe, 2007, n.p.). As the Lux Research report indicates, such instances of partnerships and joint ventures are expected to increase in the near future, as nanotechnology products and services move closer to market in a variety of sectors.

In addition to the formation of strategic alliances between many smaller companies and larger, more diversified companies, there are two particular instances of strategic alliance formation that offer an interesting depiction of companies that operate in different sectors of the economy, but which are intent on linking with one another in order to take advantage of the potential benefits arising from converging technologies. The first alliance is at the 'nano-bio' interface and, originally, consisted of the formation of an industry consortium among Dupont, Partners Healthcare and Raytheon in conjunction with MIT's Institute for Soldier Nanotechnologies (ISN). The purpose of the industry consortium is to develop health and materials-related products for the US military, based upon nanotechnology research undertaken at ISN. Currently, this joint venture includes 12 companies working in fields ranging from medical implants to personal safety equipment, and continues to accept applications for new members. By working together, these firms will be able to synthesize new developments in nano-technology with their own experience in the field of personal health-care and, in turn, improve their products and strengthen their economic viability (MIT, 2004).

With respect to the 'nano-info' interface, a similar alliance occurred in Japan in 2001 between Nissei Sangyo Company Ltd and Hitachi Ltd to form the Hitachi High-Technologies Corporation. The aim of this joint venture was to create a new industrial entity capable of augmenting Hitachi's experience in the electronics and high-technology sector with Nissei's marketing and global sales force, all in conjunction with new developments in nanotechnology. Therefore, the main goal of establishing Hitachi High-Technologies was to create an 'integrated organization ready to develop, manufacture, market and service semiconductor manufacturing equipment, biotechnology products, and other equipment and systems in nanotechnology-related fields' (Hitachi High-Technologies Corporation, 2006, p. 1). Hitachi and Nissei had the foresight to realize that nanotech-nology has the potential to revolutionize the electronics industry. In turn, these corporations have taken a significant step towards merging their different core competencies in order to create and develop innovative products. As the trend towards technological convergence continues, there is the potential for a number of fruitful relationships to be formed between different kinds of companies in different sectors of the economy.

9.3.4   Intra-firm Technological Expansion

In addition to the predominance of inter-firm strategic alliances – alliances that will continue to bring companies with different technological capabilities closer together – a fourth distinct indicator of convergence is the trend towards the internal development of new technological competencies within firms and companies. In short, this trend demonstrates that firms are beginning to reach beyond their past activities and eschew traditional technological boundaries in order to gain from the merging of nanotechnology, biotechnology, information technology and, to a lesser degree, cognitive science. One recent survey of the industry found that 'experts say that the "big two" nanotechnologies in the future will be nanoelectronics and nanobio, which will be attracting most of the startup dollars five years from now' (Red Herring, 2003, p. 5), a prognostication that is encouraging firms to re-evaluate their own, internal business practices to make certain that they have a diverse set of technological resources and qualified personnel.

This increase in intra-firm technological expansion is also occurring on an international level. Lux Research's *The Nanotech Report 2004* points out that firms are diversifying their use of different technologies, with '63% of the 30 companies comprising the Dow Jones Industrial Average (Dow) . . . currently funding R&D in nanotechnology' (Lux Research, 2004, p. xii). In addition, the ETC Group indicates that a variety of companies partaking in different economic sectors from around the world, including energy (Exxon, Mobil), IT (IBM, Lucent, Motorola), chemicals (Johnson & Johnson, Dow Chemical) and electronics (Sony, Xerox, Toshiba), have begun to invest in or undertake research in nanotechnology in order to improve their performance and become leaders in the next technology wave. As mentioned earlier, a small, but growing, component of this kind of innovation related to converging nanotechnologies is at the 'nano-cogno' intersection, where early stage research is being conducted by small start-up firms and university spin-offs aimed at 'exploiting nanotechnology materials and devices either in clinical or in basic neurosciences research' (Berger, 2007, p. 1). It is anticipated that such advances could lead companies working at the intersection of various 'cogno-bio' technologies to venture further into relevant nanotechnology research.

There are also a number of companies engaged in research and commercialization at the 'nano-info' crossing point that is closer to commercialization than research associated with nano-neuroscience. One of the most striking examples of this intersection is Intel Corporation's announcement that it has developed the next generation microprocessor chip using nanotechnology. In 2005 Intel began making chips with 'the width of one of the smallest features of a transistor' at 65 nanometres and, in early 2007, announced that 'the company is moving on to the next stage of refinement, defined by a minimum feature size of 45 nanometers' (Markoff, 2007, p. 1). Such developments are possible due to Intel's in-house and contracted nanotechnology research, which has allowed the company to develop new insulator alloys for electronics that are based on the novel properties of materials at the nanoscale. Such applied research aimed at combining nanotechnology with the needs of the IT industry has provided Intel with a first-mover comparative advantage that could help the company regain its leadership position in the field of chip and transistor innovation. Similarly, Hewlett Packard is also conducting multifaceted work in information nanotechnology. Under the auspices of HP Advanced Study Labs, the Quantum Science Research project was inaugurated under the direction of Stan Williams, a well-known innovator, with the purpose of understanding how nanotechnology fits within the context of HP's ICT products. By studying the electrical and physical properties of nanoscale structures, the Quantum Science Research project has been able to 'grow' self-assembling nanoscale wires, products that 'allow researchers to integrate a variety of sensors into conventional circuitry' (Ulrich, 2004, p. 1). Eventually, these joined technologies have the potential to take on a biotechnological aspect, as they may be used to 'build a nanowire sensor that can detect complementary fragments of DNA' or 'to create sensors that can detect minute concentrations of biological and chemical materials' (Ibid.). Historically, such a 'nano-bio-info' convergence would have been unexpected from a corporation whose main product was personal printers. However, today, HP Advanced Study Labs is at the leading edge of combining breakthroughs in various fields, all with an eye to redesigning the corporation's product line and providing the company with new kinds of expertise.

Finally, in the agriculture and food sectors there are a number of companies that are working to apply novel nanotechnologies to improve food production, processing, packaging and nutrition. For example, Nestlé is working to apply insights from nanotechnology to improve the quality of their food products. The application of such 'high' technology to a traditionally 'low' technology industry, such as food, may become one of the dominant trends over the near and long-term future. Along these lines, Nestlé has established a research centre at its headquarters in order to expand its knowledge of how material science and the physics of colloid particles impact on the structure and quality of consumable food. Specifically, part of their Food Science Department is devoted to determining the potential links between food and nanotechnology, and there is an expectation that 'researchers may soon be able to use nanotechnology to make artificial noses and mouths for tasting foods, and to make packaging that prevents microbial growth' (Baard, 2004, p. 1). Eventually, nanomaterials may be placed directly into certain foods, such as ice cream, in order to allow the manufacturer to 'control the texture, flavor release and rate at which nutrients are absorbed by the body' (Ibid.). Moreover, advances in nanotechnology will have an impact on other areas of the food industry.

For example, 'in the food-packaging arena, nanomaterials are being developed with enhanced mechanical and thermal properties to ensure better protection of foods from exterior mechanical, thermal, chemical or microbiological effects' and 'nanotechnology is also being applied to the tagging and monitoring of food items' to assure safety and security (El Amin, 2005, p. 1). These developments at the boundary of nutrition and nanotechnology may have significant impacts in years to come, as the food industry begins to apply cutting-edge, converging technology research to transform and improve its products and services.

9.3.5 Patent Citations

The last indicator of the convergence of different technologies at the nanoscale is more quantitative in nature than the previous four. Counting the number of patents – and their subsequent citations – filed in relation to intersecting branches of technology can provide evidence of a trend towards convergence. However, it is important to note that, in some cases, these data can be misleading. The time lag between the initiation of a research project, filing a patent application and a subsequent citation can range from a few months to many years; in fact, patent filing is a long and arduous process, occurring simultaneously in multiple countries, that may not be finalized until a significant lapse of time since the initial discovery or innovation. Moreover, the cross-fertilization that is occurring between scientific disciplines has only truly begun to accelerate since the early 2000s, as the idea of converging technologies has become more widespread and accepted. Finally, it is important to note that undertaking a comprehensive analysis of citations in worldwide patents is beyond the scope of this chapter. However, such an in-depth project would be valuable and would provide more substantial evidence that this convergence is occurring in a variety of scientific disciplines.

With respect to patent citations, the most useful data have emerged from studies that focus primarily on analysing information provided by the United States Patent and Trademark Office (USPTO). For instance, Roco pointed out that patent citation data provide evidence of the beginnings of a significant and ongoing convergence at the nanoscale. He argues that 'patent trends and new venture funding for 2002–2003 show an increase in the proportion of nanobiotechnology users to about 30%' (Roco, 2003, p. 1248). Roco (Ibid.) also reports that 'of 6,400 nanotechnology patents identified in 2002 at the US Patent and Trademark Office, the leading numbers [of related subjects] are for molecular biology and microbiology (roughly 1,200 patents) and for drug, bio-affecting and body treating compositions (about 800 patents), together representing about 31% of the total patents in the respective year'. A majority of these statistics arise from a large landmark study that was published in the *Journal for Nanoparticle Research* by Huang et al. (2003) that was undertaken to analyse specific patent trends that have surfaced in the nanotechnology sector. For example, the authors found that "'chemistry: molecular biology and microbiology" was revealed to be the technology field with the most influential patents' related to nanotechnology (Huang et al., 2003, p. 347). In short, an initial examination of patent filings demonstrates that technologies are beginning to converge and that they are having a widespread impact in a number of disparate fields, including chemistry, molecular biology and microbiology.

Another study, which was published in *Nanotechnology Law and Business Journal*, pointed out that in 2003 patent filings in the US alone showed a rise in citations related to nanotechnology, with such terms as Atomic Force Microscope (AFM – over 600) and dendrimer (over 100), up from their 1994 baselines of 100 for the former and only 10 for the latter. While this increase in patents citing such nanotechnology-related developments does not, in and of itself, illustrate the exact convergence of technologies at the nanoscale, it does demonstrate that nanotechnology research is becoming translated into patentable applications and products. Moreover, it is the case that the eventual applications of nanotechnology-related innovations, such as AFMs and dendrimers, possess the very real potential of application to biotechnology and IT. In particular, the main expected application of dendrimers is as 'nanoscale scaffolds', which would be capable of delivering pharmaceuticals and drug therapies to specific sites in the body. The assumption here is that any patent citing such a reference is more likely than not to have an impact in biotechnology and, therefore, offers the potential of bridging the gap between pure nanotechnology research and applied 'nano-bio' products in the future.

In fact, a more recent analysis of nanotechnology patent data found that because of the inherently interdisciplinary nature of such applications, many nanotechnology patent applications are relevant to and reviewed by a variety of centres within the USPTO, including those related to biotechnology, chemicals and electrical systems. From a policy perspective, however, the multiple relevance of most nanotechnology patent applications can cause difficulties, since different patent examiners from different review centres may be basing their deciscions on different prior art, which 'may result in the issuance of patents that would have otherwise been rejected' (Serrato et al., 2005, p. 152). In addition to these intellectual property protection concerns, there are other drawbacks that make it problematic to glean much additional information from patent citations, regardless of whether it relates to the connection between nanotechnology and biotechnology or nanotechnology and IT. With respect to nanotechnology, it was clear that up until early 2004, 'the Patent Office [had] no immediate plans to create a nanotechnology examining group', thereby hindering a researcher's ability to learn about convergence at the nanoscale because the exact nomenclature and categorization remained in flux (Koppikar et al., 2004, p. 27). In other words, this lack of an agreed-upon classification system implied that nanotechnology-related patents would remain unorganized and spread across a majority of the USPTO, making it difficult for researchers to undertake a robust bibliometric study of the convergence between nanotechnology and other disciplines. In October 2004 the USPTO decided that it was worth developing a more robust system of handling nanotechnology patents, thereby creating 'a new registration category just for nanotechnology inventions' (Feder, 2004, p. 12). While nanotechnology patent applications are still reviewed at multiple centres, this special category will allow for better tracking and measurement of innovations in nanotechnology, and will go a long way towards providing information regarding this discipline's convergence with other technologies. It is to be hoped that the gaps in the studies outlined above will spur additional patent citation analyses that attempt to understand the true scope and reach of converging technologies.

9.4   CONVERGING TECHNOLOGIES POLICY NEEDS ASSESSMENT

Having outlined some of the useful indicators that illustrate the initiation of convergence between a variety of S&T disciplines, it remains clear that a number of additional steps are needed to allow society to harness this trend. As mentioned earlier, the Roco and Bainbridge and EU reports have made a point of calling for a specific, targeted, government-sponsored research priority programme with a distinct and concentrated focus on converging technologies. However, such efforts will need to be complemented and augmented by other undertakings in order to ensure that innovation in converging technologies will have the widest possible positive impact on society. Along these lines, the following policy 'plan of action' attempts to identify and outline a number of key topics that must be taken into account as the converging technologies agenda moves forward. Through discussion of these issues – which include education reform and job training, the development of improved bibliometrics and technology assessment, concern for international collaboration and development and global public participation and engagement – this chapter pinpoints some of the gaps that need to be filled and offers potential recommendations that will contribute to ensuring that the idea of converging technologies becomes more embedded and integrated into the public policy debate. Again, these suggestions should be viewed as only a start to the policy-making process. Eventually, new and creative options for managing converging technologies will emerge, necessitating additional deliberations and the presentation of new, adaptive policies over the coming years.

First, it is clear that the convergence of technologies will require radical education reform and new investment in job training and retraining for the twenty-first century worker. The merging and intersection of disciplines will require that these developments are reflected in elementary, undergraduate and graduate education systems worldwide. As outlined earlier, some moves along these lines, especially at the graduate level, have already begun to occur. Students are increasingly being encouraged to conduct research overseas, to work within international research networks and keep abreast of cutting-edge R&D occurring around the world. However, unfortunately such programmes are not the norm; instead, the majority of S&T education continues to be within traditional disciplinary boundaries and lacks any effective means to demonstrate the interactions between different subjects. Roco emphasizes this point and notes that the only way to truly benefit from converging technologies is if the 'interdisciplinary connections reflecting unity in nature' are elucidated and revealed within the education system itself (Roco, 2003, p. 1249). Certainly, undertaking such reforms can be difficult. However, one way to solve this problem, as Roco suggests, is to reverse 'the current pyramid of learning that begins with specific techniques and formalisms in the first year of undergraduate studies and ends with a coherent understanding of physical and biological features' (Ibid.). Researchers at the UK think-tank Demos have analysed the, need for such international and interdisciplinary collaboration in their *Atlas of Ideas* project (Leadbeater and Wilsdon, 2007), suggesting that a new set of fellowships and scholarships should be made available to encourage such innovation. Perhaps the concept of converging technnologies at the nanoscale can be used as an organizing framework around which such scholarships can be structured.

In addition, workers will have to be trained and retrained and have their skills and knowledge updated in order to achieve an integrated, multidisciplinary approach to S&T. Roco (2003) notes that developments in nanotechnology alone will require about 2 million new workers by 2015, a figure that will continue to rise as the convergence between this discipline and others continues to move forward. Governments must be made aware of this impending need for new kinds of human talent and expertise and, in turn, must consciously design worker training and retraining programmes that are capable of meeting this need. Along these lines, well-regarded science advisory bodies – such as The National Academies in the

US and The Royal Society in the UK – should be regularly commissioned to put together committees with the intention of studying how best to update the S&T workforce for the twenty-first century. The ability of such review boards to offer and advance concrete recommendations for policy makers will be a necessary component of bringing this issue of worker training to the fore. In addition, these high-level reviews – which will address how to institute the changes that will be needed to bring the S&T workforce in line with the new demands of convergence – will also be able to provide government officials with quantitative data and statistics that will make it easier for decision makers to grasp the importance of this emerging trend while, simultaneously, helping these elected representatives respond to their constituencies. Similar mechanisms for such a study are available at the international level; in particular, the InterAcademy Council, based in the Netherlands, could be commissioned to undertake such a study as part of a broader investigation into the changing nature of the S&T workforce.

This conclusion with respect to education and worker training leads directly into the second recommendation, which calls for researchers in universities, government agencies and non-governmental organizations to concern themselves with developing improved bibliometric measurements and advanced technology assessment techniques that will further highlight the extent and nature of converging technologies. While some studies with a focus on quantitative bibliometrics, such as patent citations, do exist, there are few broad and well-accepted analyses that take a more comprehensive view regarding the various interfaces that have arisen between different technologies. In short, there is little work being done that attempts to quantify how these metrics can be measured across different fields and disciplines. A number of organizations, including the Washington Research Evaluation Network and the Organisation for Economic Co-operation and Development (OECD), possess experience in the generation of such bibliometrics, and it would be useful if these kinds of research evaluation organizations could apply their technological and scholarly capabilities to such a project. Undoubtedly, a number of stakeholders, from academics to policy makers to interested citizens, would be interested in gaining access to better data regarding technology convergence. In particular, grant-giving agencies, such as the NSF in the US and the research councils in the UK, would welcome such information, primarily because it could help inform their funding decisions and provide them with another dimension along which to analyse the importance and viability of competing applications. Finally, improved technology assessment methodologies have been identified as a pressing need worldwide. The OECD has already established a Working Party on Manufactured Nanomaterials and, therefore, such efforts could be expanded eventually to consider the broader issues of technology assessment with respect to converging technologies. Having such a high-level, international body begin to focus on tracking bibliometrics and other aspects of converging technologies from a global perspective would signal the importance of the notion of converging technologies for policy makers by providing them with reliable, tangible measurements on how this trend is progressing on a global scale.

A third, and quite necessary, aspect of any converging technology policy plan of action is to understand the significant international aspects of S&T and to be cognizant of the fact that converging technologies have the potential to help nations collaborate, to help countries develop and to help advance state-of-the-art research worldwide. For instance, the fact that the EU set up a high-level commission to analyse the importance of converging technologies – an idea that was initially conceptualized in the US – demonstrates the fluidity of S&T ideas across international borders and underscores how this notion is beginning to shape the way R&D is approached. Since multiple reports on the topic of converging technologies call for this notion to become a priority research area, it appears that there is considerable room for collaboration involving European and American governments working together to ensure that mutually compatible programmes are launched in conjunction with one another. Moreover, as the *Atlas of Ideas* project indicates, there is growing potential for an expanded international research programme related to converging technologies at the nanoscale (Leadbeater and Wilsdon, 2007). In conjunction with other developed and rapidly developing nations, such as Japan, Australia, China, India, Brazil and South Africa, there is the potential that the US and the EU could initiate debate on converging technologies that would be both constructive and inclusive on a global scale.

Along these lines, there must be a concerted effort by the developed world to apply the derived benefits of converging technologies to the developing world. It is clear that potentially extraordinary gains could emerge once different technologies begin to work together – gains that are most needed and would be most useful in areas of the world that are suffering from extreme poverty and degradation. In its report on the subject, *Nanotechnology and the Poor*, the Meridian Institute argues that in conjunction with other technologies, 'the pieces for the responsible use of nanotechnology for development are on the table. There is an urgent need to begin putting them together' (Meridian Institute, 2005, p. iii). One way to ensure that converging technologies are deliberately directed towards helping the poor is for countries in the developed world to sponsor a forward-thinking programme that analyses the development-related issues arising from converging technologies, perhaps under the auspices of a multilateral, internationally minded organization, such as the United Nations, the World Bank or the OECD. There is already renewed interest by these organizations to focus on the social role of emerging and converging S&T applications to address the problems of the developing world (Watkins et al., 2007; Cherry, 2007). In particular, the US could use its recent decision to rejoin the United Nations Educational, Scientific and Cultural Organization (UNESCO) as a catalyst for such a development-friendly initiative associated with converging technologies at the nanoscale. By situating such a programme within the OECD or UNESCO, the US could leverage the power and influence of these far-reaching bodies and make certain that the human development issues raised by converging technologies are placed at the forefront of the international S&T policy agenda. Though efforts along these lines are beginning – as indicated in Demos's *Nanodialogues: Experiments in Public Engagement with Science*, which describes a project aimed at examining how nanotechnology might address water problems in Zimbabwe (Stilgoe, 2007) – much more needs to be done to ensure the equitable and broad distribution of nanotechnology and converging technologies in the developing world.

Finally, it is recommended that a variety of institutions, including universities, governments, think-tanks and corporations, become committed to holding public forums and providing platforms for discussing the complex issues inherent in the onset of converging technologies. Any discussion that is held regarding the pros and cons of converging technologies will require open and honest debate, touching on a variety of issues, including morals, values, acceptable scientific practice and desired goals and end-states. However, as the ETC Group report mentions, without such public participation, there is the real chance that the benefits of converging technologies will become overshadowed by their drawbacks, as the public becomes less engaged and involved in setting priorities and guiding policy. For instance, the potentially damaging health and environmental risks associated with certain technologies – in particular, nanotechnology – must be dealt with in an open and transparent manner to avoid crises similar to those that occurred with asbestos, nuclear power and genetically modified foods. New ways of engaging the global public with these novel and inter-related developments in converging technologies at the nanoscale will be needed, and many are already beginning to emerge, including video games (NanoQuest, 2006; NanoMission, 2007), youth science competitions (FIRST LEGO League, 2006), web-based dialogues (Project on Emerging Nanotechnologies, 2007b) and interactive teaching modules (Stilgoe and Warburton, 2006). In addition, there are a number of ethical, legal and social concerns that will continue to arise with respect to certain kinds of research in nanotechnology, cognitive science and biotechnology. Public dialogues (Illinois Institute of Technology, 2006; Gavelin and Wilson, 2007) and expert conferences (Sarewitz and Karas, 2006) have already begun to address these topics, but more needs to be done in this area to adequately introduce broader segments of the population to these issues. In short, a deliberate attempt is required from all stakeholders to encourage public and citizen participation, thereby ensuring that widespread input will help shape the future impact of converging technologies.

To make certain that a variety of viewpoints are heard, the media and press must use their role as guardians of the public interest to help guarantee that the marginalized voices and previously overlooked stakeholders have the chance to come to the fore, share their views and elucidate their concerns. The importance of such contributions was underscored by James Wilsdon and Rebecca Willis, who argue in favour of encouraging broad public engagement 'upstream', namely, at the beginning of any enterprise that is related to R&D in converging technologies. By advancing this notion of 'see-through science' – which calls for the public to play an integral role in the policy and agenda-setting process – Wilsdon and Willis (2004, p. 35) make it clear that embodied in the hype surrounding the benefits of technological convergence lies 'a set of assumptions about future human and social needs that are contestable and should be debated'. In short, this kind of 'see-through science' needs to become an essential aspect of all decisions or policies taken in relation to converging technologies, and its adoption will require actions that lead to the collection of a wide number of views, the assessment of a wide range of values and input from a wide variety of sources.

9.5   CONCLUSION: CONVERGING TECHNOLOGIES, INNOVATION AND THE 'INTERNATIONAL IMPERATIVE'

It is quite evident that even though the convergence of different technologies at the nanoscale has yet to reach its peak, there are some indicators that movement along these lines is already beginning to occur. Whether it is the funding of interdisciplinary projects by government agencies, the establishment of new degree-granting programmes by universities or the development of strategic alliances between corporations, there are a number of mutually complementary ways to analyse the onset and impact of converging technologies. Nevertheless, the ability to track these trends over time and across borders is limited. While it is clear that nanotechnology innovation will arrive and become commercialized, it is less clear how well the international community is prepared to deal with these potentially transformative and disruptive developments. The multidimensional analytical framework outlined in this chapter is just a start to the necessary process of understanding how converging technologies at the nanoscale will transform the international science policy landscape. Will it help close the gaps between technologically advanced and lagging countries, or will it simply serve to reinforce these divides? What new forms of hybrid industry networks will emerge that could transform the innovation landscape? How can converging technologies spur changes and improvements in existing and emerging international institutions? What kinds of novel collaboration opportunities will these technologies create that could potentially realign competitive strategies amongst nations and industries? The hope is that future examinations of the converging technology phenomenon can make an imperative to focus on these international policy issues and suggest creative ways to address the questions outlined above.

This chapter, in particular, has identified areas that will require more work and attention in future investigations, including the development of improved and more robust bibliometrics on an international level, greater public participation worldwide in defining the underlying aims and goals of convergence and an explicit focus on international collaboration and development. This should enable a deeper understanding to emerge of how technologies converge, intersect and relate to one another in practice, as the ideas from the foundational reports examined above and others that address this subject (Roco and Montemagno, 2004; Bainbridge and Roco, 2007) expand, take hold and influence the greater S&T policy community. Moreover, as the wider adoption of the converging technologies concept increases, additional, unexpected facets related to technological convergence at the nanoscale will inevitably come to light. As new indicators – capable of expressing the reach, scope and breadth of this phenomenon – surface, it will be of paramount importance persistently and systematically to re-evaluate the notion of converging technologies at the nanoscale in an international context and attempt to understand how this emerging theme will evolve and mature as it spreads globally.

NOTE

1. Portions of this chapter are reprinted, with kind permission, from Springer Science and Business Media, from Evan S. Michelson (2006), 'Measuring the merger: examining the onset of converging technologies', in W. S. Bainbridge and M. C. Roco, *Managing Nano-Bio-Info-Cogno Innovations: Converging Technologies in Society*, Dordrecht, the Netherlands: Springer, pp. 17–71.

REFERENCES

Baard, M. (2004), 'Little things could mean a lot', *Wired Magazine,* 1 February, accessed 27 July 2007 at www.wired.com/news/technology/0,1282,62602,00.html.

Bainbridge, W. S. and M. C. Roco (ed.) (2007), *Progress in Convergence: Technologies for Human Wellbeing,* vol. 1093, New York: New York Academy of Sciences.

Berger, M. (2007), 'Nanotechnology coming to a brain near you', Nanowerk LLC, 9 July, accessed 27 July 2007 at www.nanowerk.com/spotlight/spotid=2177.php.

California NanoSystems Institute (CNSI) (2006), 'About CNSI', Los Angeles, CA: California NanoSystems Institute, accessed 27 July 2007 at www.cnsi.ucla.edu/staticpages/about-us.

Center for Biological and Environmental Nanotechnology (CBEN) (2004), 'Research overview', Rice University, Houston, TX, accessed 27 July 2007 at http://cben.rice.edu/research.cfm?doc_id=5004.

Cherry, M. (2007), 'All eyes on Addis', *Nature* **445**(25), 356–58, accessed 27 July 2007 at www.nature.com/news/2007/070122/full/445356a.html.

Chinese Academy of Sciences (2007), 'China-Korea Nanotechnology Research Center formally opens in Beijing', Nanowerk LLC, accessed 27 July 2007 at www.nanowerk.com/news/newsid=2186.php.

Cornell University (2004), 'Nanobiotechnology Center', Cornell University, Ithaca, NY, accessed 27 July 2007 at www.nbtc.cornell.edu.

Department of Agriculture (USDA) (2003), *21st Century Agriculture: A Critical Role for Science and Technology,* Washington, DC: Department of Agriculture, accessed 31 July 2007 at www.fas.usda.gov/icd/stconf/pubs/scitech2003/all.pdf.

Department of Agriculture (USDA) (2004), 'Special USDA technology report', Washington, DC: Department of Agriculture, accessed 31 July 2007 at www.csrees.usda.gov/nea/technology/in_focus/nanotech_if_special.html.

El Amin, A. (2005), 'Nanotechnology targets new food packaging products', Foodnavigator.com, accessed 31 July 2007 at www.foodnavigator.com/news/ng.asp?n=63147-nanotechnology-food-packaging-research-and-development.

Erosion, Technology and Concentration (ETC) Group (2003), *The Big Down: From Genomes to Atoms,* Winnipeg, SK: ETC Group.

ETC Group (2004), *Down on the Farm: The Impact of Nano-scale Technologies on Food and Agriculture,* Winnipeg, SK: ETC Group.

European Nanoelectronics Initiative Advisory Council (2005), *Strategic Research Agenda,* Brussels: European Commission, accessed 31 July 2007 at ftp://ftp.cordis.europa.eu/pub/ist/docs/eniac/strategic_research_agenda_full.pdf.

European Technology Platform (2006), *Nanomedicine: Nanotechnology for health – Strategic Research Agenda,* Brussels: European Commission, accessed 1 February 2007 at ftp://ftp.cordis.europa.eu/pub/nanotechnology/docs/nanomedicine_bat_en.pdf.

Feder, B. (2004), 'Tiny ideas coming of age', *New York Times,* 24 October.

FIRST LEGO League (2006), 'Welcome to the 2006 Challenge Nano Quest', accessed 31 July 2007 at www.firstlegoleague.org/default.aspx?pid=21380.

Gavelin, K. and R. Wilson (2007), *Democratic Technologies? The Final Report of the Nanotechnology Engagement Group (NEG),* London: Involve, accessed 31 July 2007 at www.involve.org.uk/negreport.

Hitachi High-Technologies Corporation (2006), 'About us', Tokyo: Hitachi High-Technologies Corporation, accessed 31 July 2007 at www.hitachi-hitec.com/global/aboutus/aboutus.html.

Huang, Z., H. Chen, A. Yip, G. Ng, F. Guo, Z. K. Chen and M. C. Roco (2003), 'Longitudinal patent analysis for nanoscale science and engineering: country, institution and technology field', *Journal of Nanoparticle Research*, **5**(3–4), 333–63.

Hullmann, A. (2006), *The Economic Development of Nanotechnology: An indicators based analysis,* Brussels: European Commission, accessed 1 February 2007 at ftp://ftp.cordis.europa.eu/pub/nanotechnology/docs/nanoarticle_hullmann_nov2006.pdf.

Illinois Institute of Technology (IIT) (2006), 'Nano luminaries Mihail Roco and Sean Murdock keynoted IIT Center on Nanotechnology and Society Nanopolicy Conference in DC', Washington, DC accessed 31 July 2007 at www.nano-and-society.org/events/event_04.09.06_news.html.

Jia, H. (2005), 'Government raises nano-tech funding', Chinadaily.com, 9 July, accessed 31 July 2007 at www.chinadaily.com.cn/english/doc/2005–06/10/content_450234.htm.

Koppikar, V., S. B. Maebius and J. S. Rutt (2004), 'Current trends in nanotech patents: a view from inside the patent office', *Nanotechnology Law and Business Journal*, **1**(1), 24–30.

Leadbeater, C. and J. Wilsdon (2007), *The Atlas of Ideas: How Asian Innovation Can Benefit Us All,* 1 February, London: Demos, accessed 31 July 2007 at www.demos.co.uk/files/Overview_Final1.pdf.

Lux Research, Inc. (2004), *The Nanotech Report 2004,* New York: Lux Research, Inc.

Lux Research, Inc. (2006), 'Nanotechnology in $32 billion worth of products: global funding for nanotech R&D reaches $9.6 billion', New York: Lux Research, Inc., accessed 31 July 2007 at www.luxresearchinc.com/press/RELEASE_TNR4.pdf.

Markoff, J. (2007), 'Intel says chips will run faster, using less power', *New York Times*, 27 January.

Massachusetts Institute of Technology (MIT) (2004), 'MIT Institute for Soldier Nanotechnologies partners – industry', Boston, MA: MIT, accessed 31 July 2007 at http://web.mit.edu/isn/partners/industry/currentpartners.html.

Meridian Institute (2005), *Nanotechnology and the Poor: Opportunities and Risks*, Washington, DC: Meridian Institute, accessed 1 February 2007 at www.nanoandthepoor.org/gdnp/NanoandPoor.pdf.

Michelson, E. S. (2006), 'Nanotechnology policy: an analysis of transnational governance issues facing the United States and China', in W. A. Blanpied and Z. Gang (eds), *Proceedings of the China-US Forum on Science and Technology Policy*, Arlington, VA: George Mason University, pp. 345–58, accessed 31 July 2007 at www.law.gmu.edu/nctl/stpp/STPolicy_Forum.php.

Miller, S. and M. C. Roco (2003), 'A new renaissance: tech, science, engineering and medicine are becoming one', *New York Law Journal,* 7 October.

NanoMission (2007), 'NanoMission home', London: Playgen, accessed 31 July 2007 at www.nanomission.org.

NanoQuest (2006), 'NanoQuest it's a small world', Dublin: Discover Science and Engineering, accessed 31 July 2007 at www.nanoquest.ie/home.html.

National Cancer Institute (NCI) (2004), 'National Cancer Institute announces major commitment to nanotechnology for cancer research', Washington, DC: National Institutes of Health, 13 September, accessed 31 July 2007 at www.nci.nih.gov/newscenter/pressreleases/nanotechPressRelease, published as

Cancer Nanotechnology Plan, Bethesda, MD: National Cancer Institute, accessed 2 June 2008 http://nano.cancer.gov/about_alliance/cancer_nanotechnology_plan.pdf.

National Science and Technology Council (NSTC) (2006), *The National Nanotechnology Initiative: Research and Development Leading to a Revolution in Technology and Industry – Supplement to the President's 2007 Budget*, Washington, DC: Office of Science and Technology Policy, accessed 2 June 2008 at www.nano.gov/NNI_07Budget.pdf.

Nordmann, A. (2004), *Converging Technologies – Shaping the Future of European Societies*, Brussels: European Communities, accessed 31 July 2007 at http://europa.eu.int/comm/research/conferences/2004/ntw/pdf/final_report_en.pdf.

Project on Emerging Nanotechnologies (2008), 'Nanotechnology Consumer Products Inventory', Washington, DC: Project on Emerging Nanotechnologies, accessed 2 June at www.nanotechproject.org/consumerproducts.

Project on Emerging Nanotechnologies (2007a), 'NanoFrontiers developing story: nanotechnology and low income nations', Washington, DC: Project on Emerging Nanotechnologies.

Project on Emerging Nanotechnologies (2007b), 'Nanotechnology and the consumer: a public dialogue', Washington, DC: Project on Emerging Nanotechnologies, accessed 31 July 2007 at www.webdialogues.net/pen/consumer.

Red Herring (2003), *ICC Report: Nanotechnology: Worth its Wait?* Mountain View, CA: Red Herring.

RIA Novosti (2007), 'State Duma adopts law on Nanotechnology Corporation', accessed 31 July 2007 at http://en.rian.ru/science/20070704/68326971.html.

Risk Assessment Unit (2004), *Nanotechnologies: A Preliminary Risk Analysis on the Basis of a Workshop Organized in Brussels on 1–2 March 2004 by the Health and Consumer Protection Directorate General of the European Commission*, Brussels: European Communities, accessed 31 July 2007 at http://ec.europa.eu/health/ph_risk/documents/ev_20040301_en.pdf.

Roco, M. C. (2003), 'Converging science and technology at the nanoscale: opportunities for education and training', *Nature Biotechnology*, **21**(10), 1247–9.

Roco, M. C. and W. S. Bainbridge (eds) (2003), *Converging Technologies for Improved Human Performance*, Dordrecht: Kluwer Academic Publishers.

Roco, M. C. and C. D. Montemagno (eds) (2004), *The Coevolution of Human Potential and Converging Technologies,* vol. 1013, New York: New York Academy of Sciences.

Sarewitz, D. and T. H. Karas (2006), *Policy Implications of Technologies for Cognitive Enhancement*, Tempe, AZ: Consortium for Science, Policy and Outcomes, Arizona State University, accessed 31 July 2007 at www.cspo.org/ourlibrary/articles/FinalEnhancedCognitionReport.pdf.

Schenker, J. L. (2007), 'Nanotech disappoints in Europe', Businessweek.com, accessed 31 July 2007 at www.businessweek.com/print/globalbiz/content/jul2007/gb2007075_546185.htm.

Serrato, R., K. Hermann and C. Douglas (2005), 'The nanotech intellectual property landscape', *Nanotechnology Law & Business Journal*, **2**(2), 150–5

Seventh Research Framework Programme (2006), 'Cooperation: nanosciences, nanotechnologies, materials and new production technologies (NMP)', Luxembourg: European Commission, accessed 27 July 2007 at http://cordis.europa.eu/fp 7/cooperation/nanotechnology_en.html.

Stilgoe, J. (2007), 'Nanodialogues: experiments in public engagement with science', London, accessed 31 July 2007 at www.demos.co.uk/publications/nanodialogues.

Stilgoe, J. and D. Warburton (2006), *Broadening our Horizons – Public Engagement with the Future of Science,* London: Science Horizons, accessed 31 July 2007 at www.sciencehorizons.org.uk/resources/broadening_our_horizons 0.pdf.

The Biodesign Institute (n.d.), *The Biodesign Institute at Arizona State University,* Tempe, AZ: Arizona State University.

The National Academies (2006), 'A matter of size: triennial review of the National Nanotechnology Initiative – prepublication Draft', Washington, DC: The National Academies Press.

The National Nanotechnology Initiative (2006), *Supplement to the President's FY 2007 Budget,* Washington, DC: Office of Science and Technology Policy, accessed 31 July 2007 at www.nano.gov/NNI_07Budget.pdf.

Ulrich, T. (2004), 'Quantum leap: reinventing the integrated circuit with molecular-scale electronics', Palo Alto, CA: Hewlett-Packard Labs, accessed 31 July 2007 at www.hpl.hp.com/news/2004/july_sept/quantum.html.

Watkins, A., E. Osifo-Dawodu, M. Ehst and B. Cisse (2007), 'Building science, technology, and innovation capacity: turning ideas into actions', *Development Outreach,* Washington, DC: The World Bank, accessed 31 July 2007 at www1.worldbank.org/devoutreach/article.asp?id=393.

Wilsdon, J. and R. Willis (2004), *See-Through Science: Why Public Engagement Needs to Move Upstream,* London: Demos.

Wolfe, J. (2007), 'Nanotech gets big in China', Forbes.com, accessed 31 July 2007 at www.forbes.com/guruinsights/2007/02/01/nanotech-china-veeco-pf-guru-in_jw_0201soapbox_inl.html.

10. European Research Framework Programmes in a global context: targets, impacts, lessons for the future

Nicholas S. Vonortas

10.1 INTRODUCTION[1]

In the 1980s and 1990s analysts were concerned with the merits of national systems of innovation (NSI): the coherence of a geographically confined system had to be reconciled with the reality of the rising forces of globalization. The ensuing heated debate between the so-called 'techno-nationalist' and 'techno-globalist' camps, however, fairly quickly ran out of steam. Fleeting ideas, such as the expectation that the role of spatially confined governments would naturally diminish and eventually wither away, proved simplistic. Other ideas, better surviving the test of time, included the perception that companies, no matter how international, have a geographic base with which they identify and from which they draw competitive advantage. After a while it seemed that neither of the techno-extremes was the right horse to back: globalization certainly affected the extent and modalities of government intervention, but in no way was it going to be true that the government would become irrelevant. Its role would change, but would remain as vital as ever.

One idea popularized by Robert Reich in the early 1990s seemed to be ahead of its time (Reich, 1992). It offered a tantalizingly simple answer to the question 'what can governments do in the presence of an increasingly footloose private sector and global capital?' Spatially confined governments, Reich claimed, should first identify the less mobile factors of production and then concentrate their efforts on trying to raise the productivity of these factors. Highly productive factors tied to a location would then attract the more mobile factors to that location. Less mobile factors were defined as including labour, physical infrastructure and the institutional organization supporting production in a country/region.

Hence, the solution to the original policy dilemma was to create a domestic environment that would make a location attractive to the internationally mobile factors of production (mainly capital). The environment to be created at home would depend on highly productive, skill-intensive, immobile factors appropriate for high-technology sectors in both manufacturing and services. Such sectors provide the high value added necessary to support high living standards. In contemporary parlance, the message is essentially to create and maintain a cutting-edge knowledge-based economy.[2]

This message was not lost on the international expert panel that was put together by the European Commission (EC) (Directorate General for Research) in 2004 to carry out the third *Five-Year Assessment of the European Union Research Framework Programmes 1993–2003* (EC, 2005). In addition to appraising the achievements and drawbacks of the framework programmes implemented over the period 1999–2003, the panel was asked to make recommendations for the remaining half of Framework Programme 6 (FP6) up to 2006 and to suggest improvements over the nature and orientation of future programmes (FP7).

This chapter summarizes the most important findings from that evaluation, focusing especially on the panel's sensitivity and attention to the role of these framework programmes in the global context. Thus, a particular view is taken of the panel's work; the chapter does not try to be comprehensive in terms of findings.[3]

The chapter unfolds as follows. Section 10.2 recounts the general socioeconomic context in which the framework programmes of the past few years have operated. Section 10.3 discusses some of the panel's main findings regarding the implementation and achievements of the programmes. Section 10.4 discusses important ways in which the framework programmes interact with other policy areas of the EU and its member states that should be taken into consideration when planning and evaluating them. Finally, Section 10.5 concludes and offers recommendations for future strategies.

10.2 CONTEXT AND CHALLENGES

The period covered by this five-year assessment (1999–2003) was an important one for Europe, and included significant developments:

- Initiation of the Lisbon process for establishing the most competitive and dynamic knowledge-based economy in the world by 2010.
- Definition of the Barcelona objectives for raising research and technological development (RTD) investment in the EU to approximately 3 per cent of gross domestic product (GDP) by 2010.

- Introduction of the concept of a European Research Area (ERA) and the launch of FP6 (2002–06), which explicitly addressed this aim.

These developments are a reflection of the greater anxiety of policy decision makers over Europe's relative position in the global economic and research landscape. It was felt that knowledge-based competition was changing fundamentally the environment in which European research and industry operate. Europe and the rest of the industrialized world could no longer take their technological leadership for granted. While Europe still maintains leadership in certain areas of industry, concern about the future arises from the 'deficit' in R&D expenditures between Europe and its main competitors,[4] the rapid expansion of European private sector R&D outside Europe and the inability to attract the best talent from around the world into Europe. There is a widespread impression in the Community that the increasing availability of high-quality, industrially relevant knowledge and efficient, market-friendly innovation environments outside Europe is contributing to a gradual loss of European competitiveness.

The panel paid attention to well publicized documents, such as the Sapir et al. (2003) and Kok et al. (2004) reports, which stress Europe's difficulties in keeping up with the fast pace of its main competitors. Europe's performance, in terms of growth, productivity and job creation, appears to be insufficient to maintain prosperity in the future. There is broad consensus that research, education and innovation are at the heart of any response to these challenges.

Meanwhile, European universities and research institutions traditionally have been able to develop and maintain the European knowledge base. In many fields this is still the case. Taken as a whole, Europe currently accounts for a larger volume of scientific publications than the US. However, only a few European universities are recognized as world leaders. This, at least in part, is a result of insufficient resources combined with the fragmented nature of the European RTD landscape. European universities and institutes have yet to respond fully to global competition for knowledge and talent. But they are in the race.

It is now well established that all parts of the triple helix are important for advancement in a knowledge-based economy. Innovation depends critically on collaborative networks involving academic and business enterprise research, as well as on the participatory involvement of intelligent government. The conventional view of a linear process of academic-based knowledge creation, subsequently picked up and exploited by industry, has given way to a new practice of interactive innovation facilitated by public/private partnerships, knowledge sharing and mutual learning.

Moreover, almost half of the member states are 'new' (ten, plus two from 2007) and in the process of transition. They must continue with efforts to establish an enterprise-friendly environment and build the conditions for a knowledge-based economy. Institutional reforms and the allocation of sufficient resources to knowledge creation and sharing are necessary steps in building a sustainable economic future. The intelligent use of structural funds combined with other EU and national instruments could provide solutions to these challenges.

Finally, the citizens of Europe are becoming concerned about the social and economic impact of scientific and technological advances and about the decision-making process that leads to them. The lack of public support is apparent in some areas. To achieve the leadership in science and technology (S&T) that is critical for future prosperity these concerns must be addressed at both European and national levels.

In order to achieve the desired objectives the panel identified four key challenges that must be addressed through coordinated actions by the EU and the member states:

- attract and reward the best talent
- create a high-potential environment for business and industrial RTD
- mobilize resources for innovation and sustainable growth
- build trust in S&T.

10.3 STRUCTURE AND ACHIEVEMENTS OF THE RESEARCH FRAMEWORK PROGRAMME

The Research Framework Programme has undergone significant changes since the early 1990s. FP3 (1990–94) was developed against the background of efforts to extend the internal market; FP4 (1994–98) took place during the period of the Maastricht Treaty and the White Paper on Growth, Competitiveness and Employment; FP5 (1998–2002) reflected increasing interest in socio-economic values; and FP6 (2002–06) promoted the ERA.

Thematic priorities have evolved over the years and budgets have risen substantially. Early framework programmes placed a lot of emphasis on information and communication technologies and energy technologies. The share of both these technology areas in the framework programmes has decreased recently in favour of industrial and materials technologies, life sciences, environment, transport and researcher training. Several other areas are being funded at significantly lower levels. The panel considered the thematic coverage of the framework programmes to be satisfactory.

The research activities and goals of FP5 and FP6 were found broadly consistent with the originally defined higher level socio-economic goals of the Research Framework Programme. This programme has now established its position as a key element of the European RTD landscape contributing to the competitiveness and competence base of the Union. Organizations from all member states participate extensively in the programme, in proportions largely related to their size and RTD capabilities. This also applies to the new member states whose organizations are achieving participation rates more or less commensurate with their populations.

Members of the panel, however, expressed their concern with what they viewed as extensive fragmentation of the framework programmes – that is, a certain lack of focus – and over determination of their lower level thematic areas from above. Reported declining industrial interest, general complaints about proposal costs, and heavy over subscription to some programmes may reflect, in part, excessive fragmentation and thematic specification. Further fragmentation could lead to marginalization in some areas and increasing frustration in the research community. Such considerations led to a call for better focus of thematic priorities in forthcoming framework programmes. More focus in terms of priorities at a higher level, in fact, can be combined with less specificity at the individual programme level.

FP6 has promoted risky research through the NEST (New and Emerging Science and Technologies) programme which supports and anticipates scientific and technological needs. Although welcome, this is still a narrow approach. The panel emphasized the importance of encouraging high-risk research in all thematic priorities, that is, by raising the degree of risk of the average project funded by the Research Framework Programme.[5] Support for long-term RTD should be enhanced.

10.3.1 Industry Participation

The reported drop off in industry participation was not apparent in the available aggregate data. Overall industry participation in FP6 was not significantly different from that in FP5, especially if Networks of Excellence are excluded. Industry participation has been relatively higher in information society technologies (IST), nanotechnology, aeronautics and space and in sustainable development. It has been relatively lower in life sciences and food quality and safety. Looking across the two programmes, industry participation in FP6 increased both as a percentage of participation and budget share in life sciences, remained about the same in environment and energy, and decreased somewhat in IST and in aerospace and transport.

The share of industry participation in FP6 funding instruments was found to be highest in Integrated Projects (IPs), followed by Specific Targeted Research Projects (STRePs) and at a substantially lower level by Coordinated Actions (CAs), Specific Support Actions (SSAs), and last and at some distance by Networks of Excellence. The differences among instruments are even more pronounced in financial terms (industry share of FP funds absorbed).

The panel felt that the original target of the Research Framework Programme to strengthen European competitiveness, over the years has been complemented by a number of socio-economic objectives, which have expanded the scope of the programme and may inadvertently have decreased its industrial focus. In fact, EC data indicate that the framework programmes examined had more participants from higher education institutions and other research institutes taken together than from industry. Industry participation should be raised above its current level. In particular, it is very important that framework programmes remain easily accessible to small technology-based firms and high-technology start-ups with strong growth potential.[6]

10.3.2 European Value Added

The expert panel received significant input on European added value from the five-year appraisal of the IST Programme, from member states' appraisals of the impacts of FP5 and from surveys of framework programme participants. This evidence consistently points to high levels of input, output and behavioural additionality. The reported sources of European added value include the augmentation of national RTD funds for research infrastructures, pooling of resources to raise RTD investment in Europe-wide issues, enhanced access to foreign resources and capabilities, facilitation of international mobility of researchers, support for EU policy including regulation, health issues and so on.

While the panel recognized these benefits, it also emphasized the importance of an explicit, consistent definition of the added value from framework programmes. The concept of European added value has been evolving. Many of the conventional benefits identified in project-level evaluations imply such value: networking, especially international networking; facilities sharing; knowledge sharing; and attaining bigger scale (critical mass) than is possible at the national level. However, concerted efforts at systematic measurement have been limited. Research is needed to develop guidelines, concrete criteria and, perhaps, checklists to be used in assessing European added value. The EC should take a leading role in developing a simple and robust definition of European added value taking into account the latest research on the need for government intervention and the need to develop lead markets for European solutions, which often involve measures from other policy domains, such as common standards and easy access to the single market.

While the principle of subsidiarity precludes the Research Framework Programme from supporting activities that would be better conducted at national level, the continuation of the ERA, the establishment of the European Research Council (ERC) and the ability to facilitate technology platforms can raise the added value of future framework programmes and will increase the importance of a clear definition of the European added value even further.

10.3.3 Implementation

The implementation of the framework programmes was not entirely smooth during the time period examined by the panel. Oversubscription, increased burdens in terms of management, complexity in proposal preparation and long and arduous negotiation have discouraged some prospective applicants. One of the basic problems underlying implementation seems to be the frequent changes in the thrust and objectives of succeeding framework programmes.

Two new funding instruments were introduced in FP6: Networks of Excellence and IPs. The effectiveness of these new instruments during the first two years of implementation was reviewed by an independent Panel of High-Level Experts, chaired by Professor Ramon Marimon, which praised the continuity preserved by the new instruments in the long tradition of transnational collaborative research in Europe. These new initiatives make it possible to set more ambitious goals in objective-driven research (IPs) and in research integration Networks of Excellence through consortia and agglomerations of researchers of the necessary critical mass. However, the Marimon Panel also pointed out several areas needing improvement. One was related to the costs and risks of participation in the new initiatives, which seemed unreasonably high for prospective industry participants, and especially small and medium-sized enterprises (SMEs) and other small and emerging groups. SMEs have found it almost impossible to be involved in Networks of Excellence and have been disadvantaged in IPs. In contrast, SMEs have fared well in STRePs[7] and CRAFT[8] projects. The need for enhanced flexibility and greater simplification in proposal submission, proposal evaluation and contract negotiation was also highlighted.

On the basis of the available evidence and consultations, the panel found the Marimon report conclusions and recommendations quite appropriate. A greater budgetary allocation was called for in future programmes for

STRePs and small consortia IPs given that such instruments are better adapted to risk taking, industry participants, participants from new member states and smaller players generally. Efforts to attract emerging research groups and the most innovative firms in Europe must be enhanced. Administrative procedures and financial rules should be significantly simplified and further improved to allow more efficiency and flexibility in implementing participation in the new instruments.

Barriers to participation can be created by inefficient management processes, ineffective communication from the Commission, inadequate information channels and lack of experience in application procedures. To the extent that application costs and risks of participation are unreasonably high, SMEs will suffer the most. Apart from these generic barriers, the effort to increase impact through substantial funding of larger projects in FP6 may create biases in favour of research groups with proven track records and well accepted, objective-driven research. New, higher risk approaches and emerging research groups may be excluded. Organizations in the new member states may run a higher risk of being excluded.

10.3.4 Mobility

Mobility programmes were recognized as highly important. Key among them is the programme of Marie Curie Fellowships, which support the training and mobility of young researchers, the transfer of knowledge towards less favoured regions of the Community and, to some extent, between industry and academia. Individual fellowships account for the majority of Marie Curie Fellowships. SMEs account for only one quarter of the minority host fellowships. French, Spanish, German and Italian (in that order) nationals topped the list of funded proposals. The UK was the most favoured member state destination for applicants.

Marie Curie Fellowships would seem to be fundamental for the achievement of the Lisbon objectives and the ERA. In order to build a knowledge-based society, Europe needs to train more researchers from within and from outside – an estimated 500 000–700 000 researchers for the first decade of the 2000s alone. To retain them, Europe must make research careers more attractive by giving researchers more autonomy and responsibility, providing science careers with greater visibility, making it easier to move across disciplinary and geographical boundaries, and increasing researchers' salaries.

On the basis of the broadly held impression that Marie Curie Fellowship activity has been an overall success, and given the very severe shortages in the qualified personnel needed to meet the Lisbon and Barcelona objectives, the panel found it reasonable to call for increased attention to this activity in future framework programmes. Increased emphasis on promoting mobility between the public and private sectors was called for.

10.3.5   Trust in Science

Finally, the panel stressed that the Research Framework Programme should continue to address the issues of trust and legitimacy of S&T in Europe and gender balance.

10.4   INTERACTION WITH OTHER POLICY AREAS

R&D promoted through framework programmes is not an end in itself, but is an important instrument for achieving a vibrant, competitive European economy. Neither the Research Framework Programme nor its components can, alone, induce the major changes in the European research and innovation system that are envisaged in the ERA and the Lisbon and Barcelona agendas. RTD investments and programmes are necessary, but not sufficient for successful innovation. The interaction of RTD policy with other policy areas is of critical importance.

RTD policy should be complemented by and coordinated with other socio-economic policies. These should include policies for competitiveness, intellectual property protection, competition and state aid, human resource policies – especially education and gender, and ethics. They should also include demand-side policies, especially public procurement of RTD and innovative goods and regulation, which can be used creatively to promote innovation and the emergence of lead markets.

The importance of competitiveness, innovation and entrepreneurial culture as major drivers of growth cannot be overemphasized. Although RTD is a critical input, innovation and competitiveness depend on many other factors for success, such as investment opportunities, the regulatory environment, the ability of economic actors to rapidly transform technology into economic goods, and access to markets for goods and services. Creating a business environment favourable to RTD, innovation and entrepreneurship is of primary importance. Europe must be able to attract the most talented individuals both from within and from outside Europe. It must also become the best location for RTD for organizations around the world. This requires the willingness of the public and private sectors to work together, the former by providing an EU-wide framework favourable to business and by investing to remedy market failures, and the latter by investing the lion's share to achieve the Barcelona RTD targets. The integrated approach to competitiveness advocated in the EC Investing in

European Research action plan promotes a whole set of legislative, coordination and stimulation measures across several policy fields, such as RTD, innovation, intellectual property protection, human resources, fiscal measures, product-market regulation, competition policy and financial markets. A systemic view of the various policy dimensions involved here is absolutely crucial.

The Aho report (2006), which was published after the conclusion of the panel's work, reinforces several of the panel's recommendations and puts forward a whole battery of proposals for action. Most notably, this report stresses the importance of demand-side factors as compared to the supply-side factors common to this field for achieving technology take-up, productivity growth and competitiveness. A balanced approach to supply- and demand-side factors is recommended.[9]

These issues are important for both Community RTD expenditures and Community services. They relate to the overall innovation environment, and the framework conditions and corresponding policies. They are also important for individual member states, which have very important roles as implementers of structural reforms and guardians of competitiveness. The coherent development of national and European policies through an open coordination process is also important. The stimulation of RTD, innovation and entrepreneurship depends to a large extent on the commitment of the member states to take the necessary decisions at national level.

Private sector RTD investment – at the core of the Lisbon strategy – depends also on many factors that lie outside the traditional realm of science, technology and innovation policy. It critically depends on key framework conditions including macroeconomic conditions, fiscal conditions, financial markets and labour markets that induce and empower companies to invest. Private RTD investment is also influenced in important ways by those policy domains that affect competition, standards and regulations, entrepreneurship, intellectual property protection, human resources and public research.

Two of these policy domains directly relate to the organization and success rate of the Framework Programme for Research: intellectual property protection and competition policy and state aid.

The intellectual property rights (IPR) system in Europe currently faces very significant challenges. One of these is the lack of a European patent, the subject of discussion for more than 30 years. The lack of a Community patent disadvantages European organizations and individuals by raising the cost of protecting their inventions in distinct national markets with disparate IPR protection regimes. The overall cost of application, maintenance and enforcement of a patent with European coverage remains significantly higher than the cost in competitor countries, such as the US and Japan. Europe lacks an IPR regime that is simple, inexpensive and efficient. The panel strongly advocated swift implementation of a European patent in one language. Another issue related to IPRs is the increasing involvement of higher education institutions and other public research institutes in the commercialization of innovation-related knowledge. Key here is the establishment of IPR rules to provide the appropriate balance and incentives to university and other public research institute personnel, especially in relation to industry collaboration and participation in public research programmes.

Competition policy promotes competitive markets. A new EU competition regulatory framework, which came into force in May 2004, revamped anti-trust and merger control regulations and was intended to reduce regulatory uncertainty by replacing national standards with a single European rule. Competition policy also addresses state aid regulation (public subsidies) (under review in 2007). While Community RTD funding alone does not constitute state aid in the meaning of Article 87(1) of the EC Treaty, the Community framework for state aid becomes applicable in cases of cumulation between Community and national funding. In such cases the cumulative public support and its impact on competition are considered.

A comprehensive review of the horizontal state aid rules is currently under way to account for the Lisbon objectives and the economic and social cohesion policy of the Union. Moreover, the World Trade Organization rules for RTD subsidies are relevant here. In order to increase its international competitiveness, the Community must apply the appropriate economic rationale. The current system under which the aid level is determined by the research phase is outdated and not in compliance with the modern conceptualization of innovation. The interactive nature of the innovation process and the importance of networking as a primary working mode for the various stakeholders should be adopted. Justification of RTD funding is well established internationally and it is therefore important that EU state aid provisions maintain a level playing field that compares with Europe's main competitors.

10.5 LESSONS FOR THE FUTURE

The panel determined that the Research Framework Programme, on the whole, has played an important role in developing the European knowledge base. The various framework programmes have corrected some of the deficiencies in the European RTD landscape and have contributed to bridging the gap between RTD and innovation.

If carefully planned and targeted, successive framework programmes could serve as a catalyst for the European science, technology and innovation system. To be successful in this role the tendency to expand the objectives (excellence, cohesion), thematic scope and modalities/instruments of the Research Framework Programme should be resisted. In differing from the objectives of national RTD activities the framework programmes should address the big European challenges with clear and transparent European added value. The tailoring for local effectiveness and take-up should be left to national or regional level programmes that must be further mobilized through the ERA process.

There is no doubt that work is needed on the demand and the supply sides, at European and at national level, for RTD policy and for related broader socio-economic policies. Europe must become a lead market for innovative new products. It must also be able to respond swiftly when substantial new economic opportunities emerge. Future framework programmes could identify such opportunities, facilitate the development of lead markets and provide the catalyst for European countries to work together to lead major global developments. One possible way to achieve this that was discussed by the panel is through the establishment of a limited number of 'technology platforms' in key technology areas.

Industry has already been active in developing large collaborative research programmes for technology platforms. Ideally, they should be industry-driven and based on public/private partnerships for both financing and execution. They should involve academic institutions, large and small companies and, when needed, participants from outside Europe. They should be designed to restore European leadership in key technologies and thereby to increase private investment in RTD in Europe. To enable them to have the intended impact technology platforms must be adequately funded and managed by pooling resources from the Research Framework Programme, national sources and industry. Technology platforms are something to consider in areas where sufficient industrial commitment in terms of financing, intellectual resources and leadership are confirmed, and significant economic potential on a global scale is identified. Adequate care, however, should be devoted to making certain that this process is not high-jacked by specific interests and short-term profit objectives.

The considerations above have culminated in the newest funding scheme in FP7, the Joint Technology Initiative (JTI). For large-scale initiatives, for which the regular instruments are insufficient, a JTI provides a dedicated legal structure on the basis of Article 171. The JTI is a new instrument, introduced in FP7, with the specific objective of implementing a programme of research in a specific technological area. The basic idea behind JTIs is that they will facilitate the pooling of financial resources from the private sector, from the member states and from the Community to support the relevant European Technology Platform research agenda. They will facilitate cooperation among all stakeholders in order to improve Europe's competitive position and respond to Europe's societal needs.

At the time of writing, the EC had recognized six areas where parts of the strategic research area could be implemented through a JTI. The details of their implementation, however, had not been consolidated. Candidates for JTIs were:

- Aeronautics and Air Transport (ACARE)
- Advanced Research and Technology for Embedded Intelligence and Systems (ARTEMIS)
- Global Monitoring for Environment and Security (GMES)
- Hydrogen and Fuel Cells
- Innovative Medicines for Europe (IMI)
- European Nanoelectronics Initiative Advisory Council (ENIAC).

Another issue of major current concern is basic research. This, of course, is an area that traditionally has received support from national governments. The immense contribution of basic research to innovation and, more generally, to socio-economic development through both research results and training of highly skilled personnel has been firmly established. While international basic research is already being carried out in Europe through various channels, including the networks and projects of the European Science Foundation, EUREKA, large basic research laboratories (CERN,[10] ESO,[11] EMBO,[12] EMBL[13]), and thematic areas of the Research Framework Programme, such support is focused on a limited number of activities and its magnitude pales in comparison to the support for scientific research and graduate education provided at national level. The compartmentalization of national programmes and support systems among member states may introduce three adverse effects at European level: insufficient competition among scientists and research teams; lack of sufficient cooperation and coordination activities; and, in some cases, lack of critical mass.

Basic research, and the organizations responsible for it, are now the subject of intense debate in Europe: the twin objectives for the ERA and for a knowledge-based economy have brought to the forefront the notion of a European basic research fund and a new organizational structure to administer it (ERC). The panel supported the establishment of the ERC and suggested that the Council needs to have sufficient resources to become a credible player in the European RTD landscape. The ERC should promote excellence in science, be cost efficient and encourage the development of world-class research environments. In order to be able to make a difference sufficient resources should be allocated to scientific fields that have a long-term impact on competitiveness and innovation. The ERC has become reality in FP7.

Finally, the panel urged the Commission to address more clearly the contribution of the framework programmes to the EU policy formulation process. EU research should play a significant role by providing new insights into the European innovation environment and the creation of lead markets for new innovations. Not least, member states can greatly assist in progressing towards the ERA. The overall effort must be calibrated against the results of regular, well-structured evaluation exercises, which, in addition to the direct impacts of the framework programmes, should address the higher level socio-economic effects and implications for the structural reform of the European research landscape and economic competitiveness. Such evaluation should seek answers to questions that cut across framework programme activities and increase understanding of portfolio impacts. *Ex ante* appraisal of future framework programme objectives should be connected to *ex post* evaluation on a regular and systematic basis, applying consistent criteria that give sufficient attention to both long-term and short-term issues.

That is to say, the new realizations about the relative role of the Research Framework Programme within the more general socio-economic context defined by the concepts of globalization and the knowledge-based economy require novel approaches in assessing the past and future expected impacts of the programme. This, again, is very much in line with trends in other parts of the world and, in particular, the US where the 'Marburger Initiative' on the Science of Science Policy calls for a better understanding of the process of technological advance and innovation and for more holistic approaches to appraising the impacts of government RTD programmes.

NOTES

1. This chapter draws quite extensively on Ormala and Vonortas (2005) which, in turn, summarized the results of the third *Five-Year Assessment of the Research Framework Programmes* 1999–2003. For the original report see EC (2005). In the main, however, the chapter depends on the views of the author who is solely responsible for any misconceptions and misrepresentations.
2. The term 'knowledge-based' does not identify only information technology, but extends to any sector that is advanced in terms of producing and/or using high technology. A knowledge-based economy is one in which the generation and exploitation of knowledge play a predominant role in the generation of wealth.
3. The chapter reflects the views and opinions of the author. For a more complete view of the panel's opinions and official position the reader is urged to consult the original report.

4. The deficit remains and, reportedly, widens. It extends to both public and private RTD expenditures. See, for example, DTI (2006).
5. Surveys of FP participants have repeatedly shown that the supported projects have similar characteristics to the average project of these organizations, for example, they are not more risky. See, for example, Atlantis Research et al. (2004).
6. That being said, it is not known why a good proportion of the European high-technology gazelles do not participate in the Research Framework Programme (Malerba et al., 2006). Avoidance of perceived bureaucratic procedures may be responsible – more than accessibility.
7. STRePs are Specific Targeted Research Projects aimed at improving European competitiveness and meeting the needs of society or Community policies. They can take the form of an RTD project to gain knowledge or improve existing products, processes or services or a demonstration project designed to prove the viability of new technologies.
8. CRAFT projects are cooperative research projects particularly suitable for SMEs.
9. While forcefully and successfully put forward, the idea of a balanced supply-demand approach is not new. The US responded similarly to its perceived competitiveness problem a decade or two ago. See Vonortas (1995).
10. CERN – European Organization for Nuclear Research.
11. ESO – European Southern Observatory.
12. EMBO – European Molecular Biology Organization.
13. EMBL – European Molecular Biology Laboratory.

REFERENCES

Aho, E. (2006), *Creating an Innovative Europe, Report of the Independent Expert Group on R&D and Innovation Following the Hampton Court Summit*, Luxembourg: Office for Official Publications of the European Communities.

Atlantis Research, Joanneum Research, K. Guy, W. Polt and N. Vonortas (2004), *FP5 Impact Assessment: Survey Conducted as Part of the Five Year Assessment of EU Research Activities (1999–2003)*, Final Report, Brussels: EC DG Research.

Department of Trade and Industry (DTI) (2006), *The R&D Scoreboard 2006*, London: DTI.

European Commission (EC) (2005), *Five-year Assessment of the European Union Research Framework Programmes 1999–2003*, Luxembourg: DG Research, Office for Official Publications of the European Communities.

Kok, W. (Chairman) High Level Group (2004), *Meeting the Challenge: The Lisbon Strategy for Growth and Development*, report of independent high-level group chaired by W. Kok, Luxembourg: Office for Official Publications of the European Communities.

Malerba, F., N. S. Vonortas, S. Breschi and L. Cassi (2006), *Evaluation of Progress Towards a European Research Area for Information Society Technologies*, Final Report, DG Information Society and Media, Luxembourg: European Commission.

Ormala, E. and N.S. Vonortas (2005), 'Evaluating the European Union's research framework programmes: 1999–2003', *Science and Public Policy*, **32**(5), 403–10.

Reich, R. B. (1992), *The Work of Nations: Preparing Ourselves for 21st Century Capitalism*, New York: Vintage.

Sapir, A., P. Aghion, G. Bertola, M. Hellwig, J. Pisani-Ferry, D. Rosati, J. Viñals and H. Wallace (2003), *An Agenda for a Growing Europe: Making the EU System*

Deliver, report of an independent high-level study group established at the initiative of the President of the European Commission, Brussels: EC.

Vonortas, N. S. (1995), 'New directions for U.S. science and technology policy: the view from the R&D assessment front', *Science and Public Policy*, **22**(1), 19–28.

11. Critical dimensions of innovation policy: challenges for Sweden and the EU

Göran Marklund

11.1 INTRODUCTION

Competition and competitiveness are at the heart of economic systems. Business firms in different nations are increasingly competing, either directly or indirectly, with foreign-based firms. Business competitiveness is essential not only to business firms, but also to the performance of national and regional economies. Policy strategies and design are an integral part of business competitiveness, since public institutions and policy are deeply and inherently embedded in all kinds of business activities – indirectly as the provider of general and specific conditions of fundamental importance for general business incentives and opportunities. And directly as the provider of markets, through public demand, and resources, through public investments and capital, which are often of critical importance for different kinds of business activities.

Business renewal is essential to sustained competitiveness in competitive business environments: without it, competition will eventually erode the very value basis of businesses (Schumpeter, 1934). Innovation is at the heart of business renewal and should be understood as the generation of new or improved businesses through the transformation of new ideas or new combinations of existing ideas into new business models, new products, new production processes or new business organizations.

Large numbers of technology and business experimentations continuously lead to new combinations and mutations of business ideas and technologies. Some innovative combinations turn out to be more competitive than others. Innovation processes are intimately associated with entrepreneurship,[1] related to business, technology and organization. This general logic of economic development, based on dynamic competition between different businesses, is often referred to as 'creative destruction' to use Schumpeter's (1943) words, although David Audretsch[2] proposes a more positive characterization of the key role of innovation and entrepreneurship, terming it 'creative construction'.

Economic development is not primarily a question of allocation of scarce resources. More fundamentally, it is a question of experimentation to innovate new sources of economic value. From a strictly accounting economics point of view, the experimentally organized (Eliasson, 1996) nature of capitalistic economic systems makes them 'notoriously wasteful' and yet they represent the most effective systems for economic development in the history of mankind. The fundamental reason for the relative dynamic efficiency of capitalist economic systems is precisely the experimentally organized nature of such systems, in which growth is generated through evolutionary search and selection processes (Beinhocker, 2006).

Business firms are always integrated into webs of interrelated business activities. They are also integrated with public institutions, such as laws, regulations and rules, and with social norms and practices of social interactions. In many cases business firms also have relationships with public or semi-public organizations, such as universities, institutes and agencies, particularly for those innovation processes that require high degrees of knowledge. Hence, the systemic nature of the relationships between private and public agents and institutions is critical in determining the direction and pace of innovation investments and their efficiency. Businesses continuously emerge and submerge along evolutionary development logics, within the multidimensional dynamic networks of innovation systems.

Geography is of key importance to economic dynamics. Resources and capabilities for production, innovation and value generation are not evenly distributed across geographic space. Hence, the world is not flat, despite what some commentators claim (Friedman, 2005), although globalization continuously integrates wider parts of the globe in the generation of economic growth and the sharing of its benefits. Differentiations and agglomerations are fundamental driving forces for economic development and the distribution of resources and wealth. In this sense, the world is 'spiky' rather than flat in terms of creativity and interactivity within innovation environments (Florida, 2005). As a consequence, competitiveness in such a globalizing world requires capacities and focus to generate such 'spikes' of dynamic excellence.

New businesses continuously replace old ones, as new business opportunities are seized or created through a dynamic web of mutually interrelated changes in demand, sales, production, technologies and competencies. They emerge in both large and small business firms and through new business start-ups. New businesses are fundamental to economic dynamics and renewal. Innovation-based businesses, almost by definition, are initially small businesses; either they emerge within existing large corporations or existing small business firms, or emerge through start-ups of new firms. New businesses are generally highly vulnerable in the early stages of their developments, mainly because their future development and profitability generally are associated with considerable uncertainties.

There are different degrees of novelty in innovations. A broad categorization of the degree of renewal generated by different innovations distinguishes between incremental and radical innovations, where incremental innovation is understood as step by step progression along established business and technology trajectories while radical innovation involves large business and technology leaps. While the former involves a relatively low degree of new knowledge and creativity, the latter involves high levels of creativity and new knowledge (Dosi, 1982).

As incremental innovation processes generally involve moderate or low uncertainties about the feasibility of success, the risks of investing in such developments are relatively low. In radical innovation processes uncertainties are often very high and the risks are therefore difficult, often impossible, to estimate. Consequently, radical innovations, which are inherently associated with the formation of new businesses, generally face substantial development challenges before they achieve viable market positions. These challenges are often referred to as 'valleys of death', since many radical innovation processes do not manage to pass all business and technology obstacles and therefore fail to reach a profitable market position.

Radical innovation and business renewal are inherently related to small business development, as entirely new businesses are inevitably small in their early stages. It should be noted, however, that new business development, even radically new business, is not restricted to the development of small business firms. New and small business can be generated by competences and activities within large business corporations, and other organizations. Nevertheless, new business development, even when developed within large corporations, is generally a small business issue in the early phases of development and it is therefore necessary to overcome serious obstacles in terms of competition for resources and competence with already established business areas. This competition is usually related to the often considerable uncertainties and risks connected to new businesses.

All kinds of innovations are important for economic competitiveness, though they play different roles in the ecology of innovation systems. Incremental innovation follows established paths of renewal within established business models and trajectories. This type of renewal is of critical importance to maintaining business firms' competitiveness and the competitiveness of business firm networks and entire industries. Radical innovation opens up new sources of economic value by breaking out of established business models and industrial trajectories, through the emergence of entirely new businesses. It forges routes towards entirely new business models and industries, which could emerge as important sources of business profits and economic growth.

Competition tends to increase in most markets, as the rate of globalization accelerates and wider areas of the world's modern economies are opened up to competition through different kinds of deregulation processes. As a consequence, the requirements for competitiveness and, particularly, the need for rapid development of new business models, products and processes are continuously increasing. Therefore, in addition to good general business conditions, rapid economic renewal requires competitive conditions for incentives, capabilities and resources related to high value adding innovation.

Public policy related to innovation and business renewal is of critical importance to the long-term competitiveness, growth and job creation of nations and regions. This chapter discusses different innovation policy strategies and schemes that are particularly relevant to some major general innovation policy challenges in Sweden and the European Union (EU). In Section 11.2 we describe some major innovation policy challenges facing Sweden and the EU. Section 11.3 discusses some policy instruments to address market formation and business formation challenges. Section 11.4 discusses policy schemes related to the challenges in science and technology (S&T) formation. Section 11.5 concludes the chapter.

11.2 INNOVATION POLICY CHALLENGES FOR SWEDEN AND THE EU

A number of factors related to innovation systems have an influence on long-term national competitiveness. We would argue that they essentially are related to four kinds of critical formation processes within innovation systems. These four typological processes are:

- market formation
- business formation
- technology formation
- science formation.

These formation processes represent different domains of driving forces for economic system dynamics and renewal. Innovation policy should focus on developing all four types of formation dynamics and the connections between them in order to effectively generate and sustain dynamic competitiveness (Figure 11.1).

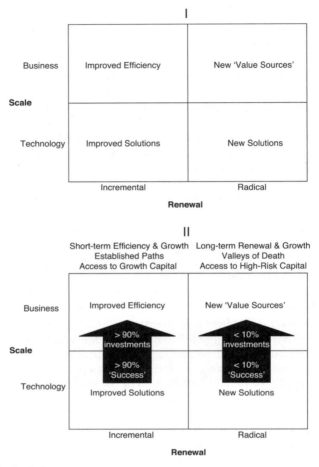

Source: Author's data.

Figure 11.1   Renewal and scale dimensions of innovation

11.2.1   Status of Innovation Policy in Government

Despite the importance of innovation and innovation policies to the dynamic competitiveness of nations, innovation policy has found it hard within most governments to establish itself as a policy field in its own right. Public policy and public sector institutions influence the conditions for innovation and competitiveness in a multitude of ways. Most policy areas and some public sector responsibilities influence these conditions, often in very important ways. However, as these impacts are seldom the main issue in deliberations over strategies related to these policy areas and public sector activities, their effects on innovation and competitiveness are often implicit and largely unintentional.

We would argue that this, admittedly highly generalized, state of innovation and competitiveness policy is both unfortunate and potentially harmful, from the perspective of the future of national prosperity, job creation and welfare. As such, it is a major general policy challenge. From the point of view of economic systems, rather than from a political administrative perspective, national and regional innovation and competitiveness policies exist whether or not they are labelled as such. Also implicit policy making is still policy making, and no policy is also a policy. Hence, innovation policies exist, whether explicit or not.

Some countries have clearly put innovation policy at the centre of plans for competitiveness and growth, most notably China and other Asian emerging economies, where strategies for competitiveness are a top priority for policy making. Other countries that prioritize innovation include Finland, whose prime minister has for long been leading a process for generating general national strategies for innovation and economic competitiveness. This example has been followed by the rapidly developing Baltic states and several former communist bloc countries. Recent policy processes initiated by the Danish national globalization council demonstrate a similar determination and expediency towards innovation policy (Danish Government, 2006), and the new American Competitiveness Initiative (ACI) is a strong demonstration of the US administration's determination to increase investments in US competitiveness (Domestic Policy Council, 2006).

In Sweden, as well as in most other highly economically developed EU countries, the priorities and administrative power of innovation and competitiveness policy have been less focused and less determined than in the countries mentioned above. We would argue that this is a major shortcoming of policy making in relation to economic growth and job creation. In fact, it is likely one of the major factors behind the EU's inability to achieve the targets of the Lisbon agenda, a failing that has been so sharply remarked upon in recent evaluations of the strategy for European competitiveness (Kok, 2004). In Sweden a national innovation strategy presented in 2005 has generated important policy impacts (Swedish Government, 2004). However, as it was developed within the Ministry of Industry and Trade and did not directly involve either the prime minister or the entire government, the full potential of the insights gained in the process has not yet been attained.

11.2.2   Innovation Policy Focus and Priorities

European and Swedish innovation related policy making is quite strongly focused on and geared towards S&T push. At the EU level this general policy trend received its clearest expression in the Lisbon agenda's target of investment in research and development (R&D) of 3 per cent of gross domestic product (GDP). Obviously, R&D investments, both private and public, are of key importance to the innovation and competitiveness of nations. However, it is seldom sufficient to set clear targets only on the input side. The innovation performance or output targets of the Lisbon agenda are considerably less specific than the input target for R&D investment.[3]

The ambitious investments in the academic sector in Sweden are not usually referred to as innovation policy, but rather as research or science policy, both of which, unlike innovation, are formally recognized policy areas. In relation to innovation, Swedish research policy has been quite strongly based, often implicitly, but sometimes also explicitly, on a 'linear' understanding of innovation and economic renewal, in which scientific discovery is regarded as the 'normal' beginning of innovation processes. For a long time, Swedish policy related to innovation and long-term growth was quite explicitly based on a general strategy of S&T push and primarily science push (Schilling, 2005).

On the other hand, Swedish policy making has also generated important long-term public-private partnerships related to R&D investments and technology-based business in Sweden, which have been key factors driving and shaping the structure and dynamics of the Swedish national innovation system. However, the generation of long-term private partnerships was, at best, only implicitly related to innovation policy ambitions, or ambitions to enhance Swedish dynamic competitiveness. Sweden is not unique in this respect in Europe. Similar public-private partnerships have been important in, for example, the UK, Germany and France.

The public policies governing the development of the public-private partnerships that have been the key driving force in technology dominating Swedish industries were primarily motivated by different kinds of 'national interests', essentially other than long-term economic growth. Defence was the main motive, but also national industry and public needs for long-distance communication and transportation in a very sparsely populated country. Another motive of importance in many areas, but particularly in relation to energy, was the arguable need for national independence in terms of available energy sources.

Despite their implicitness in relation to innovation policy and dynamic competitiveness, the emerging public-private partnerships have been instrumental in forming internationally competitive markets and businesses within key industries for Sweden. They have also been instrumental in stimulating fairly rapid growth, both economically and technologically, of initially nationally important, but internationally quite small firms into significant international players. And Sweden's ambitious research and education policies have been instrumental in backing up the emerging technology-intensive Swedish industry by providing researchers, engineers and other key higher education competences. In other words, the two lines of public policy and public sector developments were quite well matched in relation to innovation and dynamic competitiveness, despite their implicitness in relation to these ambitions.

Sweden still benefits greatly from the internationally competitive multinationals, which historically developed in Sweden and which still have important technology and business facilities in the country. In combination with sound macroeconomic policies following the severe economic crisis of the early 1990s, the competitiveness of Swedish industry has manifested itself in internationally strong national economic growth performance over the last decade. However, there are important signs of decreasing contributions from the previous key drivers of Swedish technology and business renewal – the R&D-intensive multinational corporations (MNCs) – although the trend is still limited.

As noted above, formal policy and its real impact are often very different. It was not until the late 1990s that the concept of innovation policy received any importance in Sweden. However, although innovation policy is now acknowledged as a significant policy area, it is still not recognized as a formal policy domain. Swedish policy history shows that an explicit focus on the main drivers of Swedish technological and business competitiveness in technologically dominating industries has been largely lacking. In particular, little attention has been paid to the renewal of the driving forces of key market and business formation mechanisms, which still are not a major focus of the current debate on innovation and growth policy. The essentially implicit innovation policy has continued to be quite strongly based on an S&T push strategy.

11.2.3 Need for Policy Reconsideration

An essential part of any policy development designed to enhance the role and impact of innovation policy in Sweden and the EU would need to be based on the insight that market formation and business formation are of fundamental importance to innovation and industrial renewal. This is also a general message from the European Trend Chart country report on Sweden, which points to the absence of 'incentives for radical innovation and also an inadequate use of scientific achievements [for business formation], which might hamper future economic growth and prosperity'.[4]

An increased focus on demand or pull mechanisms is warranted. However, it must be emphasized that an increased focus on market and business formation should not be developed at the expense of policies and policy measures for S&T formation. International excellence in S&T formation is a prerequisite for attracting competence and investments and should therefore be a major focus of innovation policy.

Small business innovation should be a key policy target at a time of weakening contributions of large corporations to industrial renewal, growth and job creation and at a time when small business firms are increasingly being regarded as key sources of these dynamics. As radical innovation and high value adding economic growth and job creation are inherently associated with new business formation and growth, small business innovation should be a major concern for innovation policy in Sweden and the EU.

It is important to appreciate the systemic nature of innovation systems and the importance of the dynamic relationships between large and small business firms, and the relationships between business firms and public organizations and institutions. Large companies are often key customers of small firms. Therefore, the innovation and business renewal of large corporations is generally as important as that of small business firms to the dynamics and international competitiveness of the business sectors of nations and regions. Also, different sized business firms with different histories tend to play different roles in innovation systems and can affect economic dynamics and renewal in different, but interrelated ways.

To sum up our discussion so far we would argue that there are five major policy challenges related to innovation and competitiveness facing Sweden and the EU:

- increasing the innovation pull of markets and market formation mechanisms
- accelerating business formation and renewal through radical innovation
- enhancing absorptive capabilities for high rates of incremental innovation
- attracting investments for excellence in S&T formation
- improving links between market, business, technology and science formation.

In the next two sections we discuss four categories of innovation policy schemes related to the innovation policy challenges discussed above.

Section 11.3 discusses two kinds of policy measures related to market and business formation: public innovation procurement, and award schemes for R&D and innovation. Section 11.4 describes two kinds of policy schemes related to S&T formation: tax credits for R&D investments and public-private R&D centres of excellence.

11.3   POLICY MEASURES FOR MARKET AND BUSINESS FORMATION

Policies addressing innovation and the long-term economic competitiveness of nations should consider that there are different dimensions of uncertainties and risk-reward ratios related to innovations with different degrees of renewal. Also, incremental and radical renewal involve two principally different, but highly interrelated domains of uncertainty that need to be considered: technological and business. Technological uncertainty refers to the essential functions of innovations, while business uncertainty refers to the business models and their associated profit potentials in future markets. In principle, the further the technological distance from commercialization of an idea, that is, invention, the higher the technological uncertainty, and the more radical the intended innovation in relation to existing business solutions to the same or similar problems, the higher are the business risks (Figure 11.2).

R&D investment in existing business firms tends to focus primarily on incremental innovation. The essential business rationale for this is that such investments are generally motivated by the ambition to defend the competitiveness of existing businesses. Large investments in alternative value sources based on new businesses tend to divert investments of capital and competence from existing businesses. And new business development is generally a considerably more uncertain endeavour than support for existing ones, substantially increasing the risks of failure. Hence, there are quite high disincentives for investments in radical innovation and business renewal as opposed to support for incremental innovation.

As the risks and uncertainties in radical technology and business renewal are substantial, there is generally a clear policy rationale for public measures and structures supporting such processes. Moreover, new businesses based on radical innovation generally involve disruptive breaks with existing business models and industry trajectories. Therefore, radical renewal receives weak support from existing techno-economic structures, which are based on previous investments in capital, competences and organizations. Disruption of these structures generally involves considerable costs for investors, producers and individuals employed in these industrial systems.

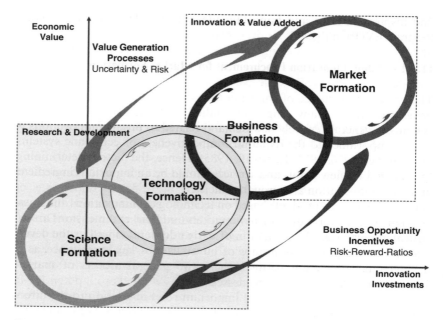

Figure 11.2   Critical formation processes in economic renewal and growth

Hence, existing incentive and power structures tend to generate obstacles to radically new paths of techno-economic development, which are exacerbated by the higher uncertainties and business risks associated with radical developments compared with incremental renewal based on relatively well-known business logics.

The international policy repertoire addressing early stages of new technology-based business formation, that is, the 'valleys of death' related to radical business renewal, is quite wide, although the definition and names of the various measures and programmes adopted in different countries vary. A variety of analogies are adopted to describe the targets and measures of such policies. One of these is seed funding, which generally refers to the public funding of early stage innovation processes before private capital can be attracted. Pre-seed funding is used to describe public funding of the stages in innovation processes that precede the stages when seed funding can be expected. Some policies refer to funding for 'verifications' of technologies and businesses. Most of these policy discussions and measures in Europe target developments in new or small businesses; initiatives supporting radical innovation in large corporations are scarce. In this respect, innovation policy makers in the EU and Sweden should find inspiration from and important ideas in the Advanced Technology Program (ATP) in the US.

11.3.1   Public Innovation Procurement for Market Formation

The critical importance of innovation-based market formation has been demonstrated by many empirical studies. The capacity of innovation systems to generate entirely new demand related to product innovations is of key importance to the dynamic competitiveness of economic systems (von Hippel, 1976, 1977; Lundvall, 1985). Hence, the factors determining the demand for new goods and services should be an important ingredient in national innovation and growth policies.

For radically new products based on technological innovations and business renewal, the formation of new markets and market dimensions are of critical importance. The formation of early adopters, as well as the developments aimed at broader groups of buyers, are of key importance, as is the dynamic interaction between these two general aspects of market formation in relation to new businesses.[5]

The public sector plays several important roles in relation to the direction, dynamics and levels of demand in economic systems. Direct demand for goods and services within public sector activities is an important part of many market formation processes. How such public demand is expressed, and its directions and character, are all important aspects of its effectiveness in stimulating innovation and business renewal. Historically, public demand for goods and services has required technology development, which has been an important factor in the development of national innovation systems in Europe. This is particularly true in the case of Sweden, as has been briefly described above. Such public demand for continuous technology formation related to major public sector needs has served as a strong driving force for market formation for national industries.

In the US, as well as in most European countries, defence-related needs have fuelled technological development and business formation. This kind of public need has also been an important driving force in the Swedish national innovation system; after World War II, as a consequence of its neutral defence policy, Sweden developed one of the biggest defence industries in the world in per capita terms. Defence-related public demand, of course, is primarily targeted to military needs. However, its long-term impact on business firm R&D and innovation capabilities has also been quite important in other countries with ambitious defence policies, such as the UK, France and Israel, and has linked public demand with the private defence industry.

Other sectors where public demand has played a major role in forming markets for the advancement of technologies and private businesses in industrialized countries are those where major infrastructural investments form the basis of development, which includes energy, transportation and communication. Public demand within these sectors has been an important basis for technology and business development in Sweden and the other OECD countries during the last century (Sörlin and Törnqvist, 2000; Marklund et al., 2004; Marklund, 2006).

An important consequence of the emergence of many European public-private relationships was that they enabled companies to sell solutions not only nationally to public agencies, but also to other countries. International deregulation processes, emphasized in Europe by the EU, have radically changed the conditions for these kinds of public-private partnerships. They have been further strengthened by EU public procurement regulations, which, in essence, are intended to protect the equal opportunities of all business firms, and particularly small business firms, in tender negotiations with public agencies. These regulations urge the need for openness, transparency and competition in public procurement. The intentions behind deregulation in Europe and the development of procurement regulations were to increase competition and promote development of the internal European market. However, the transformation process has resulted in a weakening of some of the previous public-private drivers of European innovation.

As user-producer interactions and associated market formation processes are known to be crucial for innovation investments and the success of innovation processes, effective innovation policy would generally require a well-developed user perspective on innovations and innovation processes. However, we argue that the focus on users, that is, on markets and market formation, has been quite weak in innovation policy both in the EU and in Sweden. Where public policy or public agents have been influential in forming markets for innovation in the past, these have primarily been restricted to large, nationally controlled, infrastructural investments.

Recently, a number of initiatives have been introduced in the EU and in individual European countries, including Sweden, aimed at developing new schemes for public demand to drive the formation of markets for innovative goods and services. At the EU level, such measures are primarily aimed at generating lead markets (Aho et al., 2006) for innovation, and the EU has proposed the introduction of pre-commercial procurement schemes to stimulate the emergence of these lead markets (EU, 2006). In Sweden VINNOVA has proposed a system that would require public agencies to offset at least 1 per cent of their procurement budgets to innovation procurement (Marklund and Widmark, 2007). However, in spite of promising initiatives in the UK, the Netherlands, Germany, Sweden and other EU countries, there is an absence in Europe of large-scale systems based on such policy targets.

11.3.2   Awards for Innovation and R&D

R&D and innovation award schemes generally target technology and business formation processes related to entirely new businesses, which have the potential to generate high economic benefits. As the disincentives for radical innovation investments generally are substantial, there are clear policy rationales for specific innovation policy schemes addressing this kind of business formation. R&D and innovation awards to business firms or to entrepreneurs engaged in starting up new firms can cover part or all of the costs involved in such projects. The provision of funding to cover substantial parts, or all, of the costs involved in innovation investments in radical innovation and business renewal projects is based on the rationale that:

- radical innovation is critical to the dynamic competitiveness of nations
- private investments in radical innovation are lower than socially desirable
- early stages of radical innovation projects tend to be particularly underfunded
- allocations of public funding, through grants, are based on open competitions.

Because R&D and innovation award grants are generally quite substantial, a transparent and open competition process is required. Moreover, if grants cover more than 50 per cent of project costs they generally are awarded only to small business firms, although regions and countries have different rules.

Policy measures targeting radical innovation and business renewal are essentially focused on the stages in innovation processes where new technologies are formed, as private investments are scarce or entirely lacking in these early stages of commercialization of new technologies due to the high business uncertainties and risks. Most OECD countries have competitive award schemes for providing grants for business firm R&D and innovation projects.

As the uncertainties in radical innovation are extremely high, most radical innovation processes do not result in profitable innovations. Several studies have indicated that only some 5 per cent to 10 per cent result in direct economic success. Hence, distributions within portfolios of radical innovation projects are generally highly skewed. Yet, as discussed in Section

11.1, this kind of experimentation is crucial for the dynamic competitiveness of economic systems and should therefore be supported by the best conditions and incentives. As several evaluations have shown, the overall revenues from large and well-managed portfolios of radical innovation processes can be several times higher than the total investment costs of such programmes.

Frequently, the impact of different kinds of innovation and R&D award measures and programmes is not obvious, and as serious impact evaluations are scarce despite the policy importance attached to these kinds of measures, it is often difficult to draw firm conclusions about the impacts and efficiency of many of these initiatives. There are two US programmes, however, that can be considered state-of-the-art in terms of their efficiency and impacts, which have been discussed in some detail in other chapters in this volume; the Small Business Innovation Research Program (SBIR) and the ATP. These programmes address innovation-based business formation in different, but interrelated ways. The ATP has been systematically and thoroughly evaluated in the past and SBIR has recently been evaluated in detail (Wessner, 2007). In both cases the impacts on business formation and economic renewal have been firmly established.[6]

Inspired by the SBIR, Sweden has introduced a programme called Research and Grow, and the newly transformed Innovation Bridge Foundation is offering seed funding schemes and incubators in seven regions in Sweden. Although promising, these initiatives are relatively recent and still limited in scale and, although both had forerunners in the Swedish policy system, no systematic work has been done to evaluate the impact of these policies in Sweden. The policy focus within this field in Swedish innovation policy has been considerably weaker and less persistent than in the US, where such schemes have been running and developing over several decades. To conclude, there are strong reasons to develop Swedish innovation policy further in terms of its focus and measures directed towards early stage funding of innovation processes.

11.4 POLICY MEASURES FOR S&T FORMATION

S&T formation is an essential part of innovation processes and thus of the dynamic competitiveness of firms, industries and nations. Science formation has for many years been a major concern of public policy in Sweden and in the EU, with research well established as a policy area in most governments. As a result, the main emphasis of government investments in R&D and innovation in most of Europe and in Sweden has been on investments in university-based, and university prioritized, basic research.

In parallel with the focus on public investment in basic research in universities, various other institutions have been developed for industry-motivated, or mission-oriented research. And following the rapid development of systemic perspectives on innovation and economic dynamics from the early 1990s, different kinds of innovation system or cluster-based policy measures for S&T formation have been developed. A particularly important target of these kinds of policies has been the development of schemes for generating internationally competitive public-private consortia, or R&D centres, oriented towards industrial needs.

Many countries and regions have identified highly skewed, and seemingly increasing, distributions of R&D capabilities and investments in their business sectors. This has generated increasing concern about the overall absorptive capacity for new technologies and innovation in industry. It has also raised anxieties about the high level of concentration of innovation resources in, and thereby excessive dependence on, a few R&D-intensive, and increasingly multinational, large corporations.

As a response to this situation, different kinds of policy schemes, aimed at increasing the general level and breadth of R&D investments, have been developed. The most widely used and biggest in terms of public investments are tax credit schemes for R&D investments. However, public investments designed to generate and sustain centres of excellence for R&D, generally with a considerable degree of geographical concentration, are becoming increasingly popular. In the next sub-sections we discuss the targets and impact logics of these two kinds of policy measures.

11.4.1   Tax Credits for Business Firm R&D

Tax credits for R&D investments represent a type of innovation policy measure that is becoming increasingly popular in many countries and which is designed to promote increased levels of business firm R&D in general, and levels of small business R&D in particular. The majority of the OECD countries (Sweden, Finland and Germany being notable exceptions) have tax credit schemes that promote R&D investment in business firms. In the US there are federal and state level R&D tax credit schemes; 31 states have introduced R&D tax credit systems (Wilson, 2005). And the ACI has announced that the previously provisional federal R&D tax credits will be made permanent (Domestic Policy Council, 2006). Some countries, such as Canada, have been using tax credits for several decades.

The essential idea behind R&D tax credit systems is that they should stimulate business firm R&D investments, which, without the preferential tax treatment, would otherwise not have been made. The policy logic behind the introduction and use of preferential tax treatment of business firm R&D investments is that these investments are seen as critical for the long-term competitiveness of business firms and national economies. In general, tax credit systems for R&D investments are regarded as general frameworks for stimulating business firm R&D.

In most countries R&D tax credits are complemented by different kinds of specific policy measures targeting technology and business formation, particularly radical industrial renewal. R&D tax credit schemes generally give all business firms the right to claim tax credits for R&D investments up to certain levels of R&D costs, provided these are related to real innovation projects, and classified as such in some expert review processes. There are differences among countries in terms of the share of R&D project costs allowable for small firms and large firms. However, in most cases these differences are quite small.

Essentially, R&D costs on which tax credits can be claimed are generally related to the 'renewal quality' of projects in relation to the activities of the business firm. Global innovation level criteria in terms of the market innovativeness of R&D projects are generally not involved. Generally, only a minority share, often around 20 per cent, of total R&D costs is eligible for deductions under these schemes. Qualifying for tax credits on business firm R&D generally only requires that there are some allowable costs, and the requirements related to novelty or results to be evaluated, either *ex ante* or *ex post*, are not very strict.

Apart from the general nature of tax credit schemes, the particular design of such schemes differs substantially among countries in three main ways:

- types of costs that are tax deductible
- time period for R&D cost accounting and tax crediting
- competences and organizations for evaluating eligibility for tax credits.

In most national R&D tax credit systems business profits serve as the deductible basis for taxes. This is logical from a general tax system standpoint, as taxes are normally based on added value and additional income of various kinds. However, profits can be uneven and some business firms may record negative profits for several years. This is common among business firms establishing new businesses within new emerging industries based on new technologies. Emerging technologies and industries frequently require substantial and sustained R&D investment before breakthroughs occur. Therefore, tax systems based on business profits generally have some mechanisms to allow for postponement of tax deductions until business profits are achieved.

An alternative to using business profits as the basis for tax deductions is to base tax credits on R&D labour costs. If salaries related to the R&D

projects are used to claim tax deductions, R&D investment costs immediately become deductible, and their tax base becomes less volatile over the lifetime of R&D projects than if business profits are used as the basis for taxation. This makes the incentives for R&D investments more directly related in time to the R&D investments made, which is the desired impact of these kinds of policy measures. On the other hand, the share of labour costs in total R&D costs differs considerably across industries, which may reduce or disturb the general impact of R&D tax credit schemes.

R&D represents investments in the generation of intangible assets. There are some basic agreed definitions and classifications of such investments; however, actual evaluation of the content and quality of different R&D projects is a complex accountancy task. Therefore, there is a need for special competence in the evaluation of these types of investments and in the calculation of tax credits for R&D investments. As a consequence, many countries appoint public R&D funding agencies to assess R&D projects in terms of tax allowances. Their assessments are used as the basis for the public tax authorities' final decisions.

There are few evaluations of the impacts of tax credit systems on R&D investment levels, business firm profitability and national growth in the literature, despite the fact that these innovation policy measures have been applied for many years in a number of countries. Overall, the results of those evaluations that do exist indicate that, provided these schemes are well designed and properly implemented, they can have significant and positive impacts. These evaluations indicate that R&D tax credits tend to stimulate quite broad net increases in business firm R&D investments (Hall and van Reenen, 2000; Bloom et al., 2002; Guellec and van Pottelsberghe, 2000).

Indications are that the comparatively recent Norwegian R&D tax credit scheme will be effective in increasing the number of business firms investing in R&D and the links between firm R&D and university research, particularly small business firms with no previous R&D experience (Cappelen and Soland, 2006) and between small business firms and academia (Rønneberg, 2006). These impacts may be particularly important for the absorptive capacity of small business firms not previously active in R&D.

The criteria for R&D tax credits imply that they should have an impact on innovation by reducing the eligible costs of R&D. They are therefore primarily an instrument for increasing the overall level of business firm R&D and broadening the active R&D population of business firms, both of which aspects are of particular importance for small business R&D investment. However, as there are no direct incentives involved in rewarding radical renewal, targeting investments towards certain areas or connecting users to producers of innovation, tax credit systems are unlikely to be very efficient for supporting more targeted innovation policy ambitions.

In order to level out the preferential incentive balance for R&D investments between countries, there is probably a need to introduce such schemes in countries where they do not yet exist. In this context it should be noted that R&D tax credits are only one ingredient in the much wider, and not very transparent, practices of countries and regions designed to attract business firm R&D and production through indirect and direct subsidies. The shortcomings of the World Trade Organization (WTO) and other international agreements to monitor and regulate these practices are posing challenges to the entire global system of trade and international relations, as discussed by Thomas Howell in Chapter 4 of this volume. This is a much neglected and underestimated area of innovation policy.

11.4.2   Centres of Excellence for S&T Formation

Concentrations of capabilities generally have strong geographical dimensions. The geographic concentration of international excellence in resources and capabilities for S&T formation is an essential feature of such environments. The emergence and development of spatial concentrations of competences, R&D capabilities and industrial activities have been the focus of social sciences for many years. Alfred Marshall's studies of industrial districts have been a major direct or indirect inspiration for the current flood of literature on clusters, much of which also adopts the perspectives developed by Michael Porter. A primary focus in this cluster tradition is agglomerations of related business activities. In recent years the perspectives of economists and geographers have broadened to focus also on the role and impacts of S&T structures in the emergence and development of different kinds of clusters.

Policy makers are focusing more and more on the importance of and challenges involved in promoting centres of excellence in S&T formation. There are generally strong policy rationales for stimulating the generation and sustainability of spikes of R&D and innovation capabilities, which, in the context of increasingly global competition, act as attractors for investment. A large number of initiatives has been implemented to contribute to the generation of centres of excellence in S&T. In Sweden and the EU these initiatives are increasingly characterized by a greater focus on long-term funding of centres of excellence for S&T, influenced by the emerging insights into the requirements for global competition. The policy trend towards stimulating such centres of excellence is being justified, as internationally high-performing environments work to attract capital and high value adding R&D competences and activities. The messages from social science about the key issues, challenges and impacts involved are less clear, however.

From a business perspective, the importance of centres of excellence for S&T has increased as the research or science part of business firm R&D tends to decrease and development activities related to commercialization tend to increase. This is occurring at a time when the importance and use of science as a basis for technology formation and innovation are increasing. Both these trends are related to globalization and increased global competition, which strongly argue for increased specialization, first, because global competition generates quite strong disincentives for long-term R&D investments relative to short-term business development activities and, second, because global S&T developments generate a combination of increasingly widening and more complex arrays of S&T. As a consequence, business firms are increasingly dependent on external S&T knowledge in their innovation processes and S&T environments delivering excellent S&T for innovation become relatively competitive in terms of attracting business R&D and innovation investments.

The aim of policies designed to generate or strengthen centres of excellence is to create internationally competitive environments for S&T that will breed innovation and innovation-based businesses with strong growth and job opportunities. Therefore, the connection between science formation, on the one hand, and technology formation, on the other, is generally a primary concern in most centre of excellence initiatives. The aim is to attract both the best academic research and researchers, and also leading business sector R&D capabilities, to create an environment in which the presence of institutions facilitating commercialization processes is central.

A primary focus of policies related to the stimulation of clusters in general, and to centres of excellence in particular, is the interactions between key partners or stakeholders. As interactions among private business, academic institution and public administration investment are of key importance, the focus on triple helix dynamics in policy development has increased. There is a vast policy repertoire of networking and cluster initiatives in Europe and around the world all aiming at stimulating internationally competitive centres or clusters. However, such programmes still only represent a fairly small proportion of the innovation policies in the EU and Sweden.

The Research Framework Programmes in the EU focus strongly on R&D networking and R&D performing agents in Europe, which is having a considerable impact on the R&D landscape in Europe, as the connectedness among researchers and R&D institutions increases (Ormala and Vonortas, 2005). However, recent evaluations and policy perspectives on EU competitiveness policy for S&T show that the focus on global excellence is rather weak (Kok, 2004). This is becoming a major concern in Europe, with the introduction of the Lisbon agenda for global competitiveness and the emphasis in EU policy is being redirected to S&T excellence within a global perspective. The efforts to create a European Research Area (ERA), supported by the EC Research Framework Programmes, are clear attempts in this direction. Several of the instruments in the 6th and 7th framework programmes support such developments.

All the R&D funding agencies in Sweden have established schemes for long-term funding of different kinds of centres of excellence for S&T. The pioneering VINNOVA initiative, established in 1995, has been renewed in the form of a ten-year programme called VINN Excellence Centres, which focuses on mission-oriented basic research in cooperations between academic and industrial researchers. The initiative is supported by long-term funding and continuous evaluations. An impact evaluation of the initial initiative, conducted near to the end of its ten-year term, showed that publicly co-funded, basic, mission-oriented research performed by academic-industry consortia had generated economic benefits exceeding the total costs of the programme (Arnold et al., 2004). There are similar initiatives either running, or being initiated, in several other European countries, including Finland, France, Austria and the Netherlands.

Despite the policy rhetoric on global excellence, and the emergence of many new instruments, much remains to be done in terms of prioritizing excellence in policies and initiatives in the EU and Sweden. Within the programmes directly aimed at international excellence criteria for evaluating excellence *ex ante*, as well as monitoring and *ex post* evaluations, often lack focus and rigour. Whether or not global excellence is being effectively targeted and achieved is often not clear because of the scale and scope of excellence, and problems in the benchmarking analysis of actual S&T competitiveness within various fields.

In line with the Aho report (Aho et al., 2006), we would argue that the generation and sustainability of centres of excellence for S&T formation represent a fundamental challenge for the long-term competitiveness of the EU and European countries and regions. Targeting S&T excellence on a global scale is still a major challenge for European and Swedish S&T and innovation policy, and measures and evaluation practises need to be further developed.

11.5   CONCLUSIONS

This chapter has highlighted some critical dimensions and targets of innovation policy. It has pointed to different kinds of policy measures related to different kinds of impact logics critical to innovation and business renewal, arguing that innovation policy is about stimulating the experimental economy through a series of interrelated policies. It is argued that innovation policy needs to address four different sets of formation processes in economic system dynamics simultaneously: market formation, business formation, technology formation and science formation. Insufficient incentives and structures related to any of these processes may limit the effectiveness of economic renewal and growth.

Swedish innovation policy and, to a large extent, innovation policy in other European countries has historically been focused on S&T push strategies. In Sweden ambitious investments in university education and research have fuelled academic performance. In combination with long-term public-private partnerships within nationally regulated sectors, such as defence, telecommunications, energy and transportation, the Swedish innovation system regime has historically been quite successful. In Sweden large R&D intensive firms and MNCs have developed, based on long-term public-private innovation partnerships. National public needs within the four sectors referred to above, together with expanding export opportunities, have been strong drivers of innovation-based growth in the ambitious investment decades following World War II.

In most recent decades the initially quite strong impact of innovation stimulating market formation has lost much of its driving force. This process has gone almost unrecognized in innovation policy strategies, which have not incorporated any compensating mechanisms. Also policy measures for business formation related to radical innovation remain weak, particularly compared to the US and to developments in the emerging Asian countries.

EU and Swedish innovation policy has retained its primary focus on research funding, based on the perspective that research is a fundamentally important input in the process of innovation. As innovation policy in the EU and Sweden has recognized that science is often only weakly linked to innovation, the focus on science funding has been complemented by large numbers of network schemes, aimed at generating cooperation between business firms and universities. However, the emphasis on generating internationally excellent S&T environments for the attraction of global investment and migration of competences is quite recent in Sweden and the EU.

Market and business formation processes are particularly critical for the emergence of radical innovation and business renewal within different innovation systems. These formation processes are typically characterized by important, often acute, system failures in the sense that private investment in the high-risk endeavours of radical renewal is generally considerably lower than is socially desired. There are two important general policy

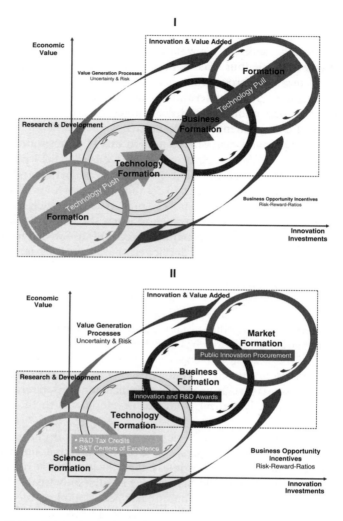

Figure 11.3   Critical targets and measures in innovation policy

areas and policy measures that are needed to stimulate radical innovation
and business renewal – public innovation procurement, and awards for
R&D and innovation.

An increased focus on market and business formation mechanisms,
together with a more determined focus on global excellence in S&T push
mechanisms, will most probably be necessary to increase and sustain the
global economic competitiveness of Sweden and the EU (Figure 11.3).

One of the main messages of this chapter is that the different kinds of measure discussed should not be perceived as a menu from which one or two courses can be selected. We want to emphasize the need for effective instruments within all four classes of policy measures, as they address different key formation processes in economic renewal. As different kinds of policy measures address different innovation process challenges which often prevail in innovation systems, they should not compete, but should be designed and implemented to complement each other in terms of their impacts on innovation in general and on small business innovation in particular.

NOTES

1. Following Schumpeter's (1934, pp. 74–80) understanding of the term entrepreneurship.
2. See Chapter 5 by David Audretsch in this volume.
3. For a summary of the Lisbon agenda see http://europa.eu/scadplus/glossary/lisbon_strategy_en.htm, (accessed 30 July 2007).
4. The European Trend Chart for Innovation, Country Report for Sweden, 2005, prepared by the European Commission Enterprise Directorate-General, accessed at www.proinno-europe.eu/docs/reports/documents/County_Report_Sweden_2005.pdf.
5. For an excellent discussion and modelling of this see Utterback (1996).
6. For one of several accounts of the continuous and ambitious evaluations of the ATP in the US see Ruegg and Feller (2003). For the most recent 25 year evaluation of the SBIR programme see National Academies (2007).

REFERENCES

Aho, E., J. Cornu, L. Georghiou and A. Subirà (2006), *Creating an Innovative Europe, Report of the Independent Expert Group on R&D and Innovation following the Hampton Court Summit*, chaired by E. Aho, January, Luxembourg: Office for Official Publications of the European Communities.

Arnold, E., J. Clark and S. Bussillet (2004), *Impacts of the Swedish Competence Centres Programme 1995–2003*, Stockholm: VINNOVA.

Beinhocker, E. D. (2006), *The Origin of Wealth – Evolution, Complexity, and the Radical Remaking of Economics*, Boston, MA: Harvard Business School Press and Random House.

Bloom, N., R. Griffith and J. Van Reenen (2002), 'Do R&D tax credits work? Evidence from a panel of countries 1979–1997', *Journal of Public Economics*, **85**, 1–31.

Cappelen, Å. and G. Soland (2006), *Skattebaserte Ordninger for å Stimulere FoU i Næringslivet – Noen Internasjonale Erfaringer*, Oslo: Statistics Norway.

Danish Government (2006), *Fremgang, Fornyelse og Tryghed, Strategi for Danmark i den Globale Økonomi – de Vigtigste Initiativer* [*Success, Renewal and Safety, Strategy for Denmark in the Global Economy – The Most Important Initiatives*], April, Copenhagen: Danish Government.

Domestic Policy Council (2006), *The American Competitiveness Initiative – Leading the World in Innovation (ACI)*, Washington, DC: Office of Science and Technology Policy.

Dosi, G. (1982), 'Technological paradigms and technological trajectories – a suggested interpretation of the determinants and directions of technical change', *Research Policy*, **11**, 147–62.

Eliasson, G. (1996), *Firm Objectives, Controls and Organization*, Boston, MA: Springer.

European Union (2006), *Pre-commercial Procurement of Innovation – A Missing Link in the European Innovation Cycle*, report of an ad-hoc National IST Directors Forum working group, Brussels, March.

Florida, R. (2005), 'The world is spiky', *The Atlantic Monthly*, October, p. 48–51.

Friedman, T. L. (2005), *The World is Flat*, New York: Farrar, Strauss and Giroux.

Guellec, D. and van Pottelsberghe de la Potterie, B. (2000), 'The impact of public R&D expenditure on business R&D', Organisation for Economic Co-operation and Development, STI working papers 2000/4, Paris.

Hall, B. and J. van Reenen (2000), 'How effective are fiscal R&D incentives? A review of the evidence', *Research Policy*, **29**, 449–69.

Kok, W. (Chairman) (2004), *Facing the Challenge – The Lisbon Strategy for Growth and Employment, Report of a EU High Level Group*, Luxembourg: Office for the Official Publications of the European Communities.

Lundvall, B-Å. (1985), *Product Innovation and User-Producer Interaction*, Aalborg, Denmark: Aalborg University.

Marklund, G. (2006), 'Swedish ICT competitiveness and the globalization of R&D', in M. Karlsson (ed.), *The Internationalization of Corporate R&D – Leveraging the Changing Geography of Innovation*, Stockholm: ITPS, pp. 129–51.

Marklund, G. and N. Widmark (2007), 'Public procurement for innovation and change', Stockholm, December.

Marklund, G., R. Nilsson, P. Sandgren, J. Granat Thorslund and J. Ullström (2004), *The Swedish National Innovation System 1970–2003*, VINNOVA analysis VA 2004:01, Stockholm.

Ormala, E. and S. Vonortas (2005), 'Evaluating the European Union's research framework programmes: 1999–2003', *Science and Public Policy*, **32**(5), 403–10.

Rønneberg, R. (2006), 'Research Council Norway', presentation of SkatteFunn at VINNOVA's annual conference in Stockholm, 17 October.

Ruegg, R. and E. Feller (2003), *A Toolkit for Evaluating R&D Investment Models, Methods and Findings from ATP's First Decade*, Gaithersburg, MD: National Institute for Standards and Technology.

Schilling, P. (2005), 'Research as a source of strategic opportunity? Re-thinking research policy developments in the late 20th century', dissertation, Umeå University.

Schumpeter, J. A. (1934), *The Theory of Economic Development*, reprinted 1983, Cambridge, MA: Transaction Inc.

Schumpeter, J. A. (1943), *Capitalism, Socialism and Democracy*, reprinted 1992, London: Routledge.

Sörlin, S. and G. Törnqvist (2000), *Kunskap för Välstånd – Universiteten och Omvandlingen av Sverige*, Stockholm: SNS Förlag.

Swedish Government (2004), *Innovative Sweden – A Strategy for Growth Through Renewal*, Ds 2004, p. 36, Stockholm: Ministry of Industry, Employment and Communications.

Utterback, J. M. (1996), *Mastering the Dynamics of Innovation*, Boston, MA: Harvard Business School Press.

Wessner, C. (2008), *An Assessment of the Small Business Innovation Research Program, National Research Council of the National Academies*, Washington, DC: National Academies Press, prepublication copy.

Wilson, D. (2005), *The Rise and Spread of R&D Tax Credits*, San Francisco, CA: Federal Reserve Bank of San Francisco.

von Hippel, E. (1976), 'The dominant role of users in the scientific instrument innovation process', *Research Policy*, **5**(3), 212–39.

von Hippel, E. (1977), 'The dominant role of the user in semiconductor and electronic subassembly process innovation', *IEEE Transaction on Engineering Management*, EM-**24**(2), 60–71.

12. Conclusion

Göran Marklund, Nicholas S. Vonortas and Charles W. Wessner

12.1 INTRODUCTION

Globalization has changed the dynamics of economic systems, business models and technological development. It is creating exceptional opportunities for new powerhouses, such as China and India, as well as for the established economies. At the same time, the forces of globalization are posing distinctly new policy challenges and opportunities. Innovation has become imperative to meet these challenges and capitalize on these opportunities.

Key innovation resources, such as research and development (R&D) investments, business operations and even human resources, have become considerably more mobile and on a global scale. As a consequence, the policy competition between nations and regions has increased in intensity and changed in nature. For policy makers, globalization is essentially a competition involving provision of the best conditions for and most efficient driving forces of innovation and long-term competitiveness.

The different contributions in this volume have addressed this transformation of the policy challenges and opportunities and discussed innovation policy strategies and measures of importance to national competitiveness and prosperity in a globalizing world. The overarching message in the chapters in this book is that national competitiveness and the prosperity it engenders are not a natural given for developed nations, such as the USA and the EU countries. Rather, ambitious and efficient innovation policies will be critical for their future competitiveness and economic development.

The foundations of competitiveness have to be continuously regenerated and restructured. And innovation, which is the basis of these foundations, often faces considerable system failures in the sense that business conditions, capital markets and tax and R&D systems do not always work to stimulate innovation and, indeed, may sometimes impede it. In fact, as uncertainties and risks are inherently associated with innovation processes, investments in innovation are generally accompanied by considerable negative incentives compared to less risky business and knowledge development endeavours.

12.2 A MULTIDIMENSIONAL PERSPECTIVE

The general conclusion that can be drawn from the contributions in this volume is that national policies for innovation, competitiveness and economic growth need to take careful account of the systemic nature of the processes of innovation and economic renewal. Hence, policy strategies and measures need to be based on a multidimensional innovation systems perspective. Several contributions emphasize the need for policy approaches, balancing supply push and demand pull strategies and measures. This suggests, for example, that R&D policy, while important, is nonetheless only one component of the complex policy mix that is necessary to create a vibrant, innovative and internationally competitive economy.

Instead of focusing on individual policy areas, innovation and competitiveness policy should focus on the dynamic efficiency of different key renewal processes in the economy. It is argued that there are four such general sets of formation processes in economic systems dynamics that need to be addressed simultaneously and integrated:

- market formation
- business formation
- technology formation
- science formation.

It is generally the case that policies within several different strategic areas have an important effect on the developments of these four types of formation processes in economic systems. And also that the dynamic efficiency of the relationships among these four key formation processes are typically a consequence of complex relationships among the policy impacts in different strategic areas.

Innovation policy should not only consider the key importance and diverse nature of different kinds of formation processes, but also the often considerable differences between specific techno-industrial innovation systems. Such differences are generally related to differences in the nature and dynamics of patterns of demand and technologies and specific agent structures and agent relationships. Hence, in addition to general strategies, innovation policy needs to address different techno-industrial innovation systems with different sets of sector specific policy measures.

Of particular importance to innovation policy are challenges related to radical innovation and industrial renewal. As incremental innovation processes generally involve moderate or low uncertainties regarding the feasibility of success, the risks of investing in such developments are relatively low. In radical innovation processes uncertainties are often high and the risks are therefore difficult to estimate.

Yet radical innovation opens up new sources of economic value by breaking out of established business models and industrial trajectories; it can engender entirely new businesses and new business models that generate important sources of business profits and economic growth. Nonetheless, there are high risks associated with radical innovation and, from a social point of view, there is a tendency to underinvest in these processes. This suggests that there is an urgent need for innovation policy strategies and measures to target radical innovation. Several of the contributions in this volume discuss both the general features of such strategies and measures and specific policy initiatives based on their objectives.

12.3   INNOVATION-BASED ENTREPRENEURSHIP

Innovation and entrepreneurship are intimately related concepts of economic dynamics. While the former refers to the new products, processes and business models representing new sources of economic value, the latter refers to the activities of agents generating creative new combinations of value. Hence, entrepreneurship is about business formation; it is the critical link between investments in new knowledge and economic growth.

Innovation-based entrepreneurship is of particular importance for economic and long-term business competitiveness and wealth creation. It should lead to increased profits and higher paid jobs. In the absence of vibrant entrepreneurship the flow and quality of innovation would be hampered. Hence, innovation policy should be targeted towards the incentives and structures that are critical for innovation-based entrepreneurship. Entrepreneurship, innovation and business formation take place in all kinds of organizations, for example, in large corporations, small business firms and new innovation-based firms, as well as in public and semi-public organizations.

A particular focus in innovation policy has been innovation and entrepreneurship in new innovative firms, for two reasons. First, they represent a critical dynamic force in economic systems, as they continuously bring flows of innovative ideas into the experimental economy. Second, supporting the innovation processes related to the creation of entirely new innovation-based firms is generally associated with specific policy challenges.

Markets and production systems are selecting among new innovation-based businesses within complex relationships and processes. Many, perhaps most of these innovative new businesses will not make significant contributions to economic growth and new jobs. However, some of them will. And because these firms often contribute in important ways to the transformation of entire industries they are a source of growth and employment insofar as a relatively high share of innovative new firms appears to have high growth rates.

Provision of a positive environment for new innovation-based business is critical to the achievement of a healthy economic system and the generation of high levels of dynamic competition. In investigations of the potential of innovation stemming from research it is frequently argued that academic entrepreneurship is central, yet the mechanisms for exploiting the results of science and technology (S&T) formation based on academic research are often underutilized.

12.4   THE EU

Several of the chapters in this book have discussed the particular innovation policy challenges of the EU. A common thread in these chapters is that EU policies generally have a strong emphasis on technology push, including relatively large investments in academic research. Innovation policy, targeting the innovation generating performance of the economy, has been considerably less emphasized in the European economic policy debate and repertoire.

The general conclusion of several contributions is that the EU and its member states should increase the emphasis on market pull mechanisms. This suggests the need for a more ambitious focus on the challenges of both market and business formation. A greater focus on innovation policy would stimulate the experimental economy, encouraging a more dynamic competitive environment.

Focusing on innovation-based entrepreneurship and new business formation is arguably critical for a more effective policy mix in Europe. In so doing, it is argued that EU policy makers should consider innovation procurement as a policy measure to improve the formation of new markets for innovation. Equal attention should be given to developing R&D and innovation award programmes, such as the American Advanced Technology Program and the Small Business Innovation Research initiative. These programmes have the advantage of providing direct incentives for radical innovation-based business formation, and for less radical, but equally valuable, creation of firms able to meet national needs across a variety of government missions.

12.5   SUPPORT FOR R&D IS PARAMOUNT

It is important to emphasize, however, that an increased focus on market and business formation in innovation policy should not be at the expense of policies and policy measures for S&T formation. Instead, it is necessary to also improve the policy strategies and measures related to its formation and to target radical renewal and the generation and sustainability of centres of excellence for research and innovation.

The contributions that discuss EU research investments argue that the targeting of world excellence in the funding of S&T has not been sufficiently emphasized in the EU. The generation of centres of excellence for research and innovation is critical to developing advanced competency in S&T in the future. Moreover, as the global locational competition over business firm R&D – and manufacturing – investments is increasing rapidly, it is important to improve the general incentive structures related to business R&D investments. This includes the agreements on trade and intellectual property rights being carefully scrutinized and rigorously enforced because, despite the World Trade Organization and other international agreements, it has been shown that there is room for aggressive policy measures designed to capture international business investments in advanced manufacturing and R&D centres. It has also been argued that for Europe and the USA to attract business R&D investments it is important to consider the establishment and further development of R&D tax credit schemes.

While the fundamental messages are simple, an effective response requires innovation at the policy level. Change is needed to encourage innovative firms that will carry the seeds of the next generation of technologies and products and provide the employment, growth and workforce gains essential to long-term growth and sustainability for the advanced economies.

There are several policy areas that need to be developed. These include:

- Greater recognition of the importance of innovation policy and the innovative firms able to renew and drive the economies of tomorrow.
- More emphasis on centres of S&T excellence, with a corresponding funding of the talent needed to develop the technologies of the future – best implemented in a flexible institutional environment.
- A focus on product development in order to address the social and environmental security needs to drive innovation during the next 20 years.
- Recognition of the importance of innovation awards as incentives to transform ideas derived in the laboratory and university to marketable products and services.

- Development of appropriate policy responses to the location of competition for R&D centres and manufacturing and distribution systems that will provide the high-technology jobs and growth industries of the future.

Index